OREGON

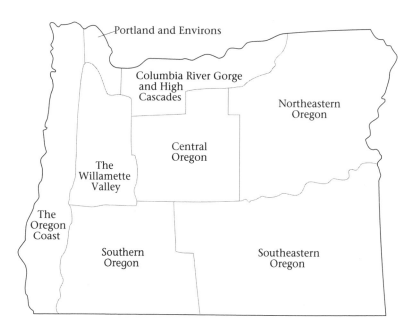

CONTENTS

To some very special little people—Bradford, P.J., and Marisa; Emily and Michael; Nathan, Jordan, and Kyle—who will one day, I trust, discover the joys of traveling off the beaten path.

And to some special big people—mom and dad, who always love traveling the byways, and good friends far and wide, kindred spirits in the joy of "shunpiking," finding out what's over there, just around the bend.

Oregon

OFF THE BEATEN PATH™

THIRD EDITION

MYRNA OAKLEY

A Voyager Book

The Globe Pequot Press

Old Saybrook, Connecticut

Cover map © DeLorme Mapping
Illustrations on page 29, 97, and 172, by Carole Drong; page 48 by Julie Lynch; all other illustrations by Elizabeth Neilson Walker.

Library of Congress Cataloging-in-Publication Data
Oakley, Myrna.
    Oregon : off the beaten path / Myrna Oakley. — 3rd ed.
        p.   cm. — (Off the beaten path series)
    "A Voyager book."
    "A guide to unique places"—Cover.
    Includes index.
    ISBN 1-7627-0071-8
    1. Oregon—Guidebooks.   I. Title. II.   Series.
F874.3.O24   1997
917.9504'43—dc21   96-40470
                                                                            CIP

Manufactured in the United States of America
Third Edition/First Printing

Oregon

OFF THE BEATEN PATH™

INTRODUCTION

Looking back a number of years ago, I remember fully discovering—and truly appreciating—the vast, diverse character of my native Oregon in the late 1960s and early 1970s, when I traveled with some forty-seven seventh-graders, several fellow teachers, and helpful parents on working field trips throughout the Beaver State.

On the Oregon coast we found eons-old seashell fossils and explored driftwood-strewn beaches and brimming tide pools; on the high desert east of the rugged Cascade Mountains we visited ancient volcano remnants, lava caves, and lava-cast forests; and we identified all the life zones, trees, vegetation, and wildflowers in between.

We trekked into the Columbia River Gorge and hiked past waterfalls and into narrow chasms, peering at thick layers of volcanic basalt supporting colonies of licorice fern, colorful lichens and mosses, and dozens of native wildflowers.

We marveled at the wide Columbia River, along whose banks Native American families fished and traded for thousands of years, the place where the first Oregon Trail pioneers, in 1843, floated belongings down the rampaging river to sites near Fort Vancouver, Oregon, and, later, Portland.

On the high desert near Bend we camped for four days and held school under the wide blue sky beneath pungent junipers on one day, then under tall, cinnamon-barked ponderosa pine on another. Surrounded by yellow blooming sagebrush, low-growing manzanita, bitterbrush, and wide-open vistas in every direction, we absorbed a new awareness of the outdoors, a new appreciation of nature's life cycles.

Some seven or eight students, arms outstretched and hands clasped, encircled an enormous ponderosa pine tree near LaPine and the Little Deschutes River. From atop Lava Butte we viewed the Cascade's highest snowcapped volcanic peaks—Mt. Washington, Mt. Jefferson, Three-Fingered Jack, Mt. Bachelor, the Three Sisters, and Mt. Hood.

With flashlights and lanterns we explored cavernous lava tubes—Skeleton Cave and Lava River Cave. We peered down into Arnold Ice Cave and learned that early Oregon pioneers chopped huge blocks of ice there and hauled them by horse and buggy to Bend for refrigeration.

At Fort Rock, an enormous volcanic remnant, we found nesting baby eagles and marveled at towering, wave-cut ledges created by ancient seas. At night, under a canopy of glittering stars, we sat around the campfire and listened to the spine-tingling poetic tales of Robert Service.

By now, traveling off the beaten path has become a well-worn habit, one shared by many fellow Oregonians as well as visitors. Our wide ocean beaches and spectacular coastline remain a favorite destination—fully preserved for everyone to enjoy. A sense of the mid-1840s pioneer past still permeates much of the state, and sections of the Oregon Trail, including the actual wagon ruts, have been identified and preserved in eastern and central Oregon.

Communities throughout the state welcome visitors to local history society museums, living history programs, and vintage homes and gardens where glimpses of Oregon's pioneer past can be seen and appreciated. Many covered bridges—and lighthouses, along the entire Oregon coast—have been preserved and can be easily located.

The safekeeping of early Oregon farms and homesteads is a continuing priority, and the battles over the protection of old-growth Douglas fir forests, as well as setting aside natural wildlife and bird-life areas to conserve them from overdevelopment, takes on that independent pioneer spirit so deeply ingrained here.

Regardless of how far off the beaten path you travel in Oregon, you'll also discover coastal and mountain lodges, inviting bed-and-breakfast inns, elegant destination resorts, quaint shops, regional vineyards and wineries, wonderful gardens, scenic natural areas, and unique eateries. I hope you enjoy this personal field trip through the Beaver State—walking in the footsteps of yesterday as well as today.

To aid you in planning your travels, a list of resources is included following the last chapter. As this book goes to press, all information is current. Should you discover other uncommon places in Oregon to recommend for future editions, please drop me a line in care of The Globe Pequot Press, P.O. Box 833, Old Saybrook, Connecticut 06475. Happy travels!

The prices and rates listed in this guidebook were confirmed at press time. We recommend, however, that you call establishments before traveling to obtain current information. Also note: Oregon now has two telephone area codes, 503 and 541.

THE OREGON COAST

1. Flora Pacifica
2. Redwood Grove Nature Trail
3. Chetco Pelican Players
4. Rogue River Mailboat Trips
5. Historic Hughes House
6. Bandon's Cheese Company
7. Faber Cranberry Farms
8. Sawdust Theatre
9. Shore Acres Gardens
10. *Marshfield Sun* Printing Museum
11. Umpqua Lighthouse and Umpqua Discovery Center
12. Dean Creek Elk Viewing Area
13. Oregon Dunes Overlook
14. Old Town Florence and South Jetty
15. Devil's Churn Wayside and Cape Perpetua
16. Sea Quest Bed and Breakfast
17. Kozy Kove Kafe
18. Yaquina Head Lighthouse
19. Keiko the Orca whale
20. Nye Beach Hotel
21. Catch the Wind Kite Shop
22. Connie Hansen Garden
23. Proposal Rock Inn
24. Dory Fleet
25. World War II Blimp Hangar Museum
26. Yurt camping
27. Manzanita News and Espresso
28. Short Sand Beach and Oswald West Park
29. Historic Seaside Promenade
30. Fort Clatsop National Monument
31. Great Oregon Beach Cleanup

THE OREGON COAST

EASTER LILIES AND CRANBERRIES

With its mild, relatively dry winters, the southern Oregon coast offers many appealing options—clamming, crabbing, hiking, fishing, beachcombing, museum hopping, and just plain solitude beckon visitors to linger awhile.

From late June to early September, fields of lilies, both Easter lilies and Oriental hybrids, nod in colorful profusion, and travelers can detour from coastal Highway 101 just south of Brookings to see them, at **Strahm's Lilies** and at ◆ **Flora Pacifica,** 15447 Ocean View Drive, Harbor 97415 (541–469–9741). Enjoy the viewing garden and several acres of flowers for cutting, such as calla lilies, astilbe, delphinium, and larkspur. You can see where the flowers are dried and made into natural swags and wreaths as well as browse the gift shop Wednesday through Saturday from 11:00 A.M. to 5:00 P.M. Before continuing north stop at the well-stocked Welcome Center (541–469–4117) located at the lovely **Harris Beach State Park,** open daily May through October.

You can then head out the Chetco River Road and spend an hour or so hiking the 1-mile ◆ **Redwood Grove Nature Trail,** located 8½ miles inland from Highway 101 and a ½-mile north of Alfred A. Loeb State Park, on the north bank of the Chetco River. Aided by the helpful interpretive brochure, you'll pass some fourteen numbered stations and identify trees, shrubs, ferns, and flowers that are characteristic of this coastal region. The centuries-old giant redwoods range between 300 and 800 years in age and may reach heights of 350 feet and girths of 25 feet.

Notice also the tanoak, a broadleaf tree that often grows with redwood. At one time tannin from the peeled bark of the tanoak was used by the Pacific Coast leather industry. You'll also identify the black huckleberry, which has bluish black fruit, and the red huckleberry, which has bright red, tart berries. Both make delicious jelly. *Note:* This nature trail is moderately difficult, as some sections are steep, but there are benches along the way. Be sure to wear sturdy shoes.

For other wilderness hiking information, stop by the Chetco Ranger Station in Brookings, at 555 Fifth Street (541–469–2196). Ask about the several recreational rentals, including the **Packer's**

2

Cabin, for primitive overnight adventures in the heart of the Chetco River forest area. This cozy cabin, located 20 miles east of town, has a woodstove, but you bring in your own water, food, and bedding. If you like your accommodations a bit more civilized, call the folks at **Oceancrest House Bed & Breakfast,** (800) 877–9741 (located near Flora Pacifica); or the friendly folks at **Holmes Sea Cove Bed & Breakfast,** (541) 469–3025, located about 3 miles north of Brookings.

Guided rafting and drift-boat fishing trips are also available on the Chetco River; information about local guides can be obtained from the ranger station or from the Brookings-Harbor Visitors' Information Center, P.O. Box 940, Brookings 97415 (503–469–3181).

Good eateries in the area include **City Grill** at 703 Chetco Avenue and **Chives Restaurant** at 1025 Chetco Avenue, both fairly new in town, and the wonderful old-timer, **Wharfside Restaurant** at 16362 Lower Harbor Road, open Tuesday to Sunday, 11:30 A.M. to 9:00 P.M. While visiting the coast, consider taking in some live local theater as well. The ◆**Chetco Pelican Players** perform throughout the year and offer contemporary as well as light comedy and melodrama—"Romance of Scarlet Gulch" was a recent offering. For current information call (541) 469–1857 or (541) 469–3834.

History buffs may want to plan a visit to the **Chetco Valley Historical Society Museum,** located in the Blake House, the oldest standing house in the Brookings-Harbor area. The vintage red-and-white structure served as a stagecoach station and trading post on the south coast during the early 1800s. On display are World War II artifacts, old photographs, and a quilt collection that includes a pioneer quilt made in 1844. The museum is located at 15461 Museum Road, 2 miles south of Brookings; its telephone number is (541) 469–6651. Notice the enormous Monterey cypress in front of the museum; one of the largest in the United States, it's 99 feet tall and measures more than 30 feet around the massive trunk. The museum is open mid-March through November, Thursday through Sunday, noon to 4:00 P.M.

If time permits, detour at **Cape Sebastion,** located just north of Brookings and Pistol River, some 5 miles south of Gold Beach. Rising 500 feet from the salty Pacific Ocean, the cape offers spectacular wide-angle views of the coastline north and south, as well as hiking trails and picnic areas. Don't be deterred by the weather; this sight is not to be missed, even on a blustery day.

For one of the best side trips on the south Curry coast, take one of the ◆**Rogue River Mailboat Trips** up the lower Rogue River. Here passengers and mail are transported in open and safe hydrojet-powered launches across ripples and easy rapids about 32 miles upriver, to Agness. Good-natured pilots point out wildlife and geological features along the way, often recounting lively tales of early river life.

Some call it Zane Grey country, for the fabled writer of westerns had a cabin in the area, where he came to fish and write in the solitude of the rushing river and forests of giant Douglas fir. A hearty lunch at rustic **Singing Springs Lodge** and the 32-mile return trip to Gold Beach complete this memorable foray into the Rogue River's pioneer past. Information about the mailboat trips and overnight options can be obtained from the Gold Beach–Wedderburn Visitors' Information Center, (541) 247–7526 or (800) 525–2334. A longer, 102-mile, round-trip excursion up into the federally designated Wild and Scenic section of the Rogue River is also available, and you could spend the night at remote **Paradise Lodge.**

As you head north on Highway 101, the coastal headlands press close to the ocean, and the highway, once a narrow Indian trail, curves along a shelf high above the waves and around Humbug Mountain to Port Orford. In 1828 mountain man Jedediah Smith trekked through the area with a dozen men and 150 horses loaded with furs obtained by trapping and trading in California. Crossing the mouth of the Rogue River, Jedediah reported in his journal that twelve horses drowned but the furs, ferried across in canoes, were saved.

At Port Orford visit the local harbor, a natural deep-water area where fishing boats are hoisted in and out of the churning waters each day with an enormous converted log boom. You'll often see the boats resting high and dry on long trailers atop the pier.

If time allows, drive about 5 miles west of Highway 101—just north of Port Orford—to **Cape Blanco State Park** to see the **Cape Blanco Lighthouse.** Constructed in the 1870s, the lighthouse is the oldest still standing on the coast, and its light still shines 21 miles out to sea. The lighthouse is open for tours April through October, Thursday through Monday, 10:00 A.M. to 4:00 P.M. Nearby, the restored ◆**Historic Hughes House,** circa

1898, sits in a small meadow above the winding Sixes River. It was built by pioneers Patrick and Jane Hughes thirty years after they'd bought the land and started a dairy ranch. Now part of the Cape Blanco State Park complex, the house is open from May to September, Thursday through Monday from 10:00 A.M. to 4:00 P.M. The turnoff to the house is about 4 miles out Cape Blanco Road. For current information call (541) 332–6774.

Of the nine original lighthouses on the Oregon coast, light beams from six of them continue to guide mariners, fishing parties, sailors, and pleasure boaters along coastal waters. Although newer technology in marine navigation—radiobeacons and such—has retired the other three lighthouses from active service, there is growing interest in preserving these vintage maritime structures as historic sites, interpretive centers, and museums. **The U.S. Lighthouse Society,** established in 1984, has supported these efforts on both coasts. The Oregon chapter of the society can be contacted at P.O. Box 600, Lakeside 97449.

The nearby **Sixes River** offers fishing for fall chinook, spring and fall sea-run cutthroat, and winter steelhead. **Cape Blanco State Park** is open from April to November and has complete facilities for day and overnight use, in addition to a primitive hiker-biker camp. A helpful booklet on Oregon's state parks and campgrounds can be obtained from the State Parks and Recreation Division, 525 Trade Street South East, Salem 97310 (503–379–6305). *Note:* There are large state campgrounds in each section of the coast that remain open all year.

In tiny Sixes, 5 miles north of Port Orford at 93316 Sixes River Road, the historic **Sixes River Hotel,** recently renovated, has developed a following for both its small restaurant and its five cozy guest rooms. The chef serves such tasty entrees as lamb with orange sauce and wasabi butter, ling cod with baby shrimp sauce, and tortellini with prawns. Everything served is fresh, including the meats, seafood, and vegetables. The dining room is open Tuesday through Sunday, 5:30 to 9:30 P.M. Call (541) 332–3900 for information and reservations.

Located at the mouth of the Coquille River, where the river surges into the Pacific Ocean, the community of Bandon is known for its cheese and its cranberries. Milk for the original Bandon Cheese and Produce Company, founded in 1927, was hauled from nearby Coquille Valley dairies by stern-wheel riverboats, and both cheddar cheese and butter were shipped to San Francisco by steamboat.

Stop at ◈ **Bandon's Cheese Company** (541–347–2456), located on Highway 101, where you can see the "cheddaring" process take place in long stainless-steel vats. Large bricks of curd are carefully flipped over and over, then stacked to allow the whey to drain so that the curd can reach its optimum cheddar texture. In the gourmet gift shop, you can sample an assortment of mouth-watering varieties—from medium and aged sharp cheddar to a zingy jalapeño Jack.

Then, too, some 900 acres of cranberry bogs are under cultivation near Bandon. The original vines were brought from Cape Cod, Massachusetts, in 1879 by pioneer grower Charles McFarlin. In those days the Coos Indians helped pick the bright red berries with wooden-toothed scoops each autumn. The Bandon community celebrates a cranberry festival each September. You can take a cranberry bog tour at ◈ **Faber Farms,** 519 Morrison Road, and also browse through a small gift shop that offers cranberry coffeecake mix and brandied cranberries among other specialty items. During the fall harvest, shop hours are 9:00 A.M. to 5:00 P.M., Monday through Saturday. Call (541) 347–4300 to reserve space on the tour.

Displays of Indian artifacts and old photos of the cranberry harvest, as well as exhibits of local history—the town burned to the ground twice, in 1914 and 1936—can be seen at the **Bandon Historical Museum,** near the harbor and **Old Town** shops and eateries. Located in a large old U.S. Coast Guard building, the museum is open Tuesday through Sunday from 10:00 A.M. to 4:00 P.M. and is well worth a stop. If time allows, from here drive a couple of blocks up to the bluff top and turn onto **Beach Loop Drive;** wind along the ocean to see enormous sea stacks and large rocks filled with colonies of seabirds. There are several places to park and walk down to the beach, one being **Face Rock State Scenic Viewpoint.** This is one of the best beach walks on the south coast.

Within walking distance of the museum, you can enjoy a stroll through Old Town shops and galleries. On Baltimore Street the bulletin board outside **Andrea's Restaurant**—a favorite with the locals—usually lists the current schedule for the **Bandon Storm Watchers.** Beginning in January, this group of storm lovers hosts a series of a dozen or more enrichment programs on

Saturdays at 3:00 P.M. at the Bandon Community Center in City Park. From "Watching Sea Birds" to "Whales and Their Eating Habits" to "Tide Pools at Low Tide," the programs feature slide shows and lectures by local experts and provide an opportunity for you to mingle with friendly Bandon folks. For the current schedule call the Bandon Visitors' Center, (541) 347–9616. Ask too about the **Bandon Playhouse**—they usually do one musical production each summer.

Nestled alongside the Coquille River, just north of Bandon's Old Town marina, the **Coquille River Lighthouse**, now a museum, celebrated its centennial in 1996. You can access the historic structure from **Bullards Beach State Park** located just north of Bandon. Walk out the jetty trail to see spectacular ocean waves crash on the rocks that edge both sides of the Coquille River as it surges into the Pacific. The large state park offers RV sites, tent sites, and space for hiker-bicycle parties and for horse campers. Contact the state reservation number, (800) 452–5687, weekdays, 8:00 A.M. to 5:00 P.M.; Bullards Beach is open year-round.

For a pleasant side trip from Bandon, head east on Highway 42 for about 15 miles to Coquille, where you can take in an old-fashioned melodrama, such as *Sweet, Sweet Revenge* or *Live Women in the Mines,* at the ◆ **Sawdust Theatre** on Saturday evenings at 8:00 P.M. during June and on Fridays and Saturdays from July through Labor Day. The community's annual Gay 90's Celebration on the first Saturday of June launches the summer season. For current information call the Coquille Visitor's Center, (541) 396–3414.

To experience some of the most magnificent scenery on the south coast, detour from Highway 101 about 10 miles north of Bandon to Charleston and then double back to Sunset Bay, Shore Acres, and Cape Arago. This area can also be accessed from Coos Bay–North Bend, farther north.

Sandstone cliffs curve around picturesque, half-moon **Sunset Bay,** atop which are easy hiking trails. At low tide walk out along the rocks on the south side to explore tide pools filled with sea anemones, tiny crab, oblong chiton, and purple sea urchins. Wear sturdy shoes for this trek so as not to take a spill on wet rocks and slippery seaweed.

There are shady picnic areas, a large overnight campground, and a safe, sandy beach at Sunset Bay. For campsite reservations call (800) 452–5687. Plan to spend an hour or so visiting nearby ◆ **Shore Acres Gardens,** once the grand turn-of-the-century estate of a wealthy south coast lumberman, Louis J. Simpson, whose prospering business had been built by his father, Asa Meade Simpson, in the late 1800s. The garden is just a mile beyond Sunset Bay.

A wooded walkway invites visitors past a display illustrating the history of Shore Acres and the Simpson family, researched by Oregon historian Stephen Dow Beckham. The beautifully restored garden features enormous beds of elegant roses, lush plantings of dahlias, exotic tree species, and a lovely sunken Japanese garden. Along the nearby sea cliff is an enclosed gazebo where the mansion once perched—an excellent place to watch for whales and to safely view the crashing waves of winter storms. You'll notice, too, many uptilted ledges and massive out-croppings—ancient geology at its best on the south coast!

Easy hiking trails and picnic areas are also available on the grounds. The park is open year-round from dawn to dusk and is decorated with thousands of lights from the second week in December through New Year's Eve. Don't miss a visit to this stunning garden.

Drive on to **Cape Arago,** at the end of the road, for another panorama of wave-sculpted bluffs, for ocean breezes, and, often, for the cacophony of barking Steller sea lions, harbor seals, and elephant seals, on Simpson's Reef. You'll find secluded picnic tables and hiking trails here as well. Year-round camping is also available at nearby **Bastendorff Beach County Park,** along with a wide sandy beach and good views of the ocean. This less-crowded spot is excellent for flying kites and for walking along the beach.

Heading past the county park back toward Coos Bay–North Bend, notice the colorful boat harbor at **Charleston;** here visitors can go crabbing from the dock area. A small visitors' center near the bridge is open May to September and can provide information about crab nets and bait; call (541) 888–2311. Charter fishing excursions are also available at the Charleston Marina. Stop at the **Coffee Hub** in the Boat Basin for specialty coffees, Italian sodas, and fresh bagels.

If you're hungry for seafood and haven't the time to catch your own, stop at **Mo's Restaurant,** located at 700 South Broadway in Coos Bay, for delicious clam chowder, slumgullion, or tasty fish-and-chips. If your taste buds cater to more natural foods, try the **Blue Heron Bistro,** which is well-known for home-baked breads, tasty soups, delicious entrees, freshly made desserts, and gourmet coffee. The cafe, located at the corner of Commercial and Highway 101, is open daily from 9:00 A.M. to 9:00 P.M. (except major holidays).

For a tour through one of the south coast's myrtlewood factories, stop at **The Oregon Connection,** at the south edge of Coos Bay. You can tour the factory, watch the production process, and see local artisans create polished bowls, trays, cups, golf putters, and other handcrafted gift items from the rough myrtlewood logs.

As an added treat, more than twelve varieties of cream and butter fudge are made here—be sure to ask for a taste of your favorite. The gift shop also stocks many Northwest wines and an assortment of local and regional gourmet foods. The factory and gift shop are open every day (except Christmas, New Year's, and Thanksgiving days) from 8:00 A.M. to 5:00 P.M.; call (800) 255–5318 for more information.

For a visit to a historic newspaper and job-printing shop on the National Register of Historic Places, plan a summertime stop at the ◆*Marshfield Sun* **Printing Museum,** located at the corner of Front Street and Bayshore Drive (Highway 101) in Coos Bay. The *Marshfield Sun* newspaper was edited and published by Jesse Allen Luse from 1891 until 1944. You'll see a Washington handpress, a Chandler and Price platen press, and nearly 200 type cases and fonts of type on the main floor of the museum.

On the upper level are exhibits on the history of printing and on early Marshfield, which was Coos Bay's former name, as well as a collection of old U.S. newspapers. The museum is open during the summer Tuesday through Saturday from 1:00 to 4:00 P.M. Special open-house tours are also scheduled during the year, and a visit during winter months can be arranged by calling the Bay Area Visitors' Information Center at (541) 269–0215 or (800) 824–8486.

On the outskirts of North Bend, history buffs can stop at the **Coos-Curry Pioneer and Historical Association Museum** at Simpson Park, 1220 Sherman Street, for a look at south coast Indian and pioneer displays, exhibits, and vintage books and scrapbooks. On the grounds you'll see an old-time railroad steam engine and antique logging equipment. Just next door is the well-stocked North Bend Visitors' Information Center (541–756–4613) along with a shady picnic area and public rest rooms. The museum is open May through September Tuesday through Saturday from 10:00 A.M. to 4:00 P.M. Call the museum at (541) 756–6320 to make arrangements to visit during winter months. Ask the staff at the visitors' center which plays are currently running at **Little Theatre on the Bay** in North Bend or at **On Broadway Theater** in Coos Bay. Little Theatre is the second-oldest community theater in the state, having begun in 1948.

Heading north from Coos Bay–North Bend, you'll drive high above the bay via **McCullough Bridge,** one of the longest bridges constructed by the Works Progress Administration along the Oregon coast. Signed into law by President Franklin D. Roosevelt, the Works Progress Administration projects provided much-needed work for thousands of Americans during the Great Depression. McCullough Bridge is nearly a mile in length and was dedicated on June 5, 1936. The channel spans rise 150 feet to accommodate ships entering and leaving Coos Bay's large protected harbor.

Motoring with ease, one forgets that scenic Highway 101, with its many bridges spanning numerous rivers, was once a windswept wilderness laced with deer and Indian trails. In the 1800s both Indians and explorers traveled on foot, on horseback, by canoe, and, later, by ferry.

Actually, the journals of early mountain man Jedediah Smith and explorer Alexander McLeod often reported progress of less than 5 miles a day through thick coastal forests, over rugged ravines and valleys, and across rushing streams, rivers, and bays. Later, a stage-line route along the beach was established and remained in use until 1916. The stage operated on a "flexible" schedule—determined by the incoming or outgoing tide!

Much of **North** as well as **South Tenmile Lake** is still accessible only by boat, its many arms reaching into Coastal Range forests. Anglers return year after year to stalk the black bass, bluegill, trout, and catfish in the lake's waters. Good boat ramps, a marina, art boutiques, motels, and campgrounds are found in and about **Lakeside** and the **Tenmile Lakes** area. Ask, too, about floating houseboat rentals and the annual bass-fishing contest held each spring. Further information can be obtained from the Lakeside Visitors' Information Center, P.O. Box 333, Lakeside 97449 (541–759–3981).

WHALE-WATCHING TERRITORY

Travel north again on Highway 101 to **Winchester Bay,** the largest salmon-fishing harbor on the Oregon coast, and discover bustling **Salmon Harbor**—where the Umpqua River meets the Pacific Ocean—by turning west toward **Windy Cove Campground.** You'll find facilities here for launching seaworthy boats and for renting crabbing and fishing equipment; you'll also find custom canning, bait, fuel, and ice, as well as information about appropriate fishing licenses.

Charter deep-sea fishing trips are available throughout most of the year at Salmon Harbor; call the harbor office (541–271–3407) or the Reedsport–Winchester Bay Visitors' Center (541–271–3495) for information and current schedules.

Continue on the loop drive, following the south shore of Salmon Harbor, to discover ◆ **Umpqua Lighthouse.** From its impressive 65-foot tower, a bright red flash is seen some 16 miles at sea, the only colored signal on the Oregon coast. You can visit the Lighthouse Museum May 1 through September 30, Wednesday to Saturday, 10:00 A.M. to 5:00 P.M.; to arrange a guided tour limited to groups of six, call Douglas County Parks and Recreation, (541) 271–4631. Camping options include **Umpqua Lighthouse State Park** or nearby **Windy Cove** (800–452–5687 for reservations); or, for RV spaces and cottages on lovely Half Moon Bay call the folks at **Discovery Point Resort,** (541) 271–3443. You could also sleep in splendid comfort aboard a replica of a stern-wheel paddleboat, *Salmon Harbor Belle* **Bed & Breakfast;** for information call (541) 271–1137.

At Reedsport you can walk along reconstructed boardwalks that are reminiscent of the industrial area that housed canneries and sawmill sheds in earlier days, and learn about the small coastal town's history at the new ◆ **Umpqua Discovery Center.** It is located near the boardwalk at 409 Riverfront Way in Old Town, just off Highway 101 (541–271–4816). The kids will enjoy peeking through the center's periscope for a 360-degree view of the Umpqua River, nearby railroad swing bridge, and jet-boat dock. You can also tour the 125-foot polar research sailing vessel, *Hero,* permanently moored here as part of an Antarctic exhibit. The center is open 10:00 A.M. to 6:00 P.M. from May 15 to September 30; winter hours are 10:00 A.M. to 4:00 P.M. except Mondays and

11

Tuesdays. Snacks are available at the Schooner Cafe on the board-walk. You can also explore the scenic Umpqua River, home to bald eagles, many gamefish species, and protected Roosevelt elk, on the 680-horsepower jet boat, *Miss Umpqua,* during summer months. For further information call the Lower Umpqua Visitors' Center in Reedsport at (800) 247–2155.

If you decide to drive east toward Roseburg and I–5 via High-way 38, be sure to pull off at the ◆ **Dean Creek Elk Viewing Area** just 3 miles east of Reedsport and near the Umpqua River. Pause at Hinsdale Interpretive Center for helpful displays and to peek through the viewing scope, then gaze out over nearly 500 acres of bottomland and 600 acres of hilly woodlands where the mammoth elk roam free. Depending on the time of day, you may also see a parade of other wildlife such as black bear, porcu-pine, coyote, and raccoon as well as many bird species.

Just south of Florence, detour at the ◆ **Oregon Dunes Over-look,** a scenic pullout area whose handicap-accessible observa-tion decks offer good views of the ocean and dunes. In the Oregon Dunes are twelve developed trails, ranging from a ¾-mile stroll along a small lagoon to a 6-mile hike through Douglas fir forests and rugged dunes. Maps and information about other accessible sand dune areas can be obtained from the well-stocked Oregon Dunes National Recreation Area Headquarters, 855 Highway 101, Reedsport 97467 (541–271–3611).

At the junction of Highway 101 and Highway 126, near the mouth of the Siuslaw River, stop and explore Florence, a thriving community of some 5,000 coast dwellers. ◆ **Old Town Flor-ence,** along the river near Bay Street, is a pleasant place to stroll and poke into charming shops, galleries, and eateries housed in some of the town's most historic buildings.

For a look at the oldest structure, walk a block or so to the cor-ner of First and Maple Streets to see the **Johnson House,** a large, two-story, white saltbox-style house that is nearly a hundred years old. Now completely renovated, it's open to travelers as a bed-and-breakfast inn, Florence's first. Along Bay Street, in Old Town, shop and eat at **Traveler's Cove Cafe;** enjoy great sun-daes and cones at **BJ's Ice Cream;** have tea and scones at **Old English Tea Company;** or stop in for a steaming cup of espresso or cappuccino at **Old Town Coffee Company.** It's just across the street from the Kite Shop and an old-fashioned gazebo in tiny **Old Town Park,** where you can sit with a view

Salmon Harbor

of the Siuslaw River and its vintage bridge, circa 1936, constructed by the Works Progress Administration.

If you haven't time to try catching your own crab but would like to see how it's done, drive or ride a bike to the ◆ **South Jetty,** walk out on the large wooden pier, and watch folks lower bait-filled crab rings into the churning waters. Here you're on the Siuslaw River estuary, where the river meets the Pacific Ocean— surging mightily against the oncoming tides. *Siuslaw* is an Indian

13

word meaning "far away waters." Most of the lakes in the area have special Indian names: *Cleawox,* meaning "paddle wood"; *Siltcoos,* meaning "plenty elk"; and *Tahkenitch,* meaning "many arms."

If you visit from November through February, look for the squadron of some 200 snowy white tundra swans that winter on the Siuslaw River's marshes near South Jetty. *Note:* It's a good idea to bring rain gear, waterproof boots, and binoculars.

If you'd just as soon ride a horse, check with the friendly folks at **C and M Stables,** located 8 miles north of Florence at 90241 Highway 101 North, to reserve a gentle steed for beach and sunset rides, dune trail rides, or winter rides. On a trusty mount follow the trail through a lush alder forest down to the dunes and beach, perhaps spying deer, ducks, swans, and geese in the dune marsh areas along the way. You might even see a stately Roosevelt elk or an elusive coyote. For reservations call (541) 997–7540. The stables are open daily from June through October but closed on Mondays and Tuesdays during winter months. Call ahead from Florence for reservations. For lodging alternatives, including bed-and-breakfast inns and economical motels, stop at the Florence Area Visitors' Center, 270 Highway 101 (P.O. Box 26000), Florence 97439; (541) 997–3128.

Before continuing on, stop for picnic foods and beverages at the large market at the junction of Highway 101 and Highway 126. For homemade jams and jellies don't pass up **Woodsman Native Nursery** just 2 miles north of Florence.

Next turn off Highway 101 at the **Darlingtonia Wayside** sign, pull into the visitor parking area, and follow the shaded trail to the boardwalk that takes you out onto a marshy bog. This is one of the few small nature preserves in the United States set aside for conserving a single native species. *Darlingtonia californica* is often called cobra lily because it captures and actually digests insects. You can see the unusual greenish-speckled tubular-shaped plants here from spring through summer and into early fall.

Your next stop is **Devil's Elbow State Park,** just beyond Cape Creek Bridge, where you can walk the forested trail over to **Heceta Lighthouse.** The lighthouse is open for touring May through September, noon to 5:00 P.M. daily and July through August, 11:00 A.M. to 6:00 P.M. on weekends. The lightkeeper's house offers three bed-and-breakfast guest rooms available Thursday through Monday. For information call the Siuslaw National Forest office, (541) 563–3211. The park's sheltered beach offers a lovely spot to picnic and to beachcomb for shells and driftwood. Offshore, the large rock "islands," part of the **Oregon Islands National Wildlife Refuge,** are transient nesting grounds for tufted puffin, cormorants, pigeon guillemots, and numerous kinds of seagulls.

By now, midway on your coastal trek, you have surely felt the magic of the ocean seeping into your bones. Emanating from the rhythmic tides and from the sound of the surf is a calmness that erases stress and causes one to relax into nature's cycles for a time. Even words like *magnificent, incredible,* and *awesome* seem inadequate to describe the wide-angle views along this stretch of the Oregon coast. It's a panoramic showstopper of the first order, and nearly every inch of it is open to the public. One such dramatic encounter is found by walking down the short trail at ◈ **Devil's Churn Wayside** to watch incoming waves as they thunder and foam into a narrow basalt fissure; this is especially dramatic on the incoming tide. *Note:* wear sturdy walking shoes and use caution here, especially with children.

For another spectacular view drive up to ◈ **Cape Perpetua** and its visitors' center, just a short distance off Highway 101, perched atop a jagged chunk of 40-million-year-old volcanic basalt. The Forest Service staff offer lots to see and do at Cape Perpetua, including six nature trails, campfire talks at Tillicum Beach, and naturalist-led hikes down to the tide pools, together with interpretive exhibits and films on marine fish, animal life, and plant life. The visitors' center is open all summer, every day, from 9:00 A.M. to 6:00 P.M.; call (541) 547–3289 for more information. Also within the area are group picnic areas, a campground, and a 22-mile self-guided auto tour.

For a pleasant bed-and-breakfast experience on the central coast, there are several possibilities in Yachats. **New England House Bed & Breakfast** offers a romantic haven with large windows that look out to the ocean and to an intimate English garden; full breakfast and lovely afternoon tea are offered to guests (541–547–4799). **Kittiwake Bed & Breakfast** offers two guest rooms with ocean views from cozy window seats, also a reading and whale-watching room (541–547–4470 or e-mail: jszewc@orednet.org). ◈ **Sea Quest Bed & Breakfast** offers five splendid guest rooms, all within 100 feet of the sandy beach and the melodious ocean surf. "Remember to pack your kite and your beach walking gear," say the innkeepers. For reservations call (541) 547–3782.

15

Try **New Morning Coffee House and Back Porch Gallery** on Highway 101 at Fourth Street for great espresso and pastries. Breakfast and lunch are offered Wednesday through Sunday. For additional information contact the Yachats Area Visitors' Center, P.O. Box 728, Yachats 97498 (541–547–3530).

Detour from Highway 101 at Waldport and meander 9½ miles east on Highway 34 to enjoy breakfast, lunch, or dinner at ◈ **Kozy Kove Kafe.** Darla and Jim O'Kane operate their floating restaurant on the Alsea River at Tidewater. They can also provide mooring, boat rentals, and fishing guides—the fall chinook salmon fishing is usually very good here. During your meal (one of Darla's specialties is smoked salmon chowder) you might spy harbor seals that have swum into the river from the ocean on the tide and, along the riverbank, wild goats and grazing deer and elk. For reservations and current hours call (541) 528–3251. At Tidewater turn at the grocery/RV park/marina; park and walk down the ramp; you won't see the "kafe" from the highway because it floats below the bank.

Continuing north again on Highway 101 for about 20 miles to Newport, two more lighthouses await—the **Yaquina Bay Lighthouse** in Yaquina Bay State Park, and the ◈ **Yaquina Head Lighthouse,** 3 miles north and 1 mile west of the highway. Both are open for touring usually from noon to 5:00 P.M. Yaquina Head's tower, rising 93 feet, is especially dramatic; you can tour the tower watch room between 9:00 A.M. and noon from mid-June to mid-September. Its light has remained active since 1873. Be sure to notice the colonies of seabirds on the offshore island here. Call (541) 265–2863 for current visitor information.

Most everyone who travels through this part of the coast will plan a stop at the **Oregon Coast Aquarium** to see ◈ **Keiko,** the famous eighteen-year-old Orca whale who was brought to Newport in 1996 from Mexico City. The Orca, with his striking black-and-white markings, starred in the movie *Free Willy*. The staff's goal is to restore Keiko to optimum health, teach him essential survival skills, and someday reunite him with his Orca pod in the waters off the coast of Iceland. Both the aquarium and the **Hatfield Marine Science Center** are located just beneath the Yaquina Bay Bridge at the south edge of town. Hours are 9:00 A.M. to 6:00 P.M. daily during summer months and 10:00 A.M. to 4:30 P.M. the rest of the year. For current information call (541) 867–3474 or try the web site at http://www.aquaruim.org.

Yaquina Head Lighthouse

To immerse yourself in central coast history, plan to stop at the **Burrows House Museum** and the **Log Cabin Museum,** both cared for by the Lincoln County Historical Society, at 545 SW Ninth Street in Newport. Both museums are open June through September from 10:00 A.M. to 5:00 P.M. daily and October through May from 11:00 A.M. to 4:00 P.M. each day but Monday. Call (541) 265–7509 for more information.

Before leaving the Newport area, you can refill your picnic basket or cooler from the carry-out section at **Canyon Way Restaurant,** which features homemade pastas, delicious breads, meat- or seafood-filled croissants, and pastries that include chocolate creations and delicious tortes. Located at 1216 SW Canyon Way, just a half-block up from the bay-front area, the restaurant is open Monday through Saturday from 11:00 A.M. to 3:00 P.M.

Another historic structure in Newport, this one located in the historic Nye Beach area, is the renovated **Sylvia Beach Hotel,** at 267 NW Cliff Street (541–265–5428). The building dates to 1910, was saved from the wrecker's ball by Sally Ford and Goodrun Cable, and is dedicated to the memory of Sylvia Beach, owner of the Shakespeare and Company Bookstore in Paris during the 1920s and 1930s and one of the twentieth century's great patrons of literature. Each of the twenty guest rooms is furnished and decorated to reflect a different well-known author.

If you'd rather sleep in less bohemian style (and if you have feline allergies), try the five-year-old ◆**Nye Beach Hotel** instead, also perched on a bluff above the Pacific. At the front desk tropical birds preen and squawk in colorful harmony, and in your room you'll find a gas fireplace, a whirlpool tub, and a down comforter on the bed. The ocean view is nonstop. You might hunker down in the cafe, on a windscreened and heated deck, for a late dinner of black-bean enchiladas, Cajun grilled oysters, or crab cakes. For hotel reservations call the staff at (541) 265–3334.

The Newport Visitors' Information Center offers travelers a toll-free number for obtaining current information about the variety of goings-on in the Yaquina Bay area; call (800) 262–7844.

Heading north again on Highway 101, you can access an optional scenic loop along the sea cliff, **Otter Crest Scenic Loop Drive,** at Otter Rock. First drive out to the bluff to peer down into **Devil's Punch Bowl,** a rounded outcropping into which the ocean thunders foamy waves: an especially dramatic display during winter storms, as well as on the incoming tide. The tiny Mo's Restaurant here offers good clam chowder, slumgullion, and fish & chips. The loop drive reconnects with Highway 101 within a couple of miles.

If you're driving through the area at low tide—you can pick up current tide tables for a nominal cost at most visitors' centers—stop at the **Inn at Otter Crest,** parking close to the ocean, just beyond the Flying Dutchman Restaurant. Walk a short path down to the beach, where you can see a fascinating array of **tide pools** formed by rounded depressions in the large volcanic rocks. Bathed by tidal currents twice each day, coastal tide pools may house a variety of species such as sea anenomes, sea urchins, goose barnacles, sea stars, sea slugs, limpets, jellyfish, and tiny crab.

Just a few precautions, however, from the naturalists: Seaweed is slippery, so you should avoid jumping from rock to rock; keep an eye on the incoming tide; watch for large "sneaker" waves that can appear out of the regular wave pattern; stay away from rolling logs, which can move quickly onto an unsuspecting tide-pooler, particularly a small child; don't remove marine creatures from the tide pools or take any live specimens with you.

Combing Oregon's driftwood-strewn beaches can yield other treasures, however, ones that *can* be taken home, such as limpet and barnacle shells, sand-dollar shells, Japanese glass floats, dried kelp, driftwood, beach rocks, and translucent agates.

If your picnic basket and cooler are full of goodies and cold beverages, consider a lunch stop at one of the most charming coastal day parks, **Fogarty Creek Wayside,** just north of Depoe Bay and Pirate's Cove. Here you can walk a path that meanders through the day-use park, alongside a small creek, and through a tunnel under the highway to a small sandy cove right on the edge of the ocean. Weather permitting, you can have your picnic with seagulls and sandpipers for company. In the park are picnic tables and rest rooms. It's a great place for families with small children.

If, however, you're driving through this section of the central coast early in the day and the ocean is flat and shimmering in the morning sun, consider stopping at the seawall in **Depoe Bay,** just south of Fogarty Creek, to see whether the gray whales are swimming past. Of the seven different kinds of whales plying the Pacific Ocean, the grays maneuver closest to the shoreline. Some 15,000 of the mammoth creatures migrate south from

November to January and return north from March to May. This 12,000-mile round-trip is the longest known for any mammal.

Equipment for **whale watching** is minimal—helpful are good binoculars, a camera and tripod, and warm clothing. Or just shade your eyes and squint, gazing west toward the horizon. You might be rewarded for your patience by seeing one of the grays "breach," that is, leap high out of the water and then fall back with a spectacular splash.

During one week in January and another week in March, about 200 volunteers at whale-watching sites all along the coast offer helpful information, brochures, maps, and assistance with spotting the gray whales. Look for the familiar logo WHALE WATCH-ING SPOKEN HERE and for the volunteers, ranging from school kids to oldsters, whose efforts are coordinated by the Oregon Parks and recreation Department (503–563–2002) and the staff at the **Hatfield Marine Science Center** in Newport.

At both Shore Acres, located west of Coos Bay–North Bend, and at Cape Perpetua, north of Florence, you can view whales from glassed-in areas and stay dry to boot. For information and a current schedule call the oceanographers and volunteers at Oregon State University Extension/Sea Grant, Hatfield Marine Science Center, 2030 Marine Science Drive, Newport 97365; (503) 867–3011.

Should you decide to stay overnight in the area, check out **Whale Inn** at Depot Bay located at 416 Highway 101 North (541–765–2789). Books from the 1920s and 1930s that match the room's theme grace the bedside stands, and antiques of every sort, from cheap to outrageous, are for sale in each of the eleven guest rooms. It's great fun.

In Gleneden Beach, tucked into the woods like Hansel and Gretel's cottage, **Chez Jeanette** offers one of the most romantic dining settings on the central coast. Fresh bread and marvelous desserts are baked every day, and the house specialties of fresh seafood, veal, and game are served with several different vegetables and two kinds of fruit. The tiny restaurant is located ½ mile south of Salishan Lodge on the Gleneden Beach Loop, 7150 Old Highway 101. Open daily for dinner from 5:30 to 9:00 P.M.; call (541) 764–3434 for reservations.

Nestled in a hillside setting of coast pine and Douglas fir, **Salishan Lodge** offers spacious and comfortable guest suites, an art gallery, a golf course, indoor tennis courts, an indoor swimming pool, and gourmet dining in the inn's three restaurants.

The wine cellar is exemplary. For further information and reservations call the staff at (800) 452–2300. Directly across Highway 101 from the lodge you'll find a lively **MarketPlace** of small boutiques, book shops, and eateries, and, at the north end, a lovely **Nature Trail** that skirts tiny **Siletz Bay.**

Following all this whale-spying and gourmet eating, stop by ◈ **Catch the Wind Kite Shop** at 266 SE Highway 101 (541–994–9500) in Lincoln City for a look at kites of all sizes, shapes, colors, and prices. It's located just across the highway from the D River Wayside beach, where, on a particularly windy day, you can watch spectacular and brightly colored kites being flown by kids of all ages. There are wheelchair-accessible rest rooms here and a visitors' information booth as well. Try **Cafe Roma** on Highway 101, near NW Fifteenth Street (541–994–6616), for homestyle soups and chowder, fresh-roasted coffees, and home-made pastries and desserts.

For helpful information about the entire Lincoln City area, stop at the visitors' center at the far north end of town, at 801 SW Highway 101 (541) 994–2164 or (800) 452–2151. Ask, too, for directions to the nearby ◈**Connie Hansen Garden**—a true plantswoman's botanical paradise; on two city lots, the garden is now lovingly cared for by a group of dedicated volunteers and is open daily. Call for current hours: (541) 994–6338.

ON LEWIS AND CLARK'S TRAIL

Leaving the bustling Lincoln City area, travelers notice a quieter, more pastoral ambience along Highway 101, which winds north from Otis toward Neskowin, Sandlake, Cape Lookout, Netarts, and Tillamook. Those who travel through this region in the early spring will see dairy cows munching lush green grass inside white-fenced fields, clumps of skunk cabbage blooming in bright yellows, and old apple trees bursting with pale pink blossoms on gnarled limbs.

Native Oregon grape crowds along the roadside, with tight clusters of bright yellow blooms; low-lying salal, with its bell-shaped delicate pink flowers, carpets forested areas; and gangly salmonberry bushes show pale white blossoms. On a coastal trek this is clearly the time to slow the pace and enjoy a kaleidoscope of springtime colors.

If your sweetheart is along you might want to spend a night

near Proposal Rock, at ✦ **Proposal Rock Inn** in the charming community of Neskowin. For reservations call the staff at (503) 392–3115. There are several restaurants and a lovely golf course in the vicinity as well. For additional information about the area, contact the Nestucca Valley Visitors' Center, P.O. Box 75, Cloverdale 97112; (503) 392–3456.

Heading north on Highway 101 detour onto **Three Capes Scenic Drive,** heading toward Pacific City so that you can watch the launching of the ✦ **Dory Fleet,** one of the coast's most unusual fishing fleets. In the shadow of **Cape Kiwanda,** a towering sandstone headland, salmon-fishers from the Pacific City area launch flat-bottomed dories from the sandy beach into the protected waters near the large, offshore rock islands where those ever-present sea birds congregate.

You could also arrive in the late afternoon to see the flat-bottomed dories return with the day's catch, skimming across the water and right onto the beach. The boats are then loaded onto large trailers for the night. Then, too, keep watch for those hardy souls who can often be spotted hang-gliding from Cape Kiwanda. If you're hungry, stop at **Grateful Bread Bakery** (34805 Brooten Road; 503–965–7337) for scrumptious baked goods and some of the coast's best breads as well as good sandwiches, take-out service, and an outside deck. For information about the dory fleet and about dory fishing trips, contact the Pacific City–Woods Visitors' Information Center, P.O. Box 331, Pacific City 97135 (503–965–6161).

Just north of Sandlake, nature trails at **Cape Lookout** offer a close-up view of a typical coastal rain forest that includes such species as Sitka spruce, western hemlock, western red cedar, and red alder. A thick tangle of salal, box blueberry, salmonberry, sword fern, and Pacific wax myrtle covers the forest floor beyond the path.

Then dig out the binoculars and stop far off the beaten path, at the tiny community of **Oceanside,** to walk on the beach and see **Three Arch Rocks.** These offshore islands, set aside in 1907 by President Theodore Roosevelt as the first wildlife preserve on the Pacific Coast, are home to thousands of black petrels, colorful tufted puffins, and penguinlike murres, along with several varieties of gulls and cormorants. The bellow of resident stellar sea lions and sea pups can often be heard as well. From 500-foot

Maxwell Point to the north, you'll often see those hang-gliders taking off into the wind. The glider pilots say that curious eagles sometimes fly along with them. *Note:* Rest-room facilities are located near the public parking area. There are small eateries here and overnight accommodations, some overlooking the ocean. For specific information contact the Tillamook Visitors' Center, 3705 Highway 101 North, Tillamook 97141; (503) 842–7525.

From Oceanside continue north to the third cape, Cape Meares, which lies about 10 miles northwest of the thriving dairy community of Tillamook. Stop to visit the **Cape Meares Lighthouse** and also walk the short trail to see the **Octopus Tree,** an unusual Sitka spruce with six trunks. Bordering the paved path to the lighthouse are thick tangles of ruby rugosa roses with large burgundy blossoms; they're especially suited to salt air and coastal mists. You may well see folks sketching or photographing the picturesque circa 1890s structure that was deactivated in 1963. A photomural display is open daily during summer months, with friendly volunteers on hand to provide historic tales about the lighthouse. You can also learn about Tillamook County's history at the incredibly well-stocked **Pioneer Museum** located in the old Courthouse building at 2106 Second Street in Tillamook. You'll see the stagecoach that carried mail in the county's early days, several vintage horseless carriages, logging memorabilia along with stuffed animals and birds, the replica of a fire lookout, and a kitchen of yesteryear. The museum is a delight for all ages to visit. Hours are Monday through Saturday, 8:30 A.M. to 5:00 P.M., and Sundays noon to 5:00 P.M. (closed Mondays during winter months). For further information contact the museum staff at (503) 842–4553.

Linger awhile longer on this less populated section of the coast to visit the world's largest clear-span wooden structure, the ❖ **World War II Blimp Hangar Museum,** and its collection of historic photographs, memorabilia, and vintage airplanes. The building, more than twenty stories high and ⅕ mile long, was the site of Tillamook's Naval Air Station from 1942 to 1948. During World War II it was essentially a blimp site. Avid airplane buffs are restoring a number of vintage aircraft, such as a F4U Corsair; a 1942 Stinson V-77 Reliant; a PBY-5A Catalina; a JZF flying boat called *The Duck*; and an MK-8, one of the famous Spitfires that helped win the Battle of Britain. You can watch the restoration process and, weather permitting, enjoy a short scenic flight in one of the vintage planes. Operated by the Port of Tillamook Bay, the museum is open daily 9:00 A.M. to 6:00 P.M. from May to October and is open until 5:00 P.M. the remainder of the year (except major holidays). It's located 2 miles south of Tillamook, just off Highway 101, at 6030 Hangar Road. Needless to say, you can't miss spotting it! The telephone number is (503) 842–1130.

Just a mile north of Tillamook, in a converted dairy barn, the **Blue Heron French Cheese Factory** offers visitors delicious French-style Brie and Camembert cheeses. You can sample not only the cheeses but a good selection of Oregon wines and can purchase other international cheeses and deli foods. The tasting room and deli are located at 2001 Blue Heron Drive, just off Highway 101; the phone number is (503) 842–8281. The establishment is open daily from 8:00 A.M. to 8:00 P.M. during summer and from 9:00 A.M. to 5:00 P.M. during winter.

If you're itching to do a bit of shopping for coastal antiques, stop first in the tiny hamlet of Wheeler and find **Laknes's Pieffenschneider Antique Mall** just across from the train depot. It's filled with an eclectic mix of vintage furniture and small collectibles. For further information contact Lorraine Laknes at (503) 368–5197. Hours are 10:00 A.M. to 6:00 P.M. Monday through Saturday.

You want to try camping on the coast but you don't have a tent? Well, not to worry, both **Cape Lookout** and **Nehalem Bay State Campgrounds** near Tillamook offer a fun alternative to setting up a tent. Try ◆ **Yurt camping** in a stationary circular domed tent with a wood floor, structural wall supports, electricity, and a skylight. In fact, six other coastal campgrounds, and several inland campgrounds, offer a number of yurts in addition to regular tent sites and RV sites. Your yurt is furnished with a bunk bed, fold-out couch, small table, and space heater; bring your own sleeping bags or bedding and your own food and cooking gear. For further information and to reserve your very own yurt, call the toll-free state campground reservation number, Reservations Northwest: (800) 452–5687.

Highway 101 soon skirts Nehalem Bay and wends through the village of Nehalem, known for crabbing and clamming and for fine fishing. Angling for silver and chinook salmon, cutthroat, native trout, and steelhead is among the best along the Nehalem

River and bay area; there's a marina here with both free boat launches and private moorages. Canoe races are held on the river each spring.

For a second antiques shopping foray, trundle into **Nehalem Antique Mall,** where you can browse among an array of antique oak furniture, old books, excellent glassware, and a plethora of intriguing collectibles offered by fifty aficionados of vintage stuff, active dealers who rent space from the mall's enthusiastic owner, Carolyn Crowe. You can also pick up a free copy of *Old Stuff,* a voluminous tabloid that contains maps and information about antiques-hunting all over Oregon and the Northwest. For further information about the area—including fishing and crabbing, bicycle and horse trails, and annual festivals—contact the Nehalem Bay Area Visitors' Center, P.O. Box 159, Eighth and Tohl Streets, Nehalem 97131; (503) 368–5100.

Highway 101 now winds past Manzanita, where you could detour for delicious marionberry muffins and coffee at cozy ◆**Manzanita News and Espresso;** for crumpets and tea at **Queen Bess Tea Room** (Laneda and Fourth Avenues); or for dinner at **Blue Sky Cafe** (154 Laneda Avenue), served Wednesday through Sunday. Then, wind high atop Neahkahnie Mountain and proceed down to one of the north coast's most hidden coves and beach areas, ◆**Short Sand Beach** and **Oswald West Park.** If you seek a truly remote camping experience, try one of the thirty-six primitive campsites at Oswald West. Alternatively, have your beachside picnic at one of the many picnic spots at Short Sand Beach.

Here you can explore the agate- and driftwood-strewn cove, snoop into shallow caves and caverns, fish or wade in an icy creek or shallow streams, peer at delicate tide pools housed in large rock depressions, and let the sounds of the surf lull you to sleep on a blanket or, better yet, in a tent with the moon and stars casting shimmering bands of light across the water.

The particulars: Park in the large designated parking area along Highway 101 and walk the ½-mile trail to the beach, through old-growth Douglas fir, coast pines, salal, salmonberry, and ferns growing in lush profusion along the way. Wheelbarrows are available at the parking area for hauling in camping gear; the primitive campsites are reached by a ¼-mile trail from the picnic area. A section of the **Oregon Coast Hiking Trail** passes through the area as well. This remote beach area is accessible only by foot, a fact that tends to keep the crowds away, and it is not wheelchair-accessible. For further information contact the State Parks Office in Portland, 3554 SE Eighty-second Avenue, Portland 97266 (503–238–7488).

Sleeping in a tent on the sand is not your thing? Well, not to worry, there are dozens of motels, cozy bed-and-breakfast inns, and a new forty-six room hostelry on the beach, **Stephanie Inn,** located at the south edge of Cannon Beach, just a few miles north via Highway 101. With your private deck, gas fireplace, VCR, terry-cloth robes, whirlpool tub, and evening turn-down service, and, after a marvelous night's rest lulled by soothing ocean sounds, when you awake to the delicious smells of fresh-brewed coffee and freshly baked breakfast breads, you'll wonder how a traveler could ask for more comfortable or civilized accommodations. For further information call the staff at (503) 436–2221.

Park the car in downtown Cannon Beach and pull on tennis shoes and warm windbreakers for a walk on the beach to nearby **Haystack Rock,** the north coast's venerable landmark that houses colonies of seabirds and myriad tide pools. Then you could browse through Cannon Beach's main street art galleries, boutiques, and bookshops, or sip hot coffee and enjoy clam chowder at cozy cafes like **Dooger's** or **The Bistro** (also on Hemlock Street).

At the north edge of Cannon Beach, access and drive the shaded winding road up to **Ecola State Park** for one of the most dramatic seascape panoramas on the north coast. In the lush 1,300-acre park, you'll see splendid examples of old-growth Sitka spruce, western hemlock forest, native shrubs, and wildflower species. Deer and elk often browse nearby, and picnic tables are tucked here and there, many sheltered from coastal breezes. The views are spectacular, particularly on blue-sky days; walk the trails along the ledges and remain safely behind the fenced areas. You can spy migrating whales during winter months and ask questions of whale-watching volunteers stationed on the bluff during mid-March. *Note:* There are rest-room facilities here. Further information about the area can be obtained from the Cannon Beach Visitors' Center located at Second and Spruce Streets, P.O. Box 64, Cannon Beach 97110. The telephone number is (503) 436–2623.

For those who want to plan hikes along the **Oregon Coast**

Trail, some of which passes through scenic Ecola State Park and **Indian Beach,** maps and current information can be obtained from the State Parks and Recreation Division, 1115 Commercial Street NE, Salem 97310. The telephone number is (503) 378–6305.

Follow Highway 101 north to one of Oregon's oldest resort towns, Seaside, where families have vacationed since the turn of the century. For a nostalgic experience park the car on any side street near the ocean and walk as far as you like on the ❖ **Historic Seaside Promenade**—a 2-mile-long sidewalk, with its old-fashioned railing restored, that skirts the wide sandy beach. Benches are available here and there for sitting, and about the only discordant note in this pleasant reminiscence—folks have walked "the Prom" since the early 1900s—may be an occasional bevy of youngsters sailing by on roller skates.

The Lewis and Clark expedition reached the Pacific Ocean in 1804, near the Seaside area, and you can see the original salt cairn—just off the south section of the Prom on Lewis and Clark Avenue—where the company boiled seawater to make salt during the rainy winter of 1805.

Standing regally on the corner of Beach Drive and Avenue A is one of Seaside's historic homes, circa 1890, now the elegant **Gilbert Inn Bed and Breakfast.** Owners Carole and Dick Rees transformed the old dowager into a bed-and-breakfast inn and offer travelers ten spacious guest suites. In the Turrett Room on the second floor, you can sleep in a queen-size four-poster amid romantic, country French–style decor.

Carole serves a marvelous breakfast that includes such delights as layered French toast with warm apricot sauce, along with the usual gourmet coffees, teas, freshly squeezed juices, and fresh fruit. For reservations contact the innkeepers at 341 Beach Drive, Seaside 97138 (503–738–9770).

For a close-up look at Lewis and Clark's 1804–06 winter head-quarters, visit ❖ **Fort Clatsop National Monument,** about 10 miles north of Seaside, near Astoria. Walk the winding path from the interpretive center to the log replica of the encampment. Here, from June to September, you can see a living-history program that includes buckskin-clad park rangers, live musket firing, boat carving, tanning, and map making—all frontier skills used by the company during that first, very rainy winter.

Within 25 miles are several sites described in the Lewis and

Clark journals. The Fort Clatsop brochure, available at the visitors' center, gives all the details and a helpful map.

Additional information about Fort Clatsop and about the annual summertime Lewis and Clark historical drama, *Journey to the Pacific,* can be obtained form the well-stocked Seaside Visitors' Information Center, 7 North Roosevelt Street, P.O. Box 7, Seaside 97138; (503) 738–6391 or (800) 444–6740.

Not far from the Lewis and Clark encampment, enterprising John Jacob Astor founded Astoria—just six years later, in 1811. Settled for the purpose of fur trading, the bustling seaport at the mouth of the Columbia River grew into a respectable city during the late 1800s. You can take a walking or a driving tour and see some of the 400 historic structures still remaining, including the historic **Astor Column** high atop Coxcomb Hill, and restored Victorian homes, many of them now open as comfortable bed-and-breakfast inns.The Astoria Visitors' Center will have a helpful list and brochures. You can also write or call for a current copy of the Oregon Bed & Breakfast Directory, P.O. Box 1283, Grants Pass 97526; (800) 841–5448.

Built in 1883 by Captain George Flavel, the **Flavel Mansion Museum** is one of the finest examples of Victorian architecture in the state. Located on Eighth Street, between Exchange and Duane Streets, this impressive structure, with its columned porches, carved gingerbread detailing, and tall cupola, is worth a visit. The mansion is open daily. For further information call the Clatsop County Historical Society at (503) 325–2203. Ask, too, about visiting **Uppertown Firefighters Museum** on Thirtieth and Marine Drive, open on weekends. Its fine collection of fire-fighting equipment dates from 1877–1963.

Fort Astoria, on Exchange Street, is a partially restored fort, originally built by Astor's Pacific Fur Company in 1811. Nearby is the site of the first U.S. post office west of the Rocky Mountains, established in 1847. For a copy of *An Explorer's Guide to Historic Astoria,* contact the Astoria/Warrenton Visitors' Information Center, 111 West Marine Drive (P.O. Box 176), Astoria 97103 (503–325–6311).

If you travel along the north coast during winter and early spring, stop and visit the **Twilight Eagle Sanctuary,** located just 8 miles east of Astoria, and $\frac{1}{2}$ mile north of Highway 30 on Burnside Road. The protected area offers prime feeding and roost-

Historic Astor Column

ing for about forty-eight eagles. You can identify the noble birds by their white heads and tails, large beaks, and yellow legs. Then, too, during all four seasons, bird lovers far and wide find one of the best places on the coast to watch an enormous variety of bird species from the viewing platform at **Fort Stevens State Park,** located 10 miles west of Astoria near Hammond. Be sure to take along your binoculars or cameras with telephoto lenses. Call (503) 861–1671 to inquire about yurts and campsites at Fort Stevens.

And, to complete your tour of the coast, you can do as many families did at the turn of the century—cross the Columbia River (now via the graceful Astoria-Megler Bridge) and drive a few miles up to the historic **Long Beach Peninsula** in Washington state. Take in the **World Kite Museum** at Third Street NW (360–542–4020) and see fascinating exhibits that show the history of kites and kite-flying and feature intriguing designs by prominent kite artists; fly kites or dig for clams on the wide sandy beach; take in the annual "Jazz and Oysters" or other concerts sponsored by the Water Music Festival; and find a great place to stay the night, such as the historic **Shelburne Inn** (360–642–2442), the charming **Gumm's Bed and Breakfast** (360–642–8887), or **Moby Dick Hotel,** a 1929 structure restored as a ten-room bed and breakfast (complete with its own small oyster farm), (360–665–4543). The Long Beach Peninsula Visitors Bureau at (800) 451–2542 can provide information about upcoming events and maps showing Seaview, Long Beach, Nahcotta, and Oysterville.

If you're looking for a way to enjoy a day at the beach and do a good deed at the same time, you can participate in one of the twice-yearly ◆ **Great Oregon Beach Cleanup** events. It's work, it's great fun, and it happens along the entire coast, from Brookings in the south to Astoria in the north. A couple of years ago beach cleanup volunteers found a plethora of stuff from a shipping accident in which forty-nine containers had washed overboard some 2,000 miles off the Oregon coast—such items as hockey gear, athletic shoes, sandals, and even Spiderman toys. Scientists tracked ocean currents for months by following the journey of thousands of tennis shoes. For current information and dates call the friendly Beach Cleanup staff at (503) 844–9571 or toll free at (800) 322–3326.

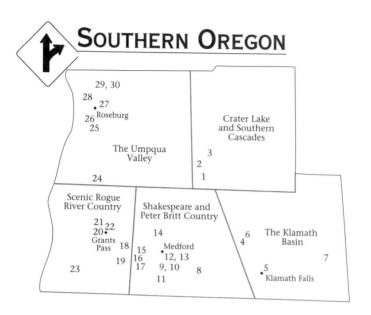

SOUTHERN OREGON

1. Crater Lake Rim Drive
2. Diamond Lake Resort
3. Chemult Invitational Sled Dog Races
4. Klamath Basin National Wildlife Refuge
5. Baldwin Hotel Museum
6. Upper Klamath Canoe Trail
7. Aspen Ridge Resort
8. Pinehurst Inn at Jenny Creek
9. Oregon Shakespearean Festival
10. Lithia Park and Japanese Garden
11. Mt. Ashland Inn
12. Jackson Hot Springs
13. Bear Creek Nature and Bicycling National Recreation Trail
14. Butte Creek Mill and Country Store
15. Under the Greenwood Tree Bed and Breakfast
16. Jacksonville Pioneer Cemetery
17. Peter Britt Music and Arts Festival
18. Willow Brook Bed and Breakfast
19. Wimer and McKee Covered Bridges
20. Rogue River
21. Pine Meadow Bed and Breakfast Inn
22. Grants Pass Grower's Markert
23. Oregon Caves National Monument
24. Wolf Creek Tavern
25. Hillcrest Vineyard
26. Wildlife Safari
27. Douglas County Museum of History and Natural History
28. The Big K Guest Ranch
29. Oakland Historic District
30. Tolley's Restaurant and Antiques

SOUTHERN OREGON

CRATER LAKE AND SOUTHERN CASCADES

Southern Oregon is a curious mixture of old ghost towns and historic landmarks combined with white-water rivers, wildlife refuges, colorful caverns, a high-altitude volcanic lake, and national forests and mountain ranges containing some of the least-known wilderness areas in the Beaver State. In Oregon's only full-fledged national park, stunning **Crater Lake** shimmers like a crystal blue jewel in the enormous caldera of 12,000-foot Mt. Mazama. More than 6,000 years ago this peak in the southern Cascade Mountains collapsed with a fiery roar, some forty times greater than the Mt. Saint Helens eruption of 1980, and formed a deep basin of 20 square miles; the lake is more than 1,500 feet deep in places, and because of numerous underground thermal springs it rarely freezes.

The 33-mile-long ◆**Crater Lake Rim Drive,** encircling the lake at an invigorating elevation of 6,177 feet, can be done in an hour or so, but to savor the 360-degree panorama and succession of splendid changing views, you'll want to plan a longer outing: Spend the whole day there, and then stay overnight in one of the several campgrounds in the area or in the venerable **Crater Lake Lodge** perched on the south rim.

You can also take a 6-mile side road from **Kerr Notch,** at the southeast corner of the rim, down to the Pinnacles, 200-foot spires of pumice and tuff (layers of volcanic ash). A 4-mile, one-way nature trail for motorists traverses Greyback Ridge, allowing a sit-down look at rock formations, native trees, and wildflowers. Within the park are some 85 miles of hiking and nature trails.

For another panoramic view take the two-hour boat trip from Crater Lake's 25-mile shoreline, accompanied by a Park Service interpreter. *Note:* The trail down to the dock at Cleetwood Cove is a very steep, 1.1-mile hike. For an easier scenic trek, try the 1-mile day hike on **Castle Crest Wildflower Trail** near Rim Village. You can hang out later at Watchman Restaurant or at Llao Rock Cafe, both at Rim Village.

Winter brings a sparkling snowy beauty to the lake, along with outdoor activities such as cross-country skiing, snowshoeing, and ski touring. For information about renting snowshoes or cross-country skis, or about winter tours—reservations are required—contact Crater Lake park staff, Crater Lake 97604; (541) 594–2511.

A Portland mountain climber and transplanted Kansan, William Gladstone Steel, visited the lake in 1885 and helped lead the crusade to save the area around the park from homesteading. He battled to have the area designated a national park, a measure approved by President Theodore Roosevelt on May 22, 1902, as the seventh such park to be established in the United States. The first horseless carriage motored up to the lake in 1905; by 1919 the spectacular Rim Drive, though just a bumpy dirt road, was a standard stop on sight-seeing rambles around the state.

William Steel was appointed the second superintendent of Crater Lake National Park in 1913, and the restored visitors' center, dating from 1934 and situated near the main headquarters building, is named in his honor. It's open daily throughout the year. A smaller visitors' center, located between the lodge and the cafeteria–gift shop, is open during the summer season from 8:00 A.M. to 7:00 P.M. daily. Additional information about lodging can be obtained from staff at Crater Lake National Park, P.O. Box 7, Crater Lake 97604. Built in the early 1900s and opened in 1915, historic **Crater Lake Lodge** has undergone complete renovation and reopened in 1995. Accommodations are available from June to early September. Call (541) 594–2511 after May 20 and (541) 830–8700 after mid-October. For campground information call the Forest Service ranger station at (541) 594–2211.

Access the Crater Lake area via Highway 97 from Bend (about 80 miles); Highway 140 from Klamath Falls (about 60 miles); Highway 62 from Medford (about 70 miles); or Highway 138 from Roseburg (about 80 miles). This last entrance closes with the first heavy snowstorm, usually in mid-October, and reopens by mid-June or July; the south entrance via Highway 62 remains open year-round.

Just north of Crater Lake National Park, at a lower elevation, is **Diamond Lake,** a smaller jewel nestled within Umpqua National Forest. Rainbow-trout season opens here the third weekend of April, and sailboats, motorboats, and canoes can be rented in advance. Moorage space is available throughout the summer and early fall, and fishing/hunting licenses can be purchased at the tackle shop.

Many campground sites, open from May through October, are found on the lakeshore; Diamond Lake and Broken Arrow Campgrounds have trailer dump stations. A well-stocked store is located near ◈ **Diamond Lake Resort.** Several lakeshore cabins are available as well—some with fireplaces and kitchens.

During winter snow lovers can take a guided snowmobile tour—ask about the special tour, including lunch, to Crater Lake—or arrange for snowcat skiing. Often space is available, but it's wise to call ahead for reservations. There's also a good "inner-tube" sledding hill for families with small children. During summer visitors enjoy horseback riding—special group rates can be arranged, and guides are also available. For further information about accommodations and winter or summer activities, write or call Diamond Lake Resort, Diamond Lake 97731 (541–793–3333).

Serious snowmobilers can obtain information about the annual **Snowmobile Jamboree,** in mid-February, from the **High Desert Stormtroopers Snowmobile Club** via Lake County Visitors' Center in Lakeview, (541) 947–6040. Or, ever dreamed about whisking across a frozen lake or snow-covered trail on a dogsled? At the **Trail of Dreams Training Camp** near Chemult, huskies train for the famous Iditarod Trail Race in Alaska by taking visitors on day trips. Reservations are made through Mt. Bachelor Reservations Department, (541) 382–2442 or (800) 829–2442. In January you can hear the cries of ". . . mush, you huskies!" at the annual ◈ **Chemult Invitational Sled Dog Races.** Chemult is located on Highway 97 south of Bend and north of Crater Lake.

Wilderness seekers, backpackers, and hikers can try climbing 8,363-foot Mt. Bailey—strenuous but worth the sweat—or the 4-mile trail to 9,182-foot Mt. Thielson. Both offer superb views of the southern Cascades, Crater Lake, and Diamond Lake. Rangers caution that summer is quite short at these alpine elevations; thus, be sure to dress adequately and to bring the proper gear, including sufficient food, water, and emergency shelter. For information about the **Pacific Crest National Scenic Trail,** which crosses the west side of the area and winds south through the wooded ridges and plateaus of Mountain Lakes Wilderness, contact the Diamond Lake Ranger Station (541–498–2531) near Toketee Falls or write the Regional Forester, P.O. Box 3623, Portland 97208.

THE KLAMATH BASIN

Continuing your exploration of southern Oregon, head south via Highway 62 or 97 toward Klamath Falls to see another region of diversity, including one of the largest wildlife and wildfowl refuges in the Northwest. Many of the roads in this area, particularly Highway 66 from "K Falls" to Ashland, were used by early mail and freight stagecoach lines between the Klamath Basin and settlements along the Rogue River, to the west.

When it was the land of the ancient Ouxkanee, or "people of the marsh," the million-acre Klamath Basin contained a vast expanse of lakes and marshes ideal for waterfowl courtship and nesting. White settlers nearly drained the area dry for farmland, but beginning in 1908, in an effort aided by the emerging conservation ethic, portions of the Klamath Basin were set aside as wildlife refuges, secure from further encroachment. The last of the area reserved in 1958, the entire region is now known as the ◈ **Klamath Basin National Wildlife Refuge.** Though their domain is much smaller than in the days of the Ouxkanee, birds and waterfowl of all species crowd enthusiastically into what remains: some 83,000 acres of marsh and shallow lakes near Klamath Falls.

For the visitor, there are countless opportunities for close-up, nondisturbing viewing of waterfowl, marsh birds, shorebirds, and upland species—along lakes and marshes, near grassy meadows and farms, among the sagebrush and juniper, near ancient lava flows, and in nearby coniferous forests.

The great thrill is seeing the early spring or fall migrations, when the sky is dark with wings and the silence pierced by much cacophonous honking—climaxing to some 7 million birds en route along the **Pacific Flyway,** which extends the entire length of North and South America. First the ducks—pintails, ruddies, mallards, shovelers, and widgeons; then the geese—Canada, snow, white-fronted, and cackling . . . to mention just a few of the more than 270 species recorded here.

In March visitors can welcome the return of the white pelicans, Klamath Falls's feathery mascot; they nest and remain here until November. Link River and Lake Ewauna at **Veteran's Memorial Park** in Klamath Falls are among the most accessible places to see these large, curious birds, with their pouched beaks.

And during winter some 500 bald eagles visit from the frozen North, attracting naturalists and bird lovers from all over to count and observe their nesting habits at the annual **Bald Eagle Conference** during the first week in January. Call (916) 667–2231 for current information.

Information about viewing sites as well as helpful maps, including one for an auto tour, can be obtained from the Klamath County Visitors' Center, 1451 Main Street, P.O. Box 1867, Klamath Falls 97601 (541–884–0666), or from the Klamath Basin Wildlife Refuge headquarters, Route 1, Box 74, Tulelake, CA 96134 (916–667–2231).

Klamath Falls, first named Linkville when founded in 1876, sits atop a geothermal area, and in early days many businesses and homes were heated by the hot water; the early native peoples used it for cooking.

The **Klamath County Museum,** at 1451 Main Street, offers exhibits and displays on the history, geology, anthropology, and wildlife of the Klamath Basin; it's open Tuesday through Saturday, 11:00 A.M. to 5:00 P.M. Also part of the museum complex, the four-story ❖ **Baldwin Hotel Museum,** a noted turn-of-the-century hostelry built in 1906 by State Senator George Baldwin, offers a look at the hotel's opulent original furnishings and early history. Located at 31 Main Street, the brick building is open for tours from June to September, Tuesday through Saturday, 10:00 A.M. to 4:00 P.M.

Maud Baldwin, well-known photographer at the turn of the century, followed her father, George, around the county and into the marshes to record on film the area's early farmland reclamation project. More than 2,000 of her vintage photographs are housed at the **Klamath County Museum.** For further information call the museum complex staff at (541) 883–4208.

Many locals claim that the best place to eat is **Saddle Rock Cafe,** where sandwiches, rotisserie chicken and ribs, freshly baked pastries, desserts, espresso, and West Coast microbrews can be ordered. Located at 1012 Main Street, the cafe is open daily 11:00 A.M. to 8:00 P.M., (541) 883–3970.

If time allows call and check out the current play or concert offerings at the **Ross Ragland Theater** housed in a renovated art deco style–building at 218 North Seventh Street; call (541) 884–0651 or 884–LIVE.

Just 30 miles north of Klamath Falls via Highway 97 is **Collier State Park and Logging Museum** (541–783–2471), where you can take a gander at the largest collection of logging equipment in the United States. Be sure to look for the huge steam locomotive—it ran on roads rather than on tracks. Be sure to stop at the Ouxkanee Lookout for a panoramic view of Spring Creek Valley and for historical information about the region. Collier Park offers both RV and tent campsites.

For a special outdoor experience, ask about the ◈**Upper Klamath Canoe Trail,** particularly the northern section where you can canoe gently along the 50-foot-wide water trail and can often see families of beavers who live in the marshes; paddle close to the bulrushes to spy their connecting trails. A mother beaver will often slap her broad foot-long tail on the water to warn her family of your presence. For canoe and kayak rentals, contact **Rocky Point Resort,** 28121 Rocky Point Road, Klamath Falls, 97601 (541–356–2287). Take Highway 140 along the west side of Upper Klamath Lake about 28 miles and turn at the signs to the resort; the put-in spot is nearby. For additional information and maps contact the U.S. Fish and Wildlife Service, 1400 West Miller Island Road, Klamath Falls 97603 (541) 883–5732.

If you decide to stay overnight in the area, check out the accommodations at Rocky Point or call **Sun Pass Ranch** located near Fort Klamath. Here, on a working ranch of one hundred acres near Wood River and Upper Klamath Lake, you can commune with cattle and horses as well as go canoeing or fishing. Guests explore hundreds of miles of nearby forest trails and back-country roads, in the winter by clamping on cross-country skis and in the summer atop mountain bikes or on guided horseback rides (there are some eleven horses at the ranch plus stables for boarding your own horse). For further information and reservations, contact Sun Pass Ranch, Highway 62 at the Wood River Bridge, P.O. Box 516, Fort Klamath (541–381–2259). Canoers can also find good floating and paddling on Crystal Creek and on Lake Ewauna in Klamath Falls.

For nearby campgrounds, hiking trails, places to fish, helpful maps, and general visitor information, stop by the Klamath Ranger District office at 1936 California Avenue in Klamath Falls (541–885–3400), open Monday through Friday from 8:00 A.M. to 4:30 P.M.

If you'd like to venture farther off the beaten path, consider treking east into the Gearhart Mountain Wilderness environs and arranging a couple of days at ◆**Aspen Ridge Resort**. This 14,000-acre working cattle ranch, owned by former Californians Steve and Karen Simmons, is accessed via Chiloquin, Sprague River Road, Highway 140, and, finally, Fish-hole Creek Road just east of Bly. But what's there to do here, you ask? Well, go horseback riding with the cowboys and learn how to manage a herd of cattle; hole up and read, go trout fishing, or mountain biking; inhale fresh air and wonderful high desert smells of sagebrush and juniper; eat hearty meals prepared by the ranch cook; then, listen to evening sounds, like the howl of coyotes or the bawl of cattle and gaze at a wide sky jam-packed with glittering stars. For more information and reservations contact Karen Simmons at P.O. Box 2, Bly 97622; (541) 884–8685 or toll free outside Oregon, (800) 393–3323.

By this time your senses will have become saturated with the wonder of Crater Lake's crystalline waters; the quietness and mystery of the southern Cascade Mountains wilderness areas will have seeped into your bones. Having experienced the breathtaking sight of a half-million or so ducks, geese, swans, white pelicans, and other waterfowl and wildlife congregating along the Pacific Flyway near Klamath Falls, you can now head further east, via Highway 395 or 140, into Oregon's Old West country; north on Highway 97, into Oregon's high desert country; or west on Highway 66, toward Ashland, Medford, and Jacksonville.

SHAKESPEARE AND PETER BRITT COUNTRY

Heading west on Highway 66 from Klamath Falls, stock up on groceries and consider holing up in one of the rustic cabins (all have kitchens) at **Green Springs Box R Ranch,** located along the historic Applegate Trail. Those weary pioneers who detoured from the Oregon Trail along this southern route in the mid-1840s often rested in this place at the 3,600-foot elevation level, near the springs and lush meadow. The ranch house, built in 1904, sits alongside the meadow, which in late spring and summer bursts with blooming wildflowers.

The ranch served originally as a stagecoach stop. Today it is a guest ranch and working cattle ranch of more than 1,000 acres, a place where you can help gather eggs from the henhouse, feed woolly spring lambs, or just relax and do nothing but soak in those marvelous southern Cascade Mountain sunrises and sunsets. You can also enjoy a sleigh ride during a winter visit or a wagon ride during the rest of the year, both activities involving a friendly pair of large Belgian horses, Willy and Waylon, harnessed and hitched and ready to go. A teamster-guide will share lively tales about the historic Applegate Trail as you tour a small pioneer village containing some of the oldest structures in southern Oregon.

For further information and reservations, write Box R Ranch, 16799 Highway 66, Ashland 97520 (541–482–1873). The ranch is located ½ mile off the highway, 39 miles west of Klamath Falls and 23 miles east of Ashland. There is also a 3,650-foot elevation airstrip nearby that can accommodate small planes; prior to use contact the FAA at (541) 378–4880.

Another option is to hole up in one of the five cozy bed-and-breakfast guest rooms at ❖ **Pinehurst Inn at Jenny Creek,** a handsomely restored, 1920-style roadhouse located just ¼ mile down the drive from the ranch house. Lunch and dinner are available in the inn's sunny dining room, on the main level; guests are served a full breakfast. Jenny Creek, well known for its brown trout fishing, bubbles alongside the inn, and you may even spy oddly shaped beaver lodges along its banks as well. For further information and reservations, contact the staff at Pinehurst Inn, 17250 Highway 66, Ashland 97520 (541–488–1002).

Highway 66 intersects with busy I–5 near Ashland, just north of Mt. Ashland and the Siskiyou Pass, which takes travelers to and from the Oregon–California border. Detour at this intersection into the bustling community of Ashland, where you can take in a southern Oregon Shakespeare tradition that dates from 1935.

In that year young professor Angus Bowmer of Southern Oregon Normal School—later renamed Southern Oregon State College—conceived the idea of producing Shakespeare's plays by reworking the walls of the town's old Chautauqua Building into an outdoor theater reminiscent of those of Elizabethan England. Convincing Ashland's city leaders took some time, but with their conditional blessing the first productions—*Twelfth Night* and *The Merchant of Venice*—took place over the Fourth of July in 1935.

The deficits from a boxing match that was scheduled to satisfy the Shakespeare skeptics were covered by the resounding success and bulging receipts from the two plays. In 1937 the ❖ **Oregon Shakespearean Festival** Association was organized as a nonprofit corporation, and in 1941 the first scholarships for actors were offered. The festival will celebrate its sixty-second year in 1997.

To complement the outdoor Elizabethan Theatre, the indoor Angus Bowmer Theatre was built in 1970 and the intimate Black Swan Theatre constructed in 1977. The three theaters anchor a large outdoor plaza, a gift shop, and ticket offices. The visitor can also poke into interesting shops and eateries along nearby Main Street.

For information about the current repertoire of traditional as well as contemporary offerings—eleven or more plays are staged from mid-February through October, ranging from *Hamlet, The Tempest,* and *Much Ado about Nothing* to the *Merry Wives of Windsor, Blithe Spirit,* and *Caberet Verboten*—write the Oregon Shakespearean Festival, P.O. Box 158, Ashland 97520 or call (541) 482–4331. *Note:* The plays staged at the superb outdoor Elizabethan Theatre run from June through October.

Ask for a complete schedule, including information about the Backstage Tour; the Exhibit Center, where you can try on a bevy of costumes, ranging from the garb of queens, kings, courtesans, and heroes to that of villains, monsters, madmen, and fools; and special festival events held throughout the nearly year-round season. A traditional, summertime feast officially opens the Shakespearean Festival season in mid-June. It's held, amid much music and colorful heraldry, in Ashland's lovely ◆ **Lithia Park.**

For a quiet respite you'll want to visit the park's exquisite ◆ **Japanese Garden,** located on a gentle slope across from the Butler-Perozzi Fountain (access from the street that skirts the park's perimeter). You'll stroll graveled paths and giant stepping-stones, perhaps pausing to sit at one of several benches placed to catch the best views of native shrubs, many tree species, and a gently flowing stream.

Along with the plays of William Shakespeare, another English tradition is alive and well in Ashland. Many comfortable bed-and-breakfast inns offer such heartwarming amenities as goose-down comforters, wine or sherry by a crackling fire in the evening, and sumptuous continental or full breakfasts. You might have home-made peach preserves, piping-hot popovers or banana muffins, Dutch babies, and a special mushroom quiche, along with gourmet coffee and teas—all served on the best china, of course.

Because of the busy theater season, it's best to make lodging reservations early. For helpful brochures contact the Ashland Visitors' Information Center, 110 East Main Street, P.O. Box 1360, Ashland 97520; (541) 482–3486. When you stop by the visitors' center—located near the Festival Center—ask about the self-guided walking tour brochure and map of historic buildings and homes, the *Inside and Outdoor Activities* guide, and winter sports information for nearby Mt. Ashland.

If the notion of sleeping in a 4,200-square-foot, handcrafted mountain log lodge sounds appealing, consider ❖**Mt. Ashland Inn,** just off the beaten path—about 16 miles south of town, on the road up to 7,528-foot Mt. Ashland. Owners Elaine and Jerry Shanafelt selected the logs from their own 160 acres of alpine wonderland at the 5,500-foot level. After cutting and stripping some 275 incense cedar logs, Jerry, an architect, coordinated the entire construction and then did all the plumbing, wiring, and finishing work.

The results are stunning. Climb up log steps to a large deck and stop for a moment to savor the wide-angle view past tall pines to the verdant slopes of the Siskiyou mountain range, the valley floor, and 14,162-foot, snowy Mt. Shasta, looming some 50 miles to the south in northern California.

An enormous stone fireplace dominates the inviting common area, beckoning guests to the cheerful fire with a good book or a glass of hot spiced cider. The aroma of fresh-baked cookies may tempt a peek into the cozy kitchen just beyond the dining area. Choose from comfortable guest rooms on the third level, each with a private bath.

Work off your delicious breakfast with an outdoor stroll or with a hike along a section of the **Pacific Crest Trail,** which crosses the inn's parking area. The trail angles through groves of ponderosa pine and red-barked manzanita up to lush alpine meadows that burst with colorful wildflowers in mid- to late summer. The wild larkspur, blue lupine, and white bear grass usually peak in August at the higher elevations.

During winter clamp on cross-country skis and enjoy a trek right from the inn's door, on the old logging roads located nearby—or try the snowshoes and sledding equipment kept handy for guests. To arrange a visit—the inn is open year-round—contact the Shanafelts at Mt. Ashland Inn, 550 Mt. Ashland Road (P.O. Box 944), Ashland 97520; (541) 482–8707.

Right next door to Ashland is **Medford,** the Rogue River Valley's industrious timber-processing and pear-packing center. Once the home of the Takelma Indians, the region changed drastically when gold was discovered near Jacksonville, just west of Medford, in 1852. Miners invaded the valley in search of fortunes in gold nuggets and were followed by early settlers lured to the valley by its fertile soil and favorable growing conditions. The fortune hunters panned and claimed, the farmers cleared and planted—and both groups displaced the peace-loving Takelma tribe.

In 1883, when the Oregon and California Railroad reached southern Oregon, a railroad station was built at Middle Ford on Bear Creek—the community of Jacksonville apparently elected not to cough up the $25,000 "bonus" for the privilege. Later a town site was platted at Middle Ford and the name shortened to Medford. Incorporated in 1885, the town took up its first order of business: to establish an ordinance that discouraged disorderly conduct. A second ordinance prevented minors from loitering at the railroad depot, and a third solemnly prohibited hogs from running loose within the town.

To recapture some of the nostalgia and history connected with the railroad's reaching into the Rogue River Valley at Medford, visit **Railroad Park,** where you can take a short train ride on the second and fourth Sundays of the month from 11:00 A.M. to 3:00 P.M. The historic park and its vintage train are located near Berrydale Avenue and Table Rock Road. Or, swing off Highway 99 between Ashland and Medford to swim or stay overnight at ❖**Jackson Hot Springs,** a wonderful, old, turn-of-the-century spa that offers renovated cottages, new suites, lush groupings of annuals and perennials, and a 50-foot by 100-foot warm mineral swimming pool. Call (541) 482–3776 for further information and for open swim times. For additional information contact the Medford Visitors' Information Center, at 101 East Eighth Street, Medford 97501; (541) 779–4847.

The **Southern Oregon Historical Society Center** also contains exhibits and historical collections and is a worthwhile addition to your travel itinerary. The center is located at 106 North Central Avenue in downtown Medford (541–773–6536) and is open from 9:00 A.M. to 5:00 P.M. weekdays and from 10:00 A.M. to 5:00 P.M. Saturdays.

Medford is loved by bicyclists for its ❖**Bear Creek Nature and Bicycling National Recreation Trail,** which meanders through town along the banks of Bear Creek. Walkers and joggers are also welcome to use the paved trail. The Old Stage Road to Jacksonville, though heavily used by automobiles, is also popular with bicyclists. Bicycles can be rented at Siskiyou Cyclery, 1259 Siskiyou Boulevard; the visitors' information center will know of other resources as well.

Detour just 10 miles north of Medford on Highway 62 to visit the historic ◆ **Butte Creek Mill** in Eagle Point. From the long wooden loading dock, step into the dim, coolish interior, where you can watch the miller at work. The tangy fragrance of wheat, rye, and corn will tantalize your nostrils, and you'll hear the faint bubbling sound of the creek, whose waters are turning two enormous millstones, 1,400 pounds each.

These giant stones were quarried in France; milled in Illinois; shipped around Cape Horn to Crescent City, on the northern California coast; and carried over the Coast Range mountains by wagon. They were first used for grinding grain here more than a hundred years ago. You can walk down to the lower level for a peek at the myriad moving belts, shafts, and pulleys—water diverted from Butte Creek activates the turbine that turns the wheels, generating power for the mill; the spent water then reenters the stream through the tail race, located below the waterwheel.

The large wooden building has perched alongside Little Butte Creek since 1872 and was one of the first flour mills built in the Rogue River Valley. It's now the only remaining gristmill still in operation in Oregon. In addition to the freshly ground flours, meals, and cracked grains, you'll find old-fashioned peanut butter, nuts, dried fruits, seeds, granolas, yeasts, raw honey, molasses, teas, and bulk spices in the adjoining ◆ **Country Store.** A great place to take the kids as well, Butte Creek Mill and its old-fashioned Country Store is open year-round Monday through Saturday from 9:00 A.M. to 6:00 P.M. There is a small museum next door, open by appointment. For further information call (541) 826–3531.

A pleasant option is to take the scenic route to the National Historic Landmark community of Jacksonville—the **Old Stage Road** off Highway 99 from the Central Point–Medford area—for a close-up view of tidy pear orchards, open-air fruit stands, and old farmsteads. During early spring the whole valley seems a canopy of luscious white pear blossoms. This eye-catching spectacle takes place from mid- to late April; call ahead to one of the visitors'

Elizabeth Neilson Walker 1990

Butte Creek Mill

information centers for current weather and bloom times.

Among the amenable bed-and-breakfast inns in the area is the historic ♦ **Under the Greenwood Tree Bed and Breakfast,** formerly a weigh station for hay and grain in the 1870s and 1880s. Situated comfortably amid enormous old oak trees and lush green lawns and gardens, the large square farmhouse was renovated by owner and world traveler Renate Ellam. Guests enjoy afternoon tea served in the common area and are often treated to a personal tour of the grounds, including the old weigh-station scales, barns, vegetable and flower gardens, resident mules, and cages of twittering songbirds on a large deck overlooking the grounds.

Four lovely guest rooms, all with private baths, offer views from the second floor. Breakfast is a tempting gourmet affair, cooked fresh each morning and accompanied by steaming hot coffee and teas. For further information and reservations, contact Renate Ellam at Under the Greenwood Tree, 3045 Bellinger Lane, Medford 97501 (541–776–0000). The inn is about midway between Medford and Jacksonville.

Following the discovery of gold in the area in 1851, the Jacksonville community emerged in a matter of weeks. The fast-and-furious life of a gold rush town took over immediately. After the first wave of several thousand gold seekers came many wagon trains loaded with settlers and their families: the future solid citizens responsible for Jacksonville's transition to an agricultural community instead of a post–gold rush ghost town.

Designated a National Historic Landmark in 1966 by the U.S. Department of the Interior, the town of Jacksonville diligently works to preserve the atmosphere of the mid-1800s. Yet one can be just a mild history buff and still enjoy a visit—park on any side street and stroll down California Street for a glimpse into the colorful past.

The clump of miners' boots, the crunch of wagon wheels pulled by mules or horses, the laughter of the saloon and dance hall queens, and perhaps a gunshot or two seem to echo here and there—through rusted hinges, around the old iron town water pump next to the 1863 Beekman Bank Building, and around the circa 1891 railway depot now housing the Jacksonville Visitors' Information Center.

You can see a small length of the original track at the corner of Fifth and C Streets. To savor an even closer feeling for Jacksonville's colorful history, trek from the old depot up E Street to the ◆**Jacksonville Pioneer Cemetery.** Situated on a small hill shaded by tall oak and madrona trees, the historic cemetery offers quiet paths into the past. Wax myrtle trails its heart-shaped leaves and small purple blossoms around vintage headstones, many of which date back to the early 1800s, and wildflowers like shooting stars and fawn lilies poke up here and there in shady nooks and crannies in early spring. Pick up a helpful map and six-page self-guided walking tour and history guide of the cemetery at the Visitors' Information Center. Don't miss this lovely spot.

The large white Courthouse Building, constructed in 1883 when the town housed the county seat—a vote to move the seat of county government to Medford was approved around 1926—is home to the **Jackson County Historical Society Museum.** Plan a visit to this fine museum, just off California Street at 206 North Fifth, with its historic collections of photographs, vintage clothing, books, and other pioneer memorabilia. Picnic tables are set on the grounds under tall, old-fashioned locust trees during summer months.

Living-history programs are offered afternoons during summer at **Beekman House,** located on California Street near the restored, circa 1854 Methodist church. Then stroll along the side streets to see more than eighty restored homes and other structures, many dating to the early 1800s, and all labeled; some have their own private gardens, which can be enjoyed from the sidewalk.

For information about other living-history exhibits and programs, contact the Jacksonville Visitors' Information Center, 185 North Oregon Street (P.O. Box 33), Jacksonville 97530 (541–899–8118).

Other old buildings, now restored, house specialty shops and boutiques, ice-cream parlors, bakeries, cafes, and tearooms. The 1863 **Jacksonville Inn** offers a good restaurant, as does the **Bella Union**—both on California Street.

Walk up First Street to the Britt Gardens, founded in 1852 by pioneer photographer, horticulturist, and vintner Peter Britt. Named in his honor, the ◆**Peter Britt Music and Arts Festival** offers a wide variety of classical, bluegrass, jazz, and dance music, the events all taking place outdoors under the stars during June, July, and August. Collect a picnic, blankets, lap robes, pillows, or lawn chairs and find just the right spot on the wide lawn (or on wooden benches) under tall Douglas fir trees for the evening's concert.

The festival has hosted such notables as Mel Tormé and Diane Schuur, Les Brown's band and the Dave Brubeck quartet, as well as classical pianist Lorin Hollander. Several evenings are devoted to bluegrass concerts, and you can also enjoy family concerts as well as participating in a wide variety of music and dance workshops.

For a helpful booklet listing the schedule and for ticket information, contact Britt Festivals, P.O. Box 1124, Medford 97501; (541) 773–6077.

For overnight stays in the Jacksonville area, try **The Touvelle House,** a stately 1916 Craftsman-style bed and breakfast at 445 North Oregon Street (541–899–8938); **Reames House Bed & Breakfast,** an 1868 restoration in a garden setting on California Street (800–207–0269); the **State Lodge,** at 830 North Fifth Street (541–899–3953); or the honeymoon cottage at **Jacksonville Inn,** 175 East California Street (541–899–1900). To avoid being disappointed, call by February or March if you plan to attend Britt Festival events.

SCENIC ROGUE RIVER COUNTRY

If time allows, take winding old Highway 99 and Highway 199 for a leisurely, 25-mile drive along the upper Rogue River to Grants Pass. You can also detour at Gold Hill to visit the **Old Oregon Historical Museum,** located at 2345 Sardine Creek Road. Containing the largest private collection in southern Oregon, the museum is generally open daily from April to mid-October. If the notion of staying overnight in a charming, restored gold miner's farmhouse sounds intriguing, call former New Yorkers JoAnn and Tom Hoeber, now happily relocated as the owners and innkeepers of ◈ **Willow Brook Bed and Breakfast,** 628 Foots Creek Road, Gold Hill 97525 (541–582–0075). Guests are welcome to use the swimming pool and hot tub. Tom has a wonderful herb garden and JoAnn spins local wools and knits colorful sweaters; ask about seeing the gentle Nubian goats, too.

If you love old covered bridges, plan to visit ◈ **Wimer Covered Bridge,** the only one in Jackson County open to vehicular traffic. Originally constructed in 1892, the current covered structure, often called "a barn over water," was built in 1927 by Jason Hartman, a county bridge superintendent. To find the vintage covered bridge, detour from the town of Rogue River about 7 miles north on East Evans Creek Road; you may also see signs of a forest fire that raged through the area during early August 1992. For information on other covered bridges in the area, call the Southern Oregon Historical Soci-

Jacksonville Pioneer Cemetery

ety library in Medford, (541) 773–6536. In Rogue River you can visit **Palmerton Arboretum** and walk a 200-foot swinging footbridge, Skevington's Crossing, that crosses Evans Creek and connects the lovely five-acre arboretum with **Anna Classick City Park.**

For an alternate route from Jacksonville, take Highway 238, which winds gently along the Applegate River, passes the hamlet of Ruch (where you'll see **Valley View Winery**—small tasting room here, open afternoons), continues past ◆**McKee Covered Bridge,** and turns north from Murphy into Grants Pass. Entering town via either route, you'll cross the Rogue River on the circa 1931 **Caveman Bridge,** which is on the National Register of Historic Places. For a list of other historic sites, write or stop by the well-stocked Grants Pass Visitors' Information Center, located at 1501 NE Sixth Street, Grants Pass 97526; (541) 476–7717.

The ◆**Rogue River** earns its nickname, "the fishingest river in the West," if you judge from the large number of folks who fish its pools and riffles year-round. The best chinook salmon angling is reported to take place from mid-April through September, whereas summer trout fishing picks up in August and again in December through March. Local tackle shops sell bait, supplies, the required licenses, and salmon/trout tags. Ask about catch regulations.

You can fish from the shore at parks along the river or hire a drift-boat guide for half-days or full days—a tradition since the early 1930s, long before an 84-mile stretch of the river, on the south coast, between Grants Pass and Gold Beach, was designated part of the **National Wild and Scenic System.** More adventurous anglers can check out the three- and four-day guided fishing trips down this section of the Rogue that are offered by licensed outfitters from September 1 to November 15; the visitors' information center will have current information.

The most common summer white-water trips use large, inflatable oar-and-paddle rafts, inflatable kayaks, drift boats, or the popular jet boats. As you drift along with an expert guide handling the oars, the Rogue River ripples, cascades, boils, churns, and spills over rocks and boulders, through narrow canyons and gorges, and along quiet, pondlike, and peaceful stretches—rimmed on both sides by forests of Douglas fir, madrona, and oak and reflecting sunlight, blue sky, and puffy white clouds from its ever-moving surface.

You can also enjoy a one-day guided raft trip on the river or a four-hour, 36-mile jet-boat excursion to **Hellgate Canyon,** stopping at OK Corral for a country-style barbecue dinner served on a large deck overlooking all that marvelous river and wilderness scenery. Local kids love to entertain jet-boat passengers by swinging out over the river on long ropes attached to bankside trees, dropping and splashing—among much clapping and raucous laughter—into the river near lovely **Schroeder County Park and Campground,** just a few miles west of downtown and off Highway 199, the Redwood Highway. For information and reservations contact **Hellgate Jetboat Excursions,** 953 SE Seventh Street, Grants Pass 97526; (541) 479–7204.

If you'd like to remain a little closer to civilization, consider spending the night at ◆**Pine Meadow Bed and Breakfast Inn.** Nestled in a pine forest with views of Mt. Walker and Mt. Sexton, guests immediately feel the stress-free, peaceful atmosphere created by innkeepers Nancy and Maloy Murdock. For starters you'll settle into a comfortable guest room decorated with early American antiques and offering sitting places such as maple rocking chairs, comfy wing chairs, or a cozy window seat with pillows. Later, enjoy a leisurely soak in the outdoor hot tub, walk or ride bicycles on shady trails and country roads, and stroll hand in hand through the couple's lovely gardens. Breakfast is perhaps most memorable because it is healthy and light, yet gourmet. You might be served, for example, a fresh veggie egg bake, country potatoes, and Morning Glory muffins along with strawberries in sour cream and brown sugar. Almost everything is fresh from the vegetable and herb garden, and the juices served are organic. For further information and reservations, contact the Murdocks at 1000 Crow Road, Merlin 97532 or call them at (541) 471–6277. The inn is located just a few miles north of Grants Pass and the Rogue River, 6 miles from I–5 via the Merlin-Galice Road.

If you're in the area on a Saturday, check out the fabulous ◆**Grants Pass Grower's Market**—the fresh-baked cinnamon rolls, breads, and pastries are to die for, not to mention the farm-fresh fruits, vegetables, and herbs. The market is set up at Fourth and F Streets, 9:00 A.M. to 1:00 P.M. Don't miss it. *Note:* You'll also find wonderful farmer's markets in Klamath Falls, Ashland, Medford, and Roseburg—check with the local visitors' information centers for locations and schedules.

Before heading north via I–5 toward Roseburg, or going west via the Redwood Highway 199 toward Cave Junction and the coast, plan a natural history stop at **Wildlife Images Rehabilitation and Education Center.** Originally started to nurse injured birds of prey back to health, the center now aids and nurtures all types of injured or orphaned wild animals, from bears and fawns to raccoons and beaver. To arrange a guided tour, available at 11:00 A.M. and 1:00 P.M. daily, call ahead, (541) 576–0222. The center is located 13 miles from town; from G Street head west to Upper River Road, then onto Lower River Road.

For another scenic side trip, take the 20-mile paved, twisting road east of Cave Junction, located 50 miles west of Grants Pass via Highway 199, up to the ◆ **Oregon Caves National Monument.** Located in the heart of the Siskiyou Mountains at an elevation of 4,000 feet, the prehistoric marble and limestone underground caverns were discovered by Elijah H. Davidson in 1874, although native peoples, of course, knew about the caves for centuries before white people arrived.

Although guided walks through the caves can be taken year-round, you may want to avoid midsummer crowds and long lines by planning a trip in either early spring or late fall, after Labor Day. Better yet, try a midwinter visit in the snowy wonderland, bringing along your snowshoes or cross-country skis.

The cave tour, somewhat strenuous, lasts about seventy-five minutes and is not recommended for those with heart, breathing, or walking difficulties; canes and other walking aids are not permitted inside the caverns. And though children under six are prohibited from entering caves, a baby-sitting service is available for a nominal fee. *Note:* The caverns are a chilly 41 degrees Fahrenheit inside; dress warmly and wear sturdy shoes.

Then, too, you could stay the night at the rustic **Oregon Caves Chateau,** built in 1934 and now on the National Register of Historic Places. It's a handsome cedar structure with twenty-two guest rooms, some overlooking a waterfall and a pond, others the Douglas fir–clothed canyon or the entrance to the caverns. The chateau's restaurant serves dinner, offering steak, seafood, chicken, and a selection of Northwest wines, with Cave Creek close by—it bubbles right through the dining room. The old-fashioned coffee shop is open for breakfast and lunch. The Oregon Caves Chateau operates from mid-June to September; for more information, write the chateau at P.O. Box 128, Cave Junction 97523 (541–592–3400).

Or, call the folks at **Kerbyville Bed & Breakfast Inn** and ask about the relaxing whirlpool bath suites. Located in the Illinois Valley and near the Oregon Caves as well as **Siskiyou, Bridgeview** and **Foris** vineyards and wineries, call the innkeepers at (541) 592–4689 for reservations. For **Kalmiopsis Wilderness** hiking trails, maps, and additional information, contact the Illinois Valley Visitors Center, P.O. Box 312, 201 Caves Highway, Cave Junction 97523; (541) 592–2631. Locals say the nearby **Wild River Brewing & Pizza Company** is a companionable spot to eat and to sample ales brewed on the premises; open daily, (541) 592–3556.

THE UMPQUA VALLEY

Early travelers came through southern Oregon in the mid-1800s by stagecoach over those rough, dusty, and sometimes muddy roads from central California on their way north to the Oregon country. The trip from San Francisco to Portland took about sixteen days, the fare being about 10 cents a mile. Stage stations were situated every 10 or so miles, and the big crimson-colored stages, built to carry the mail and as many as sixteen passengers, were an important link in the early development of the Northwest.

Completion of the railroad through the Willamette and Umpqua valleys south to California brought a sudden halt to the overland mail stage, thus marking the end of a colorful chapter in Northwest history; nevertheless, today's traveler can recapture a bit of that history. For a look at one of the oldest stage stops in the state, detour from I–5 at Wolf Creek, about 20 miles north of Grants Pass. Here you will find historic ◆ **Wolf Creek Tavern**—dating from 1857—a large, two-story, Classic Revival–style inn that is still open to travelers.

Purchased by the state and completely restored in 1979, the inn is now administered by the State Parks and Recreation Department. Hearty meals are served in the dining room, and guest rooms are available on the second floor. When you walk into the parlor, furnished with period antiques, you might notice the sunlight filtering through lace-curtained windows and imagine a long-skirted matron or young lady sipping a cup of tea while waiting for the next stage to depart.

The dining room is open to the public for breakfast, lunch, and dinner year-round (except New Year's). For information and overnight reservations, write P.O. Box 97, Wolf Creek 97497 or call (541) 866–2474.

Small hamlets and communities like Remote, Camas Valley, Days Creek, Tiller, Lookingglass, Riddle, and Glide contain many descendants of both early miners and pioneers. These folks live in the peaceful, forested valleys and remote areas of the Umpqua River and its tributaries, east and west of Roseburg, the county seat and timber community. There are a few native peoples left, too—a small community of Cow Creek Indians.

Also hidden away on the county roads—look for the bright blue Douglas County road signs with yellow numbers—and in the small valleys near Roseburg are some of the region's first vineyards and wineries. More than thirty years ago the first varietal grapes were planted by Richard Sommer at ◈ **Hillcrest Vineyard,** and from these first roots eventually emerged a thriving colony of vintners just west of Roseburg—Davidson Winery, Giradet Wine Cellars, Lookingglass Winery, Callahan Ridge Winery, Hillcrest Vineyard, Umpqua River Vineyards, and Henry Winery.

To reach the wineries, drive through the oak-dotted, rolling hills west of Roseburg. Most of these enterprises are within 20 miles of Roseburg and welcome visitors, although it's best to call ahead to make certain the tasting rooms are open; some of the vineyards are open just by appointment. The Roseburg Visitors' Center will have helpful maps and may be willing to call ahead for you. Those who want to remain on the side roads awhile longer should ask for *A Guide to Historic Barns* and *A Driver's Guide to Historic Places.* Write or stop by the visitors' center at 410 SE Spruce Street (P.O. Box 1262), Roseburg 97470, or call (541) 672–9731.

Wind over to Winston to visit ◈ **Wildlife Safari,** a 600-acre, drive-through wild-animal reserve of more than a hundred different species of animals and birds representing Africa, Asia, and other exotic areas of the world. Among the wildlife living here are the Tibetan yak, wildebeest, eland, lion, elephant, ostrich, hippopotamus, rhinoceros, and cheetah.

Since 1980 Wildlife Safari has been operated by the Safari Game Search Foundation, a nonprofit organization dedicated to preserving endangered species, conducting animal-related research, providing educational programs for elementary schools throughout the Northwest, and rehabilitating injured wildlife. A world leader in the research and breeding of cheetahs, the organization has successfully raised nearly one hundred cheetah cubs here in the past fifteen years and is one of the largest providers of cheetahs to zoos throughout the world.

The reserve is open year-round, every day from 9:00 A.M. to dusk. It offers the **White Rhino Restaurant** and Casbah Gift Shop along with a small RV park, picnic areas, and free kennels for Fido. For further information contact the staff at Wildlife Safari, P.O. Box 1600, Winston 97496 (541–679–6761). The reserve is about 4 miles west of I–5 from the Winston exit via Highway 42.

For exhibits of some of the region's natural history, as well as logging and mining equipment dating from the 1800s, detour from I–5 just south of Roseburg—at the Fairgrounds exit—to visit the ◆**Douglas County Museum of History and Natural History,** located in the large contemporary structure next to the fairgrounds. After poking around the vintage logging and mining equipment in the courtyard, be sure to look inside for the fine exhibit of old photographs. Though the photographs are yellowed with age, the weathered faces in them mirror hope and determination as well as hardship and even heartbreak; the exhibit offers a poignant look into Oregon's pioneer past. The museum is open daily from 9:00 A.M. to 5:00 P.M.; (541) 957-7007. A shady park just next door offers picnic tables and parking for recreational vehicles.

Another pleasant side trip from Roseburg weaves east on Highway 138 into the southern **Cascade Mountains.** The two-lane asphalt ribbon plays hide-and-seek with the **North Umpqua River** and with many frothy waterfalls carrying names like Toketee, Lemolo, White Horse, Clearwater, and Watson. **Watson Falls** is noted as the second highest in Oregon, a 272-foot drop down a rugged cliff; access from a well-marked ½-mile trail. The falls and nearby parking areas, beginning about 20 miles east of Glide, are well marked. A section of the scenic river, also well marked, is open just to those who love to fly-fish; the fly-fishing section between Glide and Steamboat is especially scenic. **Steamboat Inn** offers rustic cabins that overlook the chortling Umpqua River—you'll likely want to sit on the wide deck for hours and soak in the wilderness. Guests enjoy gourmet fisherman dinners in the knotty pine dining room. Reservations are a must; for further information call the inn's staff at (541) 498–2411. From here you can continue east on Highway 138 to connect with **Lemolo Lake**'s pleasantly rustic resort (541–496–0900) and its uncrowded campgrounds; with **Diamond Lake** and its wide range of fishing, camping, and resort facilities; and with **Crater Lake National Park** (see beginning of this section for details).

If you pass through the community of Glide—it's about 17 miles east of Roseburg—sometime in mid-April and notice lots of cars parked near the Community Building, stop to see whether the annual **Glide Wildflower Show** is in progress. At this show some 300 native plants and flowers from the southern Oregon region are displayed in lovely arrangements by local naturalists and wildflower lovers.

To see another section of the Umpqua River, detour west onto Highway 138 W at Sutherlin, just north of Roseburg. This meandering rural route carries travelers to ◈**The Big K Guest Ranch,** located on 2,500 acres of rolling Douglas fir forest in the Umpqua River Valley. The guest ranch complex overlooks "the loop," the biggest bend and a scenic stretch of the Umpqua River that is known for good fishing—smallmouth bass, steelhead, shad, and chinook salmon depending on the season. While the river bubbles past the ranch, through the Coast Range, and empties into the Pacific Ocean at Reedsport, the Kesterson family offers guests a number of excellent outdoor options. You can swim in the resident pool, go horseback riding, bicycle, hike, try your hand at horseshoes or the sporting-clay range, arrange for a river float trip, even go on a wild turkey hunt. Home-style fare is offered in the river-rock fireplace dining room in the main lodge; accommodations are in cozy log cabins. For further information contact the staff at (541) 584–2295 or (800) 390–2445; the guest ranch is located at 20029 Highway 138 W, Elkton 97436. The facility also hosts conferences and retreats.

Plan one last detour before entering the lush Willamette Valley region: a stop in the small community of Oakland, nestled in the picturesque hills just north of Sutherlin. About twenty-five years ago, when the area's lumber mill closed, Oakland felt an economic decline common to many timber towns throughout the Northwest. The townsfolk's response, though, was decidedly uncommon—they worked to have their circa 1852 community designated the ◆**Oakland Historic District** and placed on the National Register of Historic Places, the first such district in Oregon to be so recognized, in 1967.

Begin with a stroll on Locust Street, poking into a few of its antiques shops and boutiques. Then stop at ◆**Tolley's Restaurant and Antiques** for lunch or dinner, during which you'll be surrounded by more antiques, an old-fashioned soda fountain, and a lovely curved staircase of gleaming wood. Romantic candlelit tables are on the balcony level. The restaurant and ice-cream parlor are open daily for lunch; the intimate dining room on Tuesday through Sunday from 5:00 to 9:00 P.M. The phone number is (541) 459–3796.

Next browse through memorabilia and old photographs at the **Oakland Museum,** open daily from 1:00 to 4:30 P.M. except holidays (541–459–4531), and conclude your visit by walking farther up both sides of Locust Street to see vintage commercial structures, art galleries, antiques shops, and Victorian-style houses. Ask at Tolley's if the Oakland Gaslight Players are doing summertime melodramas in the renovated high school building at the upper end of Locust Street.

For a pleasant overnight stay call the friendly folks at **Beckley House Bed & Breakfast** located at 338 SE Second Street, Oakland 97462; (541) 459–9320. The Classic Revival Victorian was built in the late 1800s and, now renovated, offers guests two comfortable suites. Ask about the "History and Walking Tour of Oakland" brochure and for directions to covered bridges and wineries.

SOUTHEASTERN OREGON

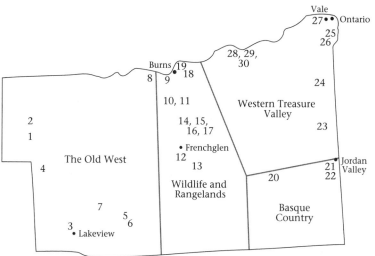

Vale
27 •• Ontario
25
26
28, 29,
30
Burns 19
8 9 18
24
10, 11
Western Treasure
Valley
2
14, 15,
16, 17
23
1
• Frenchglen
The Old West
12
4
13
21 Jordan
22 Valley
20
Wildlife and
Rangelands
7
Basque
Country
5
6
3
• Lakeview

1. Fremont Highway
2. Fort Rock State Park
3. Old Perpetual
4. Paisley Rodeo
5. Hart Mountain National Antelope Refuge
6. Hot Springs Campground
7. Abert Rim
8. Sagehen Hill Nature Trail
9. John Scharff Migratory Waterfowl Festival
10. Malheur National Wildlife Refuge
11. George M. Benson Memorial Museum
12. Frenchglen Hotel
13. Steens Mountain Loop Drive
14. Diamond Craters Natural Area
15. Hotel Diamond
16. McCoy Creek Inn
17. Kiger Mustang Viewing Area
18. Harney County Historical Society Museum
19. Lone Pine Guest Ranch
20. Rome Columns and Owyhee River
21. Jordan Valley
22. Old Basque Inn Restaurant
23. Leslie Gulch–Succor Creek
24. Lake Owyhee and Owyhee Dam
25. Nyssa
26. Keeney Pass Oregon Trail Site
27. Vale Murals
28. Juntura
29. Beulah Reservoir and Chukar Park Campground
30. Castle Rock

SOUTHEASTERN OREGON

THE OLD WEST

Southeastern Oregon is the state's "big sky" country, made up of its three largest and least-populated counties: Harney, Malheur, and Lake. The whole of many states on the East Coast could fit into this wide-open country in the Beaver State's far southeastern corner. In the 28,450-square-mile area containing just Malheur and Lake counties, there are fewer than ten people per square mile—now, that's elbow room with room to spare.

The stark, panoramic landscapes here evoke images of western movies; one can easily imagine cowboys riding "Old Red" and "Big Blue," herding cattle through sagebrush-blanketed valleys and across rushing streams and sending scouts up narrow canyons to flat-topped buttes or along alkali lakes far ahead. The horizon stretches wide in all four directions in this massive high-desert country, broken now and then by shaggy pinnacles, ridged rimrock canyons, flat-topped buttes, and massive fault-block mountains.

Hudson's Bay Company explorer-trapper Peter Skene Ogden, along with other fur traders who came in the mid-1820s, had a fairly easy trek into the region because resident Native Americans had already carved numerous trails, often following deer and antelope trails. The ancient Paiute Indians hunted, traveled the animal trails, gathered seeds, and dug camas bulbs for centuries before Ogden's party arrived in 1826.

Other white people passed through in the 1850s, during the California gold rush. Those early cattle barons then grabbed millions of acres of the southeastern desert country for rangeland in the 1870s and 1880s. The region still contains a number of the old ranches, and raising beef cattle remains one of the primary occupations—along with raising sheep, which were introduced by the immigrant Basques in the 1890s.

In 1843 Captain John C. Frémont, a topographic engineer, was sent to the territory by the U.S. government to explore the region. He is responsible for naming many of the bold features of Lake County encountered during this winter expedition. You can follow his north-south route on Highway 31, the ◆ **Fremont**

Highway, which skirts the Fremont National Forest and is accessed from Lakeview, near the Oregon–California border, or from Highway 97 just south of Bend, near LaPine.

If time allows, detour from Highway 97 at LaPine onto Highway 31 and follow the signs to ◆ **Fort Rock State Park** (about 30 miles). Rising 325 feet from the high desert floor and surrounded by miles and miles of pungent sagebrush, you get the most dramatic perspective by walking up and inside the volcanic remnant. It's more than ½ mile across inside. If you're lucky you might spot a baby eagle's nest. Notice the large wave-cut formations on the east flank, carved by aeons-old inland seas that once covered this vast region.

Although the tiny community of **Fort Rock** offers one gasoline station, a cafe, and a grocery store, it's best to also bring your own supplies such as sunscreen, wide-brimmed hats, and drinking water. The high desert gets *very* hot and dry during summer months, with temperatures in the high eighties and nineties. Stay long enough, however, to visit **Fort Rock Homestead Village Museum,** whose vintage structures date back to those original homestead days. Visit from Memorial Day weekend through September, Friday through Sunday, 10:00 A.M. to 4:00 P.M. Call (541) 576–2282 for additional information.

As you continue south on Highway 31, you could pause in Silver Lake for dinner at **Cowboy Dinner Tree,** 4 miles South Hager Mt. Road, (541) 576–2426. Friday and Saturday are steak nights, Sunday is "Tri-Tips," and Wednesday is "Cook's Choice." Just 2 miles north of Lakeview off Highway 395, visit ◆ **Old Perpetual,** a geyser that spouts about 60 feet above the ground every ninety seconds. The underground water heats to a temperature of some 200 degrees, erupting in a frothy, billowy column. Adjacent to the Sportsman Motel and rustic **Hunter's Hot Springs Resort** (541–947–2127) is a large lake that steams all year; hundreds of geese and ducks fly in to spend the night, especially during the winter, when other waters are frozen.

If you trek through the area in September, check out the **Lake County Fair,** featuring the largest and oldest amateur rodeo in the northwest, the ◆ **Paisley Rodeo.** You'll notice cowboys and cowgirls riding through the streets of nearby Paisley, a frontier town on the Chewaucan River along the Fremont Highway, and you'll also spot the old watering trough and hitching post downtown. Civilization can't be too far away, though—there's also an airstrip that accommodates small planes here. Further information and current dates for the county fair and rodeo can be obtained from the Lake County Visitors' Center, 126 North E Street, Lakeview 97630 (541) 947–6040.

If time allows, head east via Highway 140 to see whether the pelican colony is nesting at **Pelican Lake,** about 28 miles east of Lakeview. Turn north at the hamlet of Adel—a restaurant and a gas station are situated here—and proceed on a paved side road for a mile or so. This road continues another 15 miles to the small ranching community of Plush; along the way you might see Canada geese, sandhill cranes, and deer, particularly during the migrations in late fall.

For an alternate and closer route to Plush, head east from Lakeview on Highway 140 for about 15 miles, passing the small Warner Canyon Ski Area (541–947–5001). You'll reach the top of Warner Pass at 5,846 feet, then turn north and drop steeply into picturesque Warner Valley some 19 miles to Plush. This small ranching community on the edge of Hart Lake serves as the gateway to ◈**Hart Mountain National Antelope Refuge.** You'll find one store with groceries and gas here. The 275,000-acre federal wildlife refuge was established in 1930, and the mountain was named for the heart-shaped brand of a former cattle ranch located nearby; the word was apparently misspelled. Along its mountain slopes and canyons clothed with groves of graceful aspen, craggy yellow pine, and ground-hugging sagebrush flourishes one of the largest herds of prong-horn antelope in the United States. The larger mule deer, with prominent ears, are seen in the area as well.

Note: The numerous all-weather gravel roads found in this region are often bumpy, steep, and one lane wide; always have a full tank of gas, extra water, and food supplies before heading into the hinterlands. Be prepared to change flat tires as well. Diesel fuel is usually available only in the larger cities, and gas stations along remote stretches close at dusk. The high desert is unforgiving regardless of the season; days can be very hot and dry, nights chilly or freezing.

Thus well equipped, you can try out your natural-history–exploring persona and a more relaxed pace while carefully negoti-ating the narrow all-weather road north of Plush that climbs

60

steeply 27 miles to ❖ **Hot Springs Campground,** atop 7,710-foot Hart Mountain. You'll pass the National Refuge headquarters at the top and then continue a short distance to the campground, where you can immerse your road-weary body in a natural hot-water spring right next to the sky. The pool is enclosed by a block wall windbreak, roofless to let the stars in—and the night sky is virtually jammed with glittering stars. Pitch your tent, walk the short trail to the summit overlook, and watch for eagles, badgers, and wild bighorn sheep, as well as the antelope and deer that are protected here (they feed in the early morning and at dusk).

The Hart Mountain National Antelope Refuge area is also well-known to rock hounds for its agate nodules, fire opal, crystals, and sun stones. For gem-hunting locations open to the public, check with the ranger at the refuge headquarters; or pick up maps and obtain directions from the refuge visitors' information center in Lakeview (541–947–3315), particularly if you want to go to the sun-stone area. Write to the refuge manager for further information, P.O. Box 111, Lakeview 97630.

From Plush you can connect with Highway 395 by heading northwest along the hogback for about 31 miles of good all-weather dirt road. In the distance you'll see Coyote Hills and 30-mile-wide ❖ **Abert Rim** rising 2,000 feet above the plateau, filling the western horizon along the edge of Abert Lake. Its 800-foot lava cap ends in a sheer precipice.

This scarp is a nearly perfect fault, one of the largest exposed faults in the world. On huge boulders at the base are pictographs drawn by early Indians who lived in the region; arrowheads, rock foundations of primitive huts, and bleached bones have also been discovered in the area.

This southeastern region is dotted with beds of lakes formed thousands of years ago. Some lakes evaporated; others found outlets or were clogged by showers of volcanic ash. Some contain water during the brief rainy season; others are always dry; and still others retain only enough moisture to become meadows. You'll see chalky white alkali around many of the lakes' shores, as the lakes shrink during the summer months.

Head north on paved Highway 395, passing Wagontire and stopping at **Riley,** a distance of about 60 miles. Here mule deer share the browse with shaggy range bulls that look the size of locomotives. Gas up at Riley, or continue east some 25 miles on

Highway 20, stopping in the larger community of **Burns** to replenish gas and food supplies.

Just east of Riley you can detour at the state rest area and walk the ½ mile ◆**Sagehen Hill Nature Trail** to become acquainted with the native shrubs, plants, and bird species of the high desert region. At eleven self-guided stations, visitors identify big sagebrush (take a small leaf, rub it between your palms, and sniff the wonderful fragrance); bitterbrush, with its dark green leaves and yellow springtime flowers; western juniper, one of the dominant trees, its blue-green berries loved by many bird species; low sagebrush; and Idaho fescue, an important native bunchgrass that grows on the high desert.

Along the trail you may also see dwarf monkey flower, western yarrow, blue-eyed Mary, owl clover, lupine, and wild parsley. Keep an eye out for red-tailed hawks, golden eagles, turkey vultures, and prairie falcons, as well as sage grouse, mourning doves, mountain bluebirds, and Oregon's state bird, the melodious western meadowlark.

Look toward the west to spot Wagontire Mountain, Squaw Butte, and Glass Buttes. On a clear day you can see Steens Mountain to the south and east; it's composed of hundreds of layers of basalt lava that were thrust more than 1 mile above the plateau about fifteen million years ago. Directly south is **Palomino Buttes,** part of a Bureau of Land Management area for wild horses that covers about 96,000 acres. Often bands of from thirty to sixty wild horses are seen along the roads in the area.

One such area, **Palomino Buttes Horse Management Area,** can be accessed about ½ mile east of the Sagehen rest area by turning south on the gravel road labeled "Double-O." The wild horses are wary of humans, however, so binoculars and lack of noise may help you to spot them.

By now even the most confirmed city dweller should have relaxed into the quiet strength of the high desert, and the notion of becoming an amateur geologist or naturalist, even for a brief time, will seem an appealing alternative. These wide-open spaces also had an appeal for an eclectic mix of early settlers—first trappers and miners, then cowboys, cattle barons, and sheepherders, each, of course, displacing the native peoples, many of whom were ultimately sent to reservations.

The cattle barons and sheepherders were, needless to say, on less than friendly terms in those early days, and many bloody skirmishes occurred between the two groups until the federal government intervened. Today nearly 75 percent of the land in southeastern Oregon is managed by the federal Bureau of Land Management.

WILDLIFE AND RANGELANDS

If your visit to the region coincides with the early spring migration, consider taking in the ❖**John Scharff Migratory Waterfowl Festival** in Burns. Meet bird lovers from all over the Northwest, participate in guided bird-watching walks, see films and slide shows, and hear interesting lectures given by noted waterfowl experts. For dates—the festival usually takes place the first or second weekend of April—write to the Burns-Harney County Visitors' Center, 18 West D Street, Burns 97720, or call (541) 573–2636.

Burns, in its earliest years, was the capital of the old cattle empire—the surrounding areas were ruled by cattle barons like Peter French and Henry Miller—but by 1889 Burns amounted to a straggling frontier village of one dusty main street bordered by frame shacks. During the next thirty-five years, the settlers waited for the expanding railroad system to reach their town. A colorful throng gathered to see the first train arrive in September 1924—the cattle ranchers wearing Stetsons, the cowboys sporting jingling spurs on their high-heeled boots, and the Paiute Indians attired in their brightly hued native dress.

Another colorful throng, this one composed of bird species and wildlife, gathers just south of Burns near Harney and Malheur lakes on the ❖**Malheur National Wildlife Refuge.** On your way into the refuge, stop at the National Refuge headquarters for information on current road conditions and which bird species are in residence. The headquarters is located on the south shore of Malheur Lake, 40 miles south of Burns via Highways 78 and 205; the last 6 miles are gravel surfaced. The headquarters and its visitors' center are open weekdays from 8:00 A.M. to 4:30 P.M. Call (541) 493–2612; the mailing address is HC-72, P.O. Box 245, Princeton 97721. *Note:* Check water and weather conditions on the refuge when planning a visit.

While at the refuge headquarters, stop at the ❖**George M. Benson Memorial Museum,** just next door, where you can see nearly 200 beautifully mounted specimens of migratory birds. The museum is open daily.

For seminars on local history, geology, and birds and wildlife and for guided trips, folks can contact and bunk at the **Malheur Field Station,** also located just next to the National Refuge headquarters and the museum. This nonprofit "Desert Wilderness Program" is supported by twenty-two schools and by such prestigious organizations as the Audubon Society, the Nature Conservancy, and the Oregon High Desert Museum in Bend. Outdoor classes for students of all ages, from all over the region, and including Elderhostel programs for seniors sixty and older, are held here year-round.

Travelers can also bunk in one of the trailers or dorm rooms (bring your own sleeping bag) at the Malheur Field Station and can arrange for meals here as well. For information and reservations—the latter are a must, especially during spring and autumn bird migration seasons—write to Director, Malheur Field Station, Box 260-E, Princeton 97721, or call (541) 493–2629.

Use the helpful maps provided by the U.S. Fish and Wildlife Service and the U.S. Department of the Interior obtained at Refuge Headquarters as you explore this magnificent wildlife refuge, which received official approval from President Theodore Roosevelt in 1908. The lakes, ponds, marshes, mudflats, and grain crops of the refuge are now managed for the benefit of both resident and migratory wildlife. Prior to this intervention early settlers had engaged in unrestricted hunting of the birds, and plume hunters had nearly wiped out the swans, egrets, herons, and grebes to obtain and sell their elegant feathers to milliners in San Francisco, Chicago, and New York.

Continue south on Highway 205 toward **Frenchglen,** journeying on a two-lane road that will take you through the heart of the refuge, with its 185,000 acres of open water, marshes, irrigated meadows and grainfields, riparian grassy areas, and uplands. You'll first notice antelope bitterbrush, sagebrush, and western juniper, followed by quaking aspen and mountain mahogany at elevations above 4,000 feet.

Although the largest concentration of migratory birds usually occurs in March and April, many varieties can be seen throughout the year here—including the mallards, Canada geese, and greater sandhill cranes that gather noisily to feed in the **Blitzen Valley**

Frenchglen Hotel State Wayside

grainfields located just south of National Refuge headquarters, Rattlesnake Butte, and Buena Vista Ponds. Great blue herons, white pelicans, trumpeter swans, long-billed curlews, great egrets, snowy egrets, and many kinds of ducks, geese, and hawks also rest and often nest on the refuge; many of these species can also be seen on the large marshes and ponds near Burns. *Note:* Your car makes an excellent observation and photographic blind; birds will be less frightened if you stay in your car and move slowly. Use binoculars and telephoto lenses; go on your own or join a naturalist-guided tour. In any case you'll soon get used to quantities of bird talk: gabbles, honks, whistles, twitters, low quacking, and the curious rattle-honk of the sandhill cranes. This is archetypal wilderness at its best.

Just south of Malheur and Harney lakes, in the shadow of a commanding, 9,670-foot fault block known as Steens Mountain, tiny ❖**Frenchglen Hotel** sits like a miniature sentinel reminding visitors of the pioneer past. Built in the late 1870s by the early cattle baron Peter French, the hotel is now owned by the state and managed by the State Parks and Recreation

Department. Along with other bird-watchers and photography buffs, you can reserve one of the eight postage stamp–size guest rooms. The evening meal is served family style, accompanied by lively exchanges between guests about fishing exploits, bird-watching areas, wildflower finds, and ghost towns discovered in the area. Next morning the aroma of freshly brewed coffee will lure you downstairs to an enormous breakfast of such delights as giant blueberry pancakes, eggs, sausage, and huge slices of watermelon, cantaloupe, and pineapple. For information—reservations are a must, especially for meals—contact the innkeepers at Frenchglen Hotel, Frenchglen 97736; (541) 493–2825. The hotel is open from March through October.

Naturally, you'll work off this hearty morning meal by poking around the Frenchglen Mercantile; the village has a population of about ten, depending on the time of year, and the number of buildings can be counted on one hand. If you have a hardy vehicle, preferably with four-wheel drive, and want to take in spectacular vistas way off the beaten path, drive the 69-mile ❖**Steens Mountain Loop Drive,** which begins just 3 miles south of Frenchglen. *Note:* Allow two to three hours for this panoramic drive. There are two campgrounds on the north section of the loop drive.

Check with the Bureau of Land Management visitors' information trailer in Frenchglen for current road conditions—don't attempt this route in rainy or icy weather. On the one-way gravel road, the steep climb through sagebrush to juniper, through groves of quaking aspen, and into alpine wildflower-strewn meadows is deceivingly gradual.

Then you are suddenly next to the sky, at nearly 10,000 feet above the desert floor, and are pulling off at **East Rim Viewpoint** to gaze at ancient glaciated valleys and down at the Alvord Desert, more than a mile below. Keep an eye out for kestrels, golden eagles, bald eagles, prairie falcons, bighorn sheep, and deer during summer months—and black rosy finches at the summit.

If the Steens Mountain loop drive seems a bit strenuous for your automobile, consider the easier, 26-mile **Diamond Loop.** This latter trek is reached from an 18-mile side road, a section of the **Blitzen Valley Auto Tour Route,** as you head east from the Malheur National Refuge headquarters—where you can pick up a brochure for this self-guided auto tour.

On this western section of Diamond Loop, stop at ❖ **Diamond Craters Natural Area** for a self-guided hike through lava cones, ropy lava flows, cinder cones, spatter cones, and other unusual volcanic remnants scattered over several square miles. For current regional maps, auto guides, and hiking information, contact the Burns District Bureau of Land Management office, 12533 Highway 20 West, Hines 97738, or call (541) 573–5241.

At the northeast corner of Diamond Loop, you can see one of the state's oldest, most unusual structures: a round barn built a hundred or so years ago by cattle baron Peter French. It was used for breaking horses during winter months. Besides several willow and stockade fences, the only other structure remaining of French's cattle empire is the Long Barn, which you can walk through at the historic P Ranch location near Frenchglen.

From 1872, when he arrived with a herd of cattle and six Mexican vaqueros, until 1897, Peter French expanded his holdings and cattle operation to the point where he controlled nearly 200,000 acres, ran some 45,000 head of cattle and more than 3,000 horses, and built a dozen ranches encircling his domain on the west side of Steens Mountain. (Rulers of the enormous areas to the north and east were cattle barons John Devine and Henry Miller.) Peter French and his partner were fatally shot by disgruntled neighboring ranchers on the day after Christmas in 1897.

For a comfortable overnight stay about as far into the hinterlands as you can drive, located at the south end of the Diamond Loop Drive, the ❖ **Hotel Diamond** offers five small bedrooms on the second floor with baths down the hall, like the "olden days." The hostelry does extra duty as general store, deli, and post office for Diamond's six or so enthusiastic residents. These include Judy and Jerry Santillie, the couple who purchased the building in 1986 and who spent five years renovating it. Hearty family-style dinners are served to hotel guests at 6:30 P.M. or, a bit later, at 7:30 P.M. for a lighter offering of, say, salad and hearty soups. The hotel is open March through October. For information and reservations contact the Santillies at P.O. Box 10, Diamond 97722, or call them at (541) 493–1898. If the hotel is filled, check with the folks at ❖ **McCoy Creek Inn** also located near Diamond, just 12 miles east and south of Highway 205, turning east at the Diamond junction (about 40 miles south of Burns). You can choose from three guest rooms in the main house or hole up in the cozy bunkhouse just next door. Guests are invited to enjoy the hot tub as well as to roam hiking trails in **McCoy Canyon.** Breakfast is a hearty affair and a gourmet dinner is available by reservation. Contact the family of innkeepers at (541) 493–2131 days and at (541) 493–2440 evenings. *Note:* This is a working ranch so no pets are allowed.

You might also be interested in the ◆**Kiger Mustang Viewing Area** located just a few miles east and south of McCoy Creek Inn. A number of wild horses, from among the twenty different management areas in which they roam, are rounded up by Bureau of Land Management (BLM) personnel every three to four years to thin the herds. These animals are offered for adoption as part of the national **Adopt-a-Horse** program. A lively event, the **Northwest Mustang Affair** takes place at the Harney County fairgrounds in Burns, where folks who have qualified take part in the lottery drawing for the wild horses. If their number is drawn, they get to choose the mustang they wish to adopt. For further information contact the BLM office, HC 74-12533 Highway 20 West, Burns 97738; (541) 573–4400.

The ◆**Harney County Historical Society Museum** in Burns contains many informational displays and vintage photographs that allow a peek into this fascinating Old West section of Oregon. The museum, located at 18 West D Street in Burns (541–573–2636) is open from June through September, Tuesday through Saturday from 9:00 A.M. to 5:00 P.M.

If your travel schedule or the weather conditions prevent a trip from Burns into the Malheur National Wildlife Refuge and Peter French's historic Blitzen Valley, try the shorter **Lower Silvies River Valley Drive,** via Highway 78, just southeast of Burns in the scenic Harney Valley. Here you can see ducks, geese, and sandhill cranes in March and April and can observe avocets, ibis, terns, curlews, and egrets through July.

A lovely overnight option is ◆**Lone Pine Guest Ranch,** located just 3 miles east and north of Burns via Highway 20. Here the Davis family shares their spectacular view from two suites situated on the edge of a wide rim that overlooks Steens Mountain, the Silvies River and Five Mile Dam area, and the Harney Valley—the high desert at your feet. Each suite is fully self-contained with private bath, kitchenette, cozy sitting area, and wide deck. For reservations contact Fran Davis at (541) 573–2103; HC

71-51 Lone Pine Road, P.O. Box 531, Burns 97720. Children are welcome.

Before heading out of the Burns area you could also try out the following eateries: **The Powerhouse** at 305 East Monroe Street (541–573–9060); **Pine Room Cafe** on Monroe at Egan Street (541–573–6631); **Steens Mountain Cafe** at 195 North Alder Street (541–573–7226); and **Jerry's Restaurant** at 937 Oregon Avenue (541–573–7000).

From Burns you can head east on Highway 20 toward Ontario and the Oregon–Idaho border, west on Highway 20 toward Bend and central Oregon's high desert country, southwest via Highway 78 toward Jordan Valley, or continue south via Highways 78 and 95 to the Oregon–Nevada border. *Note:* Remember that distances in this remote section of the Beaver State are deceiving and that food and gasoline services are also remote and many hours apart. Always have current state maps, keep track of distances and the time of day, refill your gas tank before heading into the sagebrush and alkali desert country, and arrange ahead for overnight accommodations (unless you are camping).

BASQUE COUNTRY

At Burns Junction, about 92 miles southeast of Burns, turn east on Highway 95. After roughly 15 miles turn north on a gravel-surfaced road just beyond the hamlet of Rome (gas, groceries, and RV campsites here) and opposite the OWYHEE CANYON ROAD sign. The intriguing ◆ **Rome Columns** can be seen about 3½ miles down the dusty road. The columns are huge formations of sandstone and fossil-bearing clay from Oregon's prehistoric past that jut some 1,000 feet into the intense blue sky. Surrounded by yellow-blooming sagebrush, the creamy-colored battlements, stained with rich browns, overlook the peaceful ranch and farm valley of the nearby ◆ **Owyhee River.**

Actually, eons ago this high desert area was a lush tropical paradise, as evidenced by many species of shell and animal fossils found throughout the layers of ancient riverbeds and lake beds. Those emigrant pioneers who detoured south through this region in the early 1840s carved their names in the soft sandstone; later, the area also served as a stage stop.

Just north of the bridge, across the Owyhee River, you could turn right to the Bureau of Land Management guard station, which has a small grassy area, picnic tables, potable water, and a rest room. There is also a public boat ramp here.

Just 33 miles east of Rome, the community of ◆**Jordan Valley** sits at an elevation of 4,389 feet, virtually on the Oregon–Idaho border. This small town became the unlikely home of a band of Basque immigrants who in the 1890s left their homelands in the French and Spanish Pyrenees. The Basques, being sheepherders, also brought lambs and ewes to the Jordan Valley. By the turn of the century—and after countless bloody skirmishes—sheepherding replaced cattle ranching in this far southeastern corner of the state.

Originally an important way station on a supply line between the mining camps of California and Idaho, Jordan Valley thus became a major sheep-trading center and the home of the Basque settlers and their families. Near the old Jordan Valley Hotel in the center of town, you can see remnants of a hand-hewn stone court where early Basque townspeople played *pelota,* an energetic game similar to handball.

Stop at the ◆**Old Basque Inn Restaurant** for tasty local food; the eatery is located in town on North Highway 95 (541–586–2298) and is open daily from 6:00 to 10:00 P.M. For an overnight stay, try the Sahara Motel (541–586–2500) or the Basque Station Motel (541–586–9244). Other than camping, these two motels are the only overnight options in the Jordan Valley area.

For current information about the region, about the annual **Jordan Valley Big Loops Rodeo,** held each May, and about other colorful Basque festivals held during summer and fall, contact the Nyssa Visitors' Center, 14 South Third Street (P.O. Box 2515), Nyssa 97913; (541) 372–3091.

WESTERN TREASURE VALLEY

From Jordan Valley head north on Highway 95 about 18 miles, turning onto an all-weather gravel road that angles northwest toward ◆**Leslie Gulch–Succor Creek.** The rugged road—accessible to all but low-slung automobiles, which won't do so well—drops into a canyon where sandstone cliffs seem to loom higher, as well as to hover closer together. Their deep pinks, flamboyant purples, vibrant oranges, and flaming reds splash across the brilliant blue sky, the stark landscape littered here and there with pungent sage and bitterbrush. This scenery is guaranteed to buckle the knees of the toughest cowpoke or the most cynical urban dweller.

Miles of dirt roads and trails are available to hikers, backpackers, and off-road vehicles in the Leslie Gulch area, managed by the Bureau of Land Management. If you move quietly and carefully, you may see wild horses and bighorn sheep roaming through the canyons, as well as chukars (small partridges) dashing across dusty roadbeds and up steep talus slopes. Look for thunder eggs—oblong rocks, rough on the outside but usually containing beautiful crystal formations on the inside—at nearby **Succor Creek Canyon,** and look for agates along the banks of the Owyhee River. The best time to visit is April through June, although snow is possible in early May. Summers are hot and dry, with temperatures of 90 degrees and above, whereas by late September the nights are frosty. *Note:* There are primitive rest rooms and drinking water at the **Succor Creek Recreation Area Campground;** rest rooms and primitive camping but no water at Leslie Gulch. Check for ticks after hiking—they can carry Lyme disease. For current information check with the Vale District Office of the Bureau of Land Management, 100 Oregon Street, Vale 97918; (541) 473–3144.

A better alternative is the campground just south of Owyhee Dam at Lake Owyhee State Park, on the shores of ◆**Lake Owyhee**—about 23 miles from Adrian, off Highway 201 (Adrian is about 20 miles north of Succor Creek State Recreation Area). Another alternative is to call ahead to arrange motel-with-kitchen accommodations at **Lake Owyhee Resort,** (541) 339–2444. Services here include a small store with fishing tackle, basic food supplies, maps of reservoir and fishing areas, pontoon boat rentals, and a few cabins, as well as motel rooms.

If you plan a trip into this remote area, be sure to have a full tank of gas, plenty of food and beverages, extra containers of water, sturdy shoes, and camping gear. There are a few electrical hookups at Lake Owyhee State Park, as well as a public boat ramp and a dock. The toll-free Campsite Information center phone number is (800) 452–5687.

Be sure to stop and see the imposing ◆**Owyhee Dam,**

71

located north of the campground. Begun in 1926 and completed in 1932, the dam rises 405 feet from bedrock, is 255 feet thick at its base in the sandstone and basalt canyon, and is 30 feet thick at the top. The structure represents one of the largest and most important irrigation developments in the state, for the Owyhee River waters stored in the large lake behind the dam are used not only for year-round recreation but also to irrigate an extensive area of high desert that would otherwise remain an arid wasteland.

Near the communities of Nyssa, Vale, and Ontario—located on the Oregon–Idaho border about 45 miles north of Owyhee Dam and Lake Owyhee—you can see evidence of the Owyhee River waters bringing life to lush fields of sugar beets, potatoes, onions, and alfalfa. Notice the tall green poplars and shaggy locust trees around homesteads, then rows of fruit trees gradually giving way to wheat and grazing lands.

In ◆ **Nyssa,** a thriving community for the dairy and poultry industries, a large beet-sugar refining plant also produces and ships many tons of sugar each day. Between the three communities of Nyssa, Vale, and Ontario, you can see broad fields of blooming zinnias, bachelor buttons, and other flowers grown for the garden seed market; vegetables are grown here, too. Midsummer is a good time to see the fields of flowers in gorgeous bloom—and you might also smell the pungent, dark-green peppermint plants that cover large fields as well.

In the sagebrush-covered rimrock hills above these beautiful fields, a number of Basque sheepherders still sing and echo their distinctive native melodies while they and their sheepdogs tend large flocks. Many Mexican-American families also live in the area, as do a large number of Japanese-Americans, who resettled here following the forced internments in the area during World War II. For information and current dates for the colorful annual ethnic festivals held in the area, contact the Ontario Visitors' Center, 88 SW Third Avenue, Ontario 97914 (541–889–8012); the Nyssa Visitors' Center, 14 South Third Street (P.O. Box 2515), Nyssa 97913 (541–372–3091); and the Vale Visitors' Center, 275 North Main Street (P.O.Box 661), Vale 97918 (541–473–3800).

There is also a well-stocked State Welcome Center at the Ontario rest area on I–84 (I–80N) about ½ mile from the Oregon–Idaho border.

From nearby Nyssa travel west and north on Enterprise Avenue, which is actually a section of the Oregon Trail. Stop at the ◈ **Keeney Pass Oregon Trail Site** and look up and down the draw at the deep wagon ruts cut into the soft clay. Here you can also read about some of the hardships experienced. From Amelia Knight's diary entry dated August 5–8, 1853, for example, you'll read this: "Just reached Malheur River and campt, the roads have been very dusty, no water, nothing but dust and dead cattle all day."

For the pioneers the hot mineral springs near **Vale** were a welcome stop for bathing and washing clothes. At the **Malheur Crossing** marker, located between the bridges on the east edge of Vale, notice the deep ruts left by the heavy wagons pulling up the grade after crossing the river. Also, while in town, notice the ◈ **Vale Murals.** Painted on buildings throughout the community, the murals depict poignant scenes from the Oregon Trail journey. There's also a quaint 1890s-style Ice Cream Parlor where you could pause for cool libations.

The pioneers actually entered what is now Oregon at old Fort Boise—in Idaho, just a few miles east of Nyssa—a fur-trading post established in 1834 by the British Hudson's Bay Company. Here the wagons forded the Snake River, the settlers often having to remove the wheels before the wagons could float across. From Malheur Crossing, where the pioneers enjoyed a welcome soak in the hot springs, the wagon trains continued northwest, met the Snake River again at Farewell Bend, and then made their way through the Snake River Valley and west toward The Dalles and the most difficult river passage from there downriver to Fort Vancouver—the mighty Columbia River.

History buffs can inquire at the Ontario Visitors' Center whether the city of Boise, Idaho, located about 60 miles east, has ready for visitors its **Oregon Trail Site.** Boise boasts a large section of clearly visible ruts carved by thousands of those horse-and oxen-drawn wagons during the 1840s migration from Independence, Missouri, to the Oregon Country.

An alternate route, the old **Central Oregon Emigrant Trail,** is followed rather closely by Highway 20 east from Vale, just north of Keeney Pass. In 1845 a wagon train of some 200 pioneers, led by Stephen Meek, first attempted this route. Unfortunately about seventy members of the group died from hardship and exposure when the wagon train wandered for weeks on the high desert, bewildered by the maze of similar ridges, canyons, and washes. Meek was attempting to find a shortcut to the Willamette Valley. The survivors finally reached the Deschutes River, near Bend, and followed it to The Dalles.

Take Highway 20 toward **Burns** for a nostalgic look at more of the wagon ruts, as well as a view of the vast sagebrush desert those first pioneers struggled to cross. Later, between 1864 and 1868, the **Cascade Mountain Military Road** was laid out following the Central Oregon Emigrant Trail. This new road connected with the old **Willamette Valley Road,** which brought travelers across the central Cascade Mountains to Albany, in the lush central and northern Willamette Valley.

In those days wagon trains, some a ½-mile long, carried wool and livestock from the eastern Oregon range country to the Willamette Valley, returning with fruit, vegetables, and other food supplies. Stagecoaches, conveying both mail and passengers, added their own dramatic chapter to the history of the Cascade Mountain Military Road. Every settlement on the route drew all or part of its livelihood from this transportation link. From historians, by the way, we learn that the first automobile to cross the United States was driven over this route, in June 1905.

As travelers now speed along modern Highway 20 between Vale and Burns, a drive of about two hours, note that this same trip took two full days and one night for the stagecoaches to complete. The trip was hot and dusty, with a change of horses taking place every 15 miles. Images of a Roy Rogers or a John Wayne western movie come to mind, with a stagecoach pulled by a team of horses bumping across the sagebrush desert.

About midway between Vale and Burns, you'll pass through **Juntura,** a poplar-shaded village nestled in a small valley where the North Fork of the Malheur River joins the South Fork. Stop to see the lambing sheds near the railroad tracks. Long a major shipping point for both sheep and cattle, the entire valley and surrounding range country were once dominated by the legendary Henry Miller, one of the powerful cattle barons of the late 1800s.

You can see a shearing and dipping plant by turning south from Juntura on an all-weather gravel road and then proceeding for about 4 miles, toward the tiny community of Riverside. For camping or a late-afternoon picnic, head north from Juntura to ◆**Beulah**

Reservoir. The Bureau of Land Management's ◆**Chukar Park Campground,** situated on the North Fork of the Malheur River, has nineteen sites; the county has a primitive campground on the lake as well. *Note:* Drinking water needs to be packed in here.

About 4 miles north of the campground, find a good area for day hikes at ◆**Castle Rock,** an extinct volcano cone that rises to an elevation of 6,837 feet. For maps and further information about Chukar Park Campground, day hiking, and fall hunting in the area, contact the BLM's Vale District Office, P.O. Box 700, Vale 97918; (541) 473–3144.

Tired of camping? Well, you could call the folks at **Blue Bucket Inn at SE Ranch** and linger one more day or so in cowboy country. Here you can hole up or help out on a 2,600-acre working cattle ranch located on a scenic stretch of meadow and rangeland that borders the central fork of the Malheur River—25 miles west of Juntura and some 50 miles from Burns. The grub is good—snacks are served on arrival and dinner can be arranged at an additional charge. A full country breakfast is included. For current information call or write the innkeepers at HC68-536, Drewsy 97904; (541) 493–2375 or (541) 493–2240.

CENTRAL OREGON

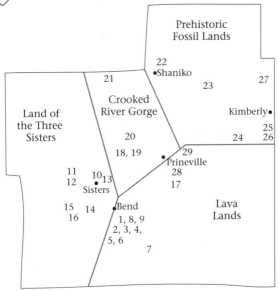

Prehistoric Fossil Lands

22
•Shaniko
21
23
27

Crooked River Gorge

Land of the Three Sisters

Kimberly•

25
20
24
26

18, 19

29
Prineville

11
12
10
13
Sisters

28
17

15
14
•Bend

Lava Lands

16
1, 8, 9
2, 3, 4,
5, 6
7

1. Pilot Butte
2. Oregon High Desert Museum
3. Lava Butte
4. Lava Cast Forest
5. Newberry Crater Auto Tour
6. Lava River Cave
7. Pine Mountain Observatory
8. Pine Tavern Restaurant
9. Deschutes Historical Center
10. Sisters Outdoor Quilt Show
11. Wizard Falls Fish Hatchery
    and Jack Creek Nature Trail
12. Black Butte Ranch
13. Cascade Country Inn
14. Cascade Lakes National Forest
    Scenic Drive
15. Three Sisters Wilderness
16. Metolius-Windigo Trail
17. Prineville Reservoir State Park
18. Redmond Smokejumper Base
19. Juniper Golf Club
20. Smith Rock State Park
21. Museum at Warm Springs
22. Historic Shaniko Hotel
23. John Day Fossil Beds
    National Monument
24. Blueberry Muffin Cafe
25. Cant Ranch Visitors' Center
26. Fish House Inn Bed &
    Breakfast
27. Corncob Ranch
28. Ochoco Lake State Park
29. Stein's Pillar

Central Oregon

Lava Lands

Carpeted with pungent sagebrush, juniper, and ponderosa pine, Oregon's central high desert country offers generous amounts of sunshine and miles of wide-open spaces at elevations of 3,000 feet and higher. Where ancient Indian fires once blazed on the shores of volcanic lakes and long-ago hunters left tracks and trails through pine and juniper forests, both Oregonians and out-of-staters now come to fish, hunt, camp, hike, and golf. Climbing high rocks and mountains, spelunking in lava-tube caves, and going alpine as well as cross-country skiing offer more adventurous outdoor pursuits as well.

The first white people to venture into central Oregon were hunters who trapped beaver for their lush pelts. Captain John C. Frémont, a topographic engineer, was sent from the East Coast to map the region in the 1840s, although both Peter Skene Ogden and Nathaniel Wyeth traveled through the area before Frémont's trek.

Lured by succulent meadows and grasses, the first immigrants to settle in the region raised cattle and sheep, and many ranches still operate in the area. Although Indian chief Paulina and his Paiute tribe fought against white settlement, peace eventually won out. Named for the old chief, the **Paulina Mountains,** rising south of Bend, offer a reminder of an important chapter in the area's colorful history.

To get your bearings when arriving in Bend—the largest city and hub of the central region—start from the downtown area and drive to the top of nearby ◆ **Pilot Butte,** at an elevation of 3,400 feet. Here you'll have a panoramic view of not only this sprawling mountain resort community, but no fewer than a dozen gorgeous snow-capped volcanic peaks to the west, in the Cascade Range. Incidentally, this is a great place to see fireworks on the Fourth of July.

The mountain peaks rise along the far horizon like vanilla ice-cream cones. Notice first the largest "double scoopers"—Mt. Jefferson, Mt. Washington, Broken Top, Three Sisters, Mt. Bachelor, and Ollalie Butte. Dusty and tired members of the pioneer wagon trains, as they lumbered across the harsh, unforgiving high desert, used to sight on Pilot Butte so as to maintain their bearings after having crossed the Snake River near the present communities of Ontario, Nyssa, and Vale in the eastern section of the state. Today the road to the top of Pilot Butte is paved, and the viewpoint area is wheelchair-accessible.

For one of the best introductions to the natural history of this vast, unique region, visit the ❖ **Oregon High Desert Museum,** just 5 miles south of Bend via Highway 97 toward Lava Butte. On the 150-acre site you can investigate a rimrock canyon, a marsh area, meadows, a flowing stream, a prehistoric cave, and other natural habitats for plants, birds, and wildlife native to the high desert. Self-guided interpretive paths shoelace in and around each life zone. You'll be able to tell a chipmunk from a ground squirrel—both have stripes along their backs, but the chipmunks have stripes on their cheeks, too—before arriving at the main entrance of the orientation center. "It's the relationship between people, the animals, and the desert habitat that we hope visitors come to understand and appreciate," said Donald Kerr, the museum's original founder and former director.

Beginning the project with a seed grant of $5,000 in 1977, Kerr and his staff—with the help of educators, private citizens, and businesspeople throughout the Northwest—raised several million dollars for the development of this extraordinary living museum. A dedicated group of volunteers from Bend and many surrounding communities donate countless hours to help maintain the grounds and develop year-round educational programs for children and adults.

Watch mischievous river otters frolic in their indoor-outdoor pool; pet friendly porcupines like "Cuddles" and "Thistlebritches"; and peer into the trunk of a ponderosa pine and hear museum staff and volunteers tell about gopher snakes, birds of prey, or desert weather patterns.

The latest group of exhibits at the museum complex can be seen in the **Earle A. Chiles Center,** offering a nostalgic dawn-to-dusk walk through eight historic scenes portraying sights, sounds, and authentic memorabilia of the setting of the West. You'll hear desert bird songs, wind and rain, and water rushing through an old mine sluice; you'll see the glow of a blacksmith's fire; and you'll smell the wood and leather in the saddlery.

For a schedule of workshops and special events offered year-round, contact the Oregon High Desert Museum, 59800 South

Highway 97, Bend 97702 (541–382–4754). The museum is open daily, except on major holidays, from 9:00 A.M. to 5:00 P.M. Enjoy, too, browsing in the Silver Sage Trading Store and having a snack in Rimrock Cafe.

For another panoramic view of the region, continue south from Bend along Highway 97 for about 10 miles to ◆ **Lava Butte,** stopping first at the **Lava Lands Visitors' Center** at its base for an intriguing look at the region's volcanic past. Colorful, animated displays simulate natural phenomena such as a volcanic eruption and an earthquake. Outdoors you can also walk the **Trail of the Molten Land** or the **Trail of the Whispering Pines,** both short self-guided treks near the visitors' center. Managed by the Deschutes National Forest, the well-stocked center is open daily (weather permitting) from 9:00 A.M. to 4:00 P.M.; the telephone number is (541) 593–2421.

The road leading up to 500-foot Lava Butte, the extinct reddish-brown volcanic cone looming above the visitors' center, is steep but well paved with red cinder rock, and there's a large parking area at the top. With camera or binoculars in hand, walk the easy self-guided trail around the top of the butte for spectacular views of ancient lava fields to the north and south and of those ever-present ice-cream-cone mountain peaks.

You're now gazing at a vast area in which folks have lived for more than 9,000 years. The earliest visitors probably came from the Great Basin area of Idaho and Utah to hunt and gather food. About 7,000 years ago the eruptions of Mt. Mazama—now Crater Lake, to the south—and nearby Mt. Newberry produced about 200 times the amount of ash, pumice, and debris created by the eruption of Mount St. Helens in Washington State in 1980. As you continue walking around the rim of Lava Butte, you can also see the Paulina Mountains, Newberry Crater, and the latter's two alpine lakes, Paulina and East Lakes, directly to the south and east.

If time allows, continue a few miles south on Highway 97 and take the 10-mile side trip into ◆ **Lava Cast Forest,** winding east through ponderosa pine, bitterbrush, and manzanita on a red cinder gravel road into the high-desert hinterlands. Access from Highway 97, turning east on Forest Service Road 9420, just opposite the Sun River turnoff. Pick up an illustrated guide at the beginning of the paved trail and enjoy twelve descriptive stops along the easy 1-mile trek. As you walk the path, notice the characteristic cinnamon-colored bark of the tall ponderosa pine; then, as you reach the sunny, open lava plain, notice the smaller version of the pine, nature's own bonsai, or dwarf, trees.

Though short and stunted—struggling to grow in the "a a" (AH-ah) lava, with its rough, jagged, and clinkerlike surfaces—the trees may actually be very old, their root systems enlarged to help fight the extreme environment. You'll also see dead trees bleached white by the desert weather, stark skeletons hunched in the black lava. During spring, flowering wild currant and bitterbrush ornament the volcanic landscape with pale pinks and yellows. Look, too, for red Indian paintbrush and rock pentstemons blooming in crevices and crannies.

Take a moment to imagine how those wagon trains and early pioneers could possibly have crossed the inhospitable lava fields of the high desert during the mid-1840s and the 1850s. The trappers, hunters, and Indians who preceded them were probably better off on foot or horseback, in comparison with having to guide the bulky, oxen- or horse-pulled covered wagons. The rough "a a" lava surely holds many heart-wrenching memories, particularly of mothers with small children, of those early crossings.

Peer into vertical and horizontal tree casts that about 6,000 years ago were enormous pines engulfed with slow-moving molten lava from **Mt. Newberry.** At station 9 along the trail you can actually see the source of the lava flow, toward what remains of the mountain, to the southeast. The rounded cylindrical casts are the only remnants of the lush forest that once clothed Mt. Newberry's slopes. Station 11 offers another grand view of the other snow-capped peaks in the Cascade Mountain Range, to the west.

Although there is no potable water at Lava Cast Forest, there are a couple of picnic tables, as well as an outdoor rest room, in the shade of tall ponderosa pine. You'll also find a few benches along the trail, affording sunny spots for a picnic lunch in the company of those intriguing tree casts, oddly shaped pine bonsais, and other specimens of plant life. Be sure to pack drinking water or canned beverages, especially on warm summer days, when temperatures can climb to the eighties or nineties.

Further information about this geologic phenomenon can be obtained from the Deschutes National Forest headquarters in Bend, at 1645 Highway 20 East, or call (541) 388–2715. The office is open year-round, Monday through Friday, from 7:45 A.M. to 4:30 P.M.

81

For a closer look at the remains of Mt. Newberry, drive to the start of ◆**Newberry Crater Auto Tour,** just 8 miles south of the Lava Cast Forest and Sun River turnoffs, and wind about 13 miles up to a pair of high mountain lakes bulging with trout—Paulina and East Lakes. When 9,000-foot Mt. Newberry collapsed in a fiery roar thousands of years ago, a large caldera, 4 to 5 miles across, was formed; it was blocked by further eruptions, creating two lakes rather than the single lake exemplified by, say, Crater Lake to the south.

East Lake is known for producing some of the largest trout ever caught in the United States; both German brown and eastern brook trout weighing in at more than twenty-five pounds have been reeled in here by dedicated anglers. Both lakes have campgrounds and boat docks, and both offer fishing boats and motors for rent. East Lake Resort offers rustic accommodations (541–536–2230) and the campground here offers lakeside views. At **Paulina Lake** there is also a rustic lodge, as well as rowboats and fishing equipment for rent. Because legal seasons, bag limits, and types of tackle are highly variable, anglers who want to get licenses to fish the many lakes and rivers in central Oregon are advised to obtain current copies of the official regulations from the Oregon Department of Fish and Wildlife, P.O. Box 59, Portland 97207; (541) 229–5403.

Although the first white person to see the two lakes was explorer Peter Skene Ogden, in 1826, he didn't find those wily trout. Fish were introduced into both lakes years later by the State Fish and Game Department; the fish hatchery is on the Metolius River near Sisters and Black Butte. The mountain was named for John Strong Newberry, a physician and noted geologist who, in 1855, accompanied the Williamson expedition to explore possible railroad routes through the central section of the state.

As you bask in the warm sun on the boat dock at Paulina Lake at a level of 6,331 feet, inside Newberry's crater, notice the large peak looming some 2,000 feet higher into the deep blue sky—that's **Paulina Peak,** also named for the Paiute Indian chief Paulina. If you're itching to bring your horse to the high desert, you'll find riding trails here, too, and you can bunk at the nearby **Chief Paulina Horse Camp.** For a bit more comfortable lodging, you can stay at **Paulina Lake Lodge** in one of a dozen rustic knotty-pine housekeeping cabins. The lodge restaurant serves lunches and dinners and a Saturday night barbecue. For information and reservations call (541) 536-2240; the address is P.O. Box 7, LaPine 97739. The resort is open summers for fishing and December through March for snowmobiling and cross-country skiing.

If the campgrounds here are full, try larger **LaPine State Park** along the **Deschutes River** just a few miles south and west of Highway 97, in the LaPine Recreation Area. For reservations call the state toll-free number, (800) 452-5687; the park number is (541) 382-3586. Incidentally, on the last Saturday in July, in the park's log amphitheater, you can hear melodious four-part harmony from singers who gather here each year for a Barbershop Quartet Concert.

Before retracing your route back to Highway 97, detour on the marked Forest Service side road located between the two lakes to see the large lava flow of glassy black obsidian used by native peoples to fashion arrowheads and other implements; lovely **Paulina Creek Falls** is close by as well. During winter the main paved road into the lakes is plowed for the first 10 miles to the Sno-Park parking area, allowing for backcountry snowmobiling and cross-country skiing; Sno-Park permits can be purchased in Bend or LaPine. This entire 56,000-acre geologic area has been designated the **Newberry National Volcanic Monument.**

While exploring Oregon's high-desert country, you must go spelunking in at least one lava cave. The most accessible is ◆ **Lava River Cave,** located in **Lava River Caves State Park,** just off Highway 97 north of Sun River and Lava Cast Forest. With lantern in hand—lanterns are available for a nominal fee at the park entrance station—and sturdy shoes on your feet, proceed toward the cave's yawning entrance. The trail drops over volcanic rocks, bridged by stairs, leading to the floor of the first large, cool chamber. There you might see stalactites and stalagmites of ice, which often don't melt completely until late June or early July.

Negotiate another stairway up to the main tunnel and walk the winding passageway, your lantern reflecting ghostly shadows all along the way. The enormous cave is in places nearly 60 feet high and 50 feet wide, larger than the tunnels beneath New York's Hudson River. Conversations echo from the cave's farthest recesses, returning as eerie voices from the darkness.

Geologists explain that the great cavernous tunnel, which runs

83

for about 5,000 feet through solid lava, was once the course of a molten lava river. Along the walls are remnants of the lava current—slaggy crusts in some places, rounded and overhanging cornicelike shelves in other places, marking the various levels of old volcanic streams. Notice the walls coated with a glaze of varying smoothness and, from the ceiling, "lavacicles," volcanic stalactites formed by dripping lava.

Lava River Cave, located about 12 miles south of Bend, is open from May through September, from 9:00 A.M. to 4:00 P.M. daily. Picnic facilities are available in the park, but no drinking water is provided. *Note:* Temperatures inside the lava caves range from 30 to 45 degrees, so be sure to dress warmly. Avid spelunkers can obtain information about **Skeleton Cave** and **Wind Cave,** both near Bend, from the Deschutes National Forest headquarters in Bend, (541) 388–2715, or from the staff at Lava Lands Visitor Center just a mile north of Lava River Cave.

Novice spelunkers should note the following safety tips: Explore caves in a group, never alone; bring an ample supply of light sources—a lantern and/or a powerful flashlight for each member of the party; take candles and matches; dress warmly—lava caves are rarely warmer than 45 degrees, even on hot summer days.

For another spectacle, this one next to the nighttime sky at the 6,300-foot level, head east from Bend via Highway 20 about 35 miles to ❖**Pine Mountain Observatory,** where you can snoop at the moon, the planets, star clusters, nebulas, and galaxies through a 15-inch research telescope managed by students and instructors from the University of Oregon. In addition to the 15-inch telescope are two other Cassegrain telescopes, with mirrors of 24 and 32 inches, respectively, that are used by the staff to collect data on the planets and stars.

Just beyond the Millican gas station, turn south on the all-weather gravel road, take the right fork near the base of the mountain, and wind 9 miles up to the parking area next to the sky. Though the Pine Mountain Observatory is usually open Friday and Saturday, May through September, with viewing at dusk, visitors are asked always to call ahead—(541) 382–8331, after 3:00 P.M.—to make arrangements before driving out to the observatory. Stargazers are advised to wear warm clothing, bring flashlights, and dim their cars' headlights as they approach the parking area.

For information about star party locations in other areas of the state, contact the Rose City Astronomer's hot line in Portland at (503) 255–2016.

Before leaving the Bend region, consider having lunch or dinner at one of Bend's oldest eateries, the ✦**Pine Tavern Restaurant,** overlooking **Mirror Pond** on the Deschutes River near **Drake Park.** Several 125-foot ponderosa pines grow right in the middle of the pond-side dining room. A mere 250 years old, the cinnamon-barked trees blend nicely with the room's rustic decor and have been growing right through the roof for about fifty years. Especially tasty are the warm sourdough scones, similar to Indian fry bread, delicious with honey butter. Located downtown, at 967 NW Brooks, the restaurant is open for lunch Monday through Saturday from 11:30 A.M. to 2:30 P.M., for dinner every day from 5:30 to 10:00 P.M. For dinner reservations call (541) 382–5581.

While in the downtown area, stop by the ✦**Deschutes Historical Center,** situated at Wall and Idaho Streets in the 1914 Reid School building that was placed on the National Register of Historic Places in 1979. Among the fine displays are old farm tools; well-used pioneer crockery; native arrowheads; thunder eggs, Oregon's state rock; and a 530-page chronicle of the region's early history that was compiled by sifting through old family records and census data. The center is open Tuesday through Saturday; call (541) 389–1813 for current hours.

If you have a canoe, save time for a leisurely paddle with a gaggle of swans, mallards, and Canada geese on Mirror Pond at lovely Drake Park. You could also call the staff at Bend Metro Parks and Recreation for information about canoeing classes, held during spring, summer, and fall. The address is 200 Pacific Park Lane, Bend 97701; or you can call the staff at (541) 389–7275.

For delicious baked goodies, and for breakfast or lunch, stop at **Westside Bakery,** located just west and south of Drake Park at 1005 NW Galveston Avenue (541–382–3926). Or have breakfast or lunch at one of the downtown eateries such as **Alpenglow,** 1040 NW Bond Street (541–383–7676).

For helpful brochures and information about overnight lodging in the Bend area, contact the Central Oregon Welcome Center, 63085 North Highway 97, Suite 104, Bend 97701; (541) 389–8799.

LAND OF THE THREE SISTERS

Heading west from Bend on Highway 20, you'll find that the Three Sisters—**South Sister, Middle Sister,** and **North Sister**—form a stunning mountain backdrop against the deep blue sky of central Oregon as you make your way to Sisters, Black Butte, and the headwaters of the Metolius River. The snowy peaks form an elegant trio; you could even imagine them enjoying a sisterly gossip session over cups of hot steaming espresso or lattes!

If you haven't yet had supper, you could stop by the **Tumalo Feed Company,** a family steak house and old-fashioned saloon. For reservations call (541) 382–2202. The eatery is located just off Highway 20 in Tumalo, about 4 miles northwest of Bend.

Or you can check out several good options in Sisters—**Coyote Creek Cafe,** in Three Winds Shopping Center at the western edge of town, open daily 7:00 A.M. to 10:00 P.M. (541–549–9514); **Depot Deli** and **Hotel Sisters** in the center of town; and **Miller's Mountain Harvest Store,** at 110 South Spruce Street (541–549–5781) for fresh fruit, natural foods, and microbrews.

The community of **Sisters,** transformed into an Old West tourist town with wooden boardwalks and Western-style storefronts, is filled with interesting shops, lovely boutiques, and old-fashioned eateries. Hotel Sisters is one of the few early structures remaining, now restored as an 1880s-style restaurant (541–549–7427). The hotel's colorful saloon looks as though it came right off a western-movie set.

In mid-July take in the spectacular ◆ **Sisters Outdoor Quilt Show** and in late September hang around for the **High Mountain Dixieland Jazz Festival;** call the Sisters Visitors' Center, (541) 549–0251, for current information.

If time allows, detour about 5 miles west of Sisters to see the headwaters of the Metolius River, bubbling directly from the lower north slopes of Black Butte near Camp Sherman. The entire length of the Metolius River offers fishing access, along with homey, rustic campgrounds and river cabins. At the ◆ **Wizard Falls Fish Hatchery,** a few miles downriver from Camp Sherman, you can see where those wily trout are raised to stock the more than one hundred lakes in the high Cascades. The Metolius is well known to fly-fishers for its enormous wild trout, and nearby **Lake Billy Chinook,** behind Round Butte Dam, offers some of the best kokanee, or landlocked salmon, troll fishing in the region.

Walk along the ¼-mile **❖ Jack Creek Nature Trail** near Camp Sherman to see native plants and wildflowers thriving in a lush, spring-fed oasis that contrasts with the dry, open forest floor strewn with long pine needles and ponderosa pinecones the size of large baseballs. Peer over the footbridge at Camp Sherman to spot some of the largest trout you've ever laid eyes on, playing hide-and-seek in the clear waters of the Metolius.

If you're looking for a quiet retreat some distance from civilization, consider **❖ Black Butte Ranch,** located just south of the Metolius River headwaters. Nestled on some 1,800 acres of ponderosa pine forest and lovely meadows at the base of 6,436-foot Black Butte—a volcanic cone whose warm innards keep it virtually snow-free all year—the area was, from the late 1800s to about 1969, a working cattle ranch and stopping-off place for sheep and wool coming from eastern Oregon across the Cascade Mountains to the Willamette Valley. Today you can stroll or bicycle along paths that wend around guest quarters, condominiums, and private vacation residences. If you play golf or tennis, you can choose from two 18-hole golf courses and nineteen open-air tennis courts. Or you can paddle a canoe on the small lake just beyond the restaurant and dining room; nestle in front of a friendly fire and watch the squirrels dash about the ponderosa pine just outside a wide expanse of windows; or curl up for a snooze amid the utter quiet in this peaceful spot.

For further information and reservations at Black Butte Ranch during all four seasons, call (541) 595–6211. During winter, you can bring Nordic ski gear and enjoy cross-country treks on those flat meadows, which are covered with snow from November through March.

Just west of Sisters on Highway 126, you may see a number of woolly llamas in large grassy meadows belonging to the 350-acre Patterson Ranch. Gentle creatures with high intelligence and great curiosity, the llamas are raised here, at one of the largest llama-breeding ranches in North America. You can stop by the roadside to see them.

For information about guided llama hikes, contact the friendly folks at **Oregon Llamas,** P.O. Box 6, Camp Sherman 97730; (541) 595–2088. The Sisters Area Visitors' Center at 231 East

Hood Street, Suite D, P.O. Box 430, Sisters 97759 (541–549–0251) will also have helpful information about the area and its accommodations. For example, a lovely bed-and-breakfast option would be ✦ **Cascade Country Inn** located next to the small Sisters Airport—the runway can accommodate two- and four-seater private aircraft. The comfortable guest rooms have names like "My Heart's Delight," "Granny's Garden," "Mi Amor," and "Country Fair" and are decorated accordingly with fresh colors, wonderful prints and chintzes, soft pillows, and cozy sitting places. The inviting common room on the main floor offers a large bay window with comfy window seat, soft cream Berber rugs, 1930s-style upholstered chairs, and a floral sofa and matching love seat along with small tables and chairs of white pine where breakfast is served. For information and reservations write to Cascade Country Inn, P.O. Box 834, Sisters 97759 or call (541) 549–4666. Ask about the charming hideaway out in the hangar that's decorated with vintage airplane memorabilia.

The Cascade Mountains form an effective weather barrier, with their forested foothills, sparsely clad higher slopes, and snowy volcanic peaks extending down the midsection of the Beaver State and siphoning those heavy rain clouds from the Pacific Ocean to the west. Most of this moisture falls as snow in the high Cascades from November through April, leaving less moisture for the high-desert regions east of the mountains. Spring snowmelt gurgles into hundreds of lakes, creeks, and streams, tumbling down the mountainsides to larger rivers that find their way to the Pacific Ocean, completing the eternal cycle.

As they made the first wagon train crossing of the central Cascades south of Bend across Pengra, later renamed **Willamette Pass,** toward Eugene in late fall 1853, those emigrants who crossed the lonely high desert found that the first snows of late autumn had already whitened most of the mountain peaks. With 300 wagons, the half-starved, weary group was nearly stranded in the high country until guided safely to Eugene by resident pioneers who had earlier begun to open the route over the pass.

Years before, around 1826, botanist David Douglas, sent by the British Hudson's Bay Company, trekked through these forests. Early records describe him carrying a pack on his back, a gun across his shoulder, and a "shaggy terrier at his heels." Apparently Douglas's skill at shooting birds in flight and magically producing fire from the heavens—by way of a magnifying lens—kept the local Indians "at an admiring distance."

Your visit to the high Cascades wouldn't be complete, however, without including the 87-mile **❖ Cascades Lakes National Forest Scenic Drive,** which meanders along the same routes as the native peoples, botanist Douglas, and explorers like John Frémont, Nathaniel Wyeth, Peter Skene Ogden, and Kit Carson traversed. Designated a National Forest Scenic Byway in 1989, this highway loop from Bend to the **Wickiup Reservoir** was once called Century Drive. In 1920 the original Indian trails, horse trails, and wagon roads were finally replaced by a main wagon road from Bend to Sparks Lake and the Elk Lake area.

Today you can take the well-paved cinder road to wind your way through ancient lava beds to 6,000-foot **Mt. Bachelor** and down through pine forests, skirting more than a dozen alpine lakes—Sparks, Elk, Big Lava, Little Lava, Cultus, Little Cultus, Deer, North Twin, and South Twin—on whose shores are many campgrounds and places from which to fish. Fly-fishing-only lakes include **Davis, Sparks,** and **Fall River.** At Cultus and Little Cultus lakes, an interesting mixture of ponderosa pine, Douglas fir, white fir, white pine, sugar pine, and spruce grows along the road into the lake area; here, too, are some of the few places along the drive that offer shallow sandy beaches.

There are summer hiking and camping areas at most of the lakes, as well as winter cross-country ski trails along the route; during winter, visitors enjoy skiing into Elk Lake, where rustic **Elk Lake Lodge** remains open year-round. Good sources for maps and information are the Deschutes National Forest Headquarters in Bend and the Central Oregon Visitors' Center in Bend (541–382–8334).

Because of heavy snowfall in winter and early spring, the Cascade Lakes Scenic Drive is closed past the entrance to the **Mt. Bachelor Ski Area** parking lot from mid-November until late May. You can enjoy driving along this historic route from June through October, accessing it from the north, near Bend, or from the south, near LaPine and the Wickiup Reservoir near Highway 97.

During summer months visitors can ride one of the Mt. Bachelor ski chairlifts for grand top-of-the-mountain views of more than a dozen snowy peaks, of shaggy green forests, and of sparkling mountain lakes. It's a stunning panorama.

Located just west of Elk Lake and directly south of McKenzie Pass, the 247,000-acre ◆ **Three Sisters Wilderness** offers more than 250 miles of trails that skirt alpine meadows, sparkling streams, glittering patches of obsidian, ancient lava flows, old craters, and dozens of small lakes, as well as glaciers at higher elevations. About 40 miles of the **Pacific Crest National Scenic Trail** runs through this vast region, which in the late 1950s was set aside as a wilderness.

Protected by the National Wilderness Preservation Act of 1964, the Three Sisters Wilderness—along with more than 15 million acres of other land so designated across the United States—permits visitors to travel only by foot or by horse—no vehicles are allowed. Oregon has set aside thirteen such wilderness areas, seven of them located from south to north in the Cascade Mountains.

Like the early mountain men, explorers, and naturalists, experienced and well-equipped backpackers will often stay out for four or five days at a time in the high country, letting the wilderness saturate every pore and limb. The Three Sisters Wilderness is accessible from mid-July through October for hiking and from November through June for snow camping and cross-country skiing. Snow often reaches depths of 20 feet or more at the higher elevations, and hikers may encounter white patches up to the first week of August.

Most of the high mountain lakes are stocked with eastern brook, rainbow, and cutthroat trout. From Lava, Elk, and Sparks lakes, you can access trails into the Three Sisters Wilderness, walking just a short distance if time doesn't allow an overnight trek with backpacks and tents.

During summer and fall, you might enjoy seeing the high mountain country on horseback, just as explorers like Lewis and Clark, John Frémont, and Kit Carson did in the early 1800s. The ◆ **Metolius-Windigo Trail,** built in the 1970s by horse lovers in cooperation with the Sisters, Bend, and Crescent ranger districts staff, offers a network of riding trails, as well as campsites with corrals. The Metolius-Windigo Trail runs through the spectacular alpine meadow and high backcountry from Sisters toward Elk Lake and then heads south, following Forest Service roads and sections of the **Old Skyline Trail,** toward **Crescent Lake** and **Windigo Pass,** located off Highway 58, about 60 miles south of Bend.

For horse campers the familiar crackling warmth of a morning fire mixes well with hands that hold mugs of hot coffee before breaking camp and saddling up. The creak of saddle leather punctuates the crisp morning air; the clop of the horses' hooves echoes through the pines; the air smells fresh and clean. Most horse campers are lured by both the wilderness and the simple joys of riding, and many assist hikers in the **Adopt-a-Trail** program. The Forest Service provides materials and consultation, whereas various hiking and trail-riding groups maintain or build new trails.

For information about guided horseback trips and about the **Central Oregon Equestrian Trails** organization, contact the Sisters Area Visitors' Center (541–549–0251).

CROOKED RIVER GORGE

About a million years ago, lava spilled into the Crooked River canyon upriver near the community of Terrebonne and flowed nearly to Warm Springs. As you drive though this area, stop at **Peter Skene Ogden Wayside,** just off Highway 97, and peer into a 300-foot-deep rocky chasm where the Crooked River, at its base, is still searching for that old canyon. It is more than an awesome sight.

If time allows, drive into the Crooked River Gorge via Highway 27 from Prineville to the large ◆**Prineville Reservoir State Park**—a gorgeous drive into the heart of the gorge and, at its base, the ancient river. There are campgrounds on the lake, which offers fishing throughout the year, including ice fishing in winter. For more information contact the Prineville–Crook County Visitors' Center, 390 North Fairview (P.O. Box 546), Prineville 97754; (541) 447–6304. And if you're a rock hound, ask about the annual Thunderegg Days held during mid-summer. To access Prineville head east from Redmond for about 20 miles on Highway 126.

Of the nation's nine smokejumper bases, eight are located in the Northwest, and one, ◆**Redmond Smokejumper Base,** is based at the Redmond Air Center, just off Highway 97 and near Redmond. If you call ahead for tour information (541–548–5071), you may get to watch trainees jump from the practice

91

tower in their full smokejumping regalia as well as see how the parachutes and harnesses are repaired, rebuilt, and repacked. Head east via Sisters Avenue, the road out to the Juniper Golf Course, to the airfield's entrance. Note, however, that spring and fall are the best times to arrange a visit; the base may be closed to guests if a summer fire emergency occurs.

Speaking of golf, the ◆**Juniper Golf Club** welcomes all travelers who enjoy the game. Call ahead for a tee time (541–548–3121) for either nine or eighteen holes of golf under a vibrant blue sky and with lush green fairways lined with ponderosa pine, pungent juniper (one of the aromatic cedars), and yellow flowering sagebrush. Wednesday is women's day from 8:00 to 11:00 A.M.; Thursday is men's day from noon to 5:00 P.M. Avid golfing buffs claim that there are more than 216 holes on some fifteen golf courses in the Central Oregon area. For a complete list contact the Redmond Visitors' Center, 446 Southwest Seventh, Redmond 97756. The telephone number is (541) 923–5191.

Then, too, you could detour at Terrebonne, a few miles north of Redmond, and drive out to spectacular ◆**Smith Rock State Park** to watch the rock climbers before heading north on Highway 97 toward Madras and the Warm Springs Indian Reservation. The rock climbing at Smith Rock is considered some of the best and most challenging anywhere in the world. As you crane your neck upward to watch the brightly Lycra-clad men and women scale the vertical reddish-colored rock inclines, you may hear words of encouragement in more than a dozen languages—from French, Italian, and German to Swedish, English, and Japanese.

Free climbing, the most popular form of rock climbing, allows only the use of the rock's natural features to make upward progress; however, safety ropes are allowed to stop a fall. You'll notice climbers on the ascent using just their hands and feet to perch on small outcroppings or to clutch narrow crevices as they carefully negotiate a route to the top; the object is to climb a particular section, or route, "free" without using the safety ropes.

If rock climbing is your thing, for information and instruction contact First Ascent Climbing School in Redmond, (541) 548–5137.

You'll find shady places to picnic here, as well as an easy, ten-minute trail you can walk down to the meandering Crooked River. Then cross the footbridge for a close encounter with those enormous, almost intimidating vertical rocks that nature has painted in shades of deep red-orange, vibrant browns, and pale creams. Be sure to stay a safe distance from the climbers, because loose chunks of rock can dislodge and plummet to the ground. The best picture-snapping view of Smith Rock and the Crooked River, by the way, is from the far end of the parking area, near the turnaround—an absolute showstopper at sunrise or sunset. *Note:* A forest fire swept through the area during summer 1996; although the view is still awesome, it will take several years for Mother Nature to repair the scorched juniper trees.

Located in the heart of the Warm Springs Indian Reservation, **Kah-Nee-Ta Resort** is nestled alongside the Warm Springs River at the base of another bright copper-and-amber canyon just a few miles from the community of Warm Springs. The moment you turn off Highway 26 and wind down from stark rimrock ridges and sparsely clad hills into the multicolored canyon, city cares will seem far away. The area easily recalls scenes from a well-worn Zane Grey novel or a colorful Charlie Russell painting.

The charm of Kah-Nee-Ta owes as much to its culture as to its unique rimrock setting. A sense of the Native American past permeates the air, while the unobstructed desert landscape encourages a gentle sifting away of those citified cobwebs. Long walks are a must here—meander down a paved path next to the Warm Springs River, which bubbles alongside the Village, and catch whiffs of pungent sage, bitterbrush, and juniper.

For further information and reservations, contact the staff at Kah-Nee-Ta, P.O. Box K, Warm Springs 97761; (541) 553–1112.

With a massive stone entry shaped like a tribal drum and brick walls fretted with a traditional native basket pattern, the ❖ **Museum at Warm Springs** resonates with the cultural past and present of the three Native American tribes—Wasco, Warm Springs, and Paiute—who live in this spectacular rimrock canyon near the Deschutes River. The museum is one of the premier tribal-owned museums in the United States, and visitors can see one of the most extensive collections of Native American artifacts on a reservation. Be sure to stand in the song chamber, where you can hear traditional chanting. Many Indian elders hope that the museum will be an important link to the younger members of the Confederated tribes, teaching them, as well as visitors, about their languages, religions, and cultures. Located just off Highway 97 in Warm Springs, on Shitake Creek, the museum is open from

8:00 A.M. to 5:00 P.M. daily. For further information contact the staff at (541) 553–3331.

PREHISTORIC FOSSIL LANDS

Shaniko, located at the junction of Highways 97 from the Bend-Redmond-Madras area and 218 from the John Day area, was an important shipping point for wheat, wool, and livestock at the turn of the century. The bustling town at the end of the railroad tracks was filled with grain warehouses, corrals, loading chutes, cowboys, sheepherders, hotels, and saloons. Known as the Wool Capital, the town was named for August Scherneckau, whom the Indians called Shaniko and whose ranch house was a station on the old stage route from The Dalles to central Oregon.

The last of the battles between the cattle ranchers and the sheep ranchers were fought near Shaniko in the mid-1850s; for some twenty-five years the former resisted what was considered an invasion of their territory by "those ornery sheepherders." The sheep won, however, and still dominate the rangelands on the high desert. In fact you should be prepared to wait a considerable amount of time for flocks of the woolly critters to cross various highways throughout the region when the herds are moved to and from mountain pastures in both spring and fall.

Although Shaniko is mostly a ghost town today, a few energetic citizens are breathing new life into the old frontier village. The ◆ **Historic Shaniko Hotel,** no longer tired and weather-beaten, has been renovated by Jean Farrell and his wife, Dorothy—transplants from the Salem area. A wide plank porch once again wraps around both sides of the redbrick hotel, graceful arched windows sparkle in the morning sun, and oak doors with new glass panels open into a lace-draped, plant-filled lobby that holds one of the original settees and an antique reception desk. The oak banister, refinished and polished, still winds up to the second floor.

Hanging brass plaques also identify sixteen refurbished guest rooms, each named for an early Shaniko pioneer. Shiny brass lamps have replaced bare light bulbs; plush carpeting covers floors that earlier sported tired, cracked linoleum; firm mattresses offer rest in place of creaky old springs; lovely linens and floral spreads grace beds that once offered mismatched and worn blankets; and new private bathrooms keep guests from having to trek to the far end of the hall.

What's there to do in Shaniko? Well, mosey over to the gas station and buy a soft drink; capture with a camera or paintbrush the weathered romance of the old school, the jail, and city hall or the water tower and the hotel; peer into old buildings and wonder who lived there; or just sit on the porch swing and reflect about the days when Shaniko bustled with cowboys, ponies, sheepherders, sheep, train whistles, and steam locomotives.

The hotel restaurant, open daily from 7:00 A.M. to 9:00 P.M., serves moderately priced meals. For further information and reservations, contact the Farrells and their staff at the Historic Shaniko Hotel, Shaniko 97057; (541) 489–3415 or (541) 489–3441.

Hopefully, you refilled your picnic basket and cooler in Bend, Redmond, or Madras before heading to Shaniko and can now continue east on Highway 218 for about 20 miles, driving into the ◆**John Day Fossil Beds National Monument** area. Stop to see the Palisades of the **Clarno Unit,** just east of the John Day River. Not only the leaves but also the limbs, seeds, and nuts of the tropical plants that grew here forty to fifty million years ago are preserved in the oldest of the Cenozoic era's layers, the Clarno formation, named for Andrew Clarno, an early white settler who homesteaded here in 1866. The formation is a mudflow conglomerate that has been battered by eons of weather; you'll notice the unusual leftovers—eroded pillars, craggy turrets, top-heavy pedestals, natural stone bridges, and deep chasms. Walk up the slope from the picnic area to stand amid these intriguing shapes and notice pungent-smelling sagebrush and junipers dotting the otherwise barren hills where a tropical forest once grew. *Note:* There is no fresh drinking water here. And although they usually hide in rock crevices, keep an eye out for the Western Pacific rattlesnake while you're in this area.

According to analysis of the bone and plant fossils unearthed here, first by a cavalry officer and then by Thomas Condon, a minister and amateur paleontologist who settled in The Dalles in the 1850s, an ancient lush tropical forest covered this region. This humid life zone of eons past contained palm, fig, cinnamon, hydrangea, sequoia, and ferns, together with alligators, primitive rhinoceroses, and tiny horses. As you walk along the interpretive **Trail of the Fossils,** notice the many leaf prints in which every vein and tooth has been preserved in the chalky-colored hardened clays.

When Condon first learned of the area, through specimens brought to The Dalles, he explored it and found other hidden clues to Oregon's past. In 1870 he shipped a collection of fossil teeth to Yale University, and during the next thirty years many of the world's leading paleontologists came to Oregon to study the John Day fossil beds. Three large units in the region, encompassing more than 14,000 acres, were designated a national monument in 1974 and are now under the direction of the National Park Service. The digging and collecting of fossil materials are coordinated by two Park Service paleontologists, and evidence of new species of prehistoric mammals continues to surface as the ancient layers of mud, ash, and rock are washed and blown away by rain and wind each year. The **Hancock Field Station,** located on the Clarno Unit and near the small community of Fossil and the John Day River, offers outdoor workshops and fossil-hunting field trips for kids of all ages during the summer; you can obtain information from the **Oregon Museum of Science and Industry** in Portland by calling (503) 797–4000.

If you discover some interesting fossil remains while exploring the area, the park staff encourages reporting their locations so that the findings can be identified and cataloged into the computer.

To visit the **Painted Hills** unit, continue on Highway 218 to Fossil, head south past **Shelton Wayside** and Campground—a lovely oasis and a good picnic spot—and turn onto Highway 207 toward Mitchell, a total of about 60 miles. Find the turnoff to the Painted Hills just a few miles west, then continue 6 miles north to the viewpoint.

The vast array of cone-shaped hills you'll see here are actually layer upon layer of volcanic ash from those huge mountains such as Newberry and Mazama, once looming to the south, that each collapsed in a fiery roar thousands of years ago. Some of the layers of tuff are stained a rich maroon or pink, others are yellow-gold, and still others are black or bronze. The colors are muted by late afternoon's golden light and at sunset turn a deep burgundy. As you behold this barren, surrealistic landscape, you'll blink and wonder whether you aren't really looking at a marvelous water-color or oil painting.

For a closer view of the brilliantly colored bands of tuff, walk

Old farmhouse near Shaniko

along the ½-mile trail from the overlook, or drive to nearby
Painted Cove Trail. *Note:* Remember to take plenty of fresh
drinking water with you into both the Clarno and the Painted
Hills units.

Later, returning to Mitchell, you might plan a coffee break at
◆ **Blueberry Muffin Cafe,** located right on Highway 26. Here
friendly conversation is offered along with breakfast, lunch, and
dinner. The cafe is open Monday through Saturday from 6:30
A.M. to 7:00 P.M. and Sunday from 7:00 A.M. to 7:00 P.M.; the
phone number is (541) 462–3434.

Continuing east about 30 miles, stop at **Picture Gorge** before
turning north on Highway 19 for a couple of miles to the
◆ **Cant Ranch Visitors' Center.** At Picture Gorge you can
easily see the oldest to youngest major formations, all marching
across the landscape in orderly layers of mud, ash, and rock—the
Picture Gorge Basalt, about fifteen million years old; Mascall Formation, about twelve million years old; and the narrow ridge on

top, named the Rattlesnake Formation, about three million years old. You can easily see where the two oldest formations were tilted southward together and eroded before the rattlesnake formation was laid down across them, horizontally.

Plan a stop at the **Cant Ranch** Visitors' Center, where fossil replicas and actual specimens from the three units are displayed and identified. You can also watch park staff prepare the fossils for exhibiting, and you can ask questions about the specimens you find and report. In the orchard nearby a collection of farm implements from the ranch is being restored, and in the main ranch house one of the rooms has been set aside to look just as it did some sixty years ago, complete with original furnishings and an arrangement of Cant family photos. The visitors' center is open from about mid-March through October from 9:00 A.M. to 6:00 P.M. Drinking water is available at Cant Ranch and also at the Foree Deposit area in the nearby **Sheep Rock Unit;** both facilities are also wheelchair accessible. Additional information and maps are available from the John Day Fossil Beds National Monument staff; the address is HCR82, Box 126, Kimberly 97848; (541) 987–2333.

Campgrounds in the area include those at **Shelton Wayside State Park;** the **Clyde Holiday Wayside** on Highway 26 near Mt. Vernon about 30 miles east of the Cant Ranch Visitors' Center; and the primitive camping areas in the **Strawberry Mountain Wilderness** south of John Day and Canyon City. Current camping information is also posted in each unit of the park.

The ❖ **Fish House Inn Bed & Breakfast** in nearby Dayville offers three comfortable guest rooms in the main house, a 1908 bungalow, and a small cottage that sleeps four. During warm weather, innkeepers Mike and Denise Smith serve a hearty breakfast outdoors under the trees. "We serve our own blend of freshly roasted gourmet coffee, too," adds Denise. The Smiths also offer facilities for several RVs and a few tent sites. Within walking distance is the John Day River, a city park with a tennis court, a small cafe, and several country stores. For reservations contact the couple at P.O. Box 143, Dayville 97825 or call (541) 987–2124.

There are a limited number of motels and restaurants in Mount Vernon and Mitchell; more can be found in Prineville or in John Day, about 5 miles east of Mt. Vernon. For current information contact the Grant County Visitors' Information Center, 281 West

Main Street, John Day 97845; (541) 575–0547 or (800) 769–5664.

By now, however, you may be hankerin' for a cattle ranch experience. There's one close by, just north of Dayville via Highway 19 toward Kimberly and Spray. You could call the folks at ◆ **Corncob Ranch,** a 5,000-acre working cattle ranch that's been in operation since 1892. Rockey and Rahlie Goodell offer travelers a cozy but spacious cabin with kitchen that sleeps six. Activities here include horseback riding on 30 miles of trails on the ranch, bass fishing in the ranch pond or trying your luck in the nearby John Day River, hunting for quail and chukars, hiking and mountain biking, swimming in the ranch pool, or simply holing up with a good read. For more information, including river rafting opportunities, call the Goodells at (541) 468–2071. The ranch is located 6 miles from the community of Spray.

If you head west from Mitchell toward Prineville and Redmond, completing the western loop into high-desert fossil country, plan to picnic or camp at ◆ **Ochoco Lake State Park,** just on the western edge of the **Ochoco National Forest.** Notice the stands of western larch, often called tamarack, a tall graceful conifer with lacy needles that turn bright lime green in the fall. An interesting side trek is the 10-mile drive on mostly gravel-surfaced Forest Service road to see ◆ **Stein's Pillar.** The basalt pillar rises some 250 feet from the forest floor, ancient layers of clay jutting into the deep blue sky. For information about hiking and camping in the area, contact the Ochoco National Forest, P.O. Box 155, Prineville 97754; (541) 447–6247. Access the road to Stein's Pillar just across the highway from the Ochoco Lake State Park turnoff.

For information about motel accommodations, contact the Prineville–Crook County Visitors' Information Center, 390 North Fairview, Prineville 97754. The telephone number is (541) 447–6304.

NORTHEASTERN OREGON

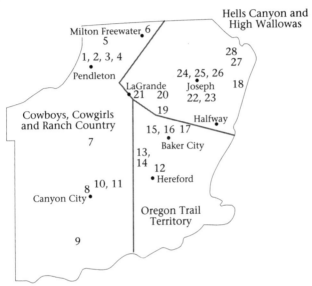

Hells Canyon and
High Wallowas

Milton Freewater 6
5

1, 2, 3, 4
Pendleton

28
27

24, 25, 26
Joseph   18

LaGrande
21   20
22, 23

19

Halfway

Cowboys, Cowgirls
and Ranch Country

15, 16 17

7

Baker City

13,
14   12

Hereford

8 10, 11

Canyon City

Oregon Trail
Territory

9

1. Pendleton Underground
2. Living Heritage Tours
3. Pendleton Woolen Mill
4. The Inn on Main Street Bed & Breakfast
5. Baker's Bar M Ranch
6. Frazier Farmstead Museum and Gardens
7. Lehman Hot Springs
8. Grant County Museum & Oxbow Trade Co.
9. Ponderosa Cattle Company and Guest Ranch
10. Strawberry Mountain Inn
11. DeWitt Depot Museum
12. Fort Reading Bed & Breakfast
13. Sumpter Valley Narrow Gauge Railroad
14. Sumpter Bed & Breakfast
15. Geiser Grand Hotel
16. Oregon Trail Regional Museum
17. National Historic Oregon Trail Interpretive Center
18. Hells Canyon National Recreation Area
19. Haines Steak House
20. Union County Museum and Cowboy Heritage Collection
21. Stang Manor Inn
22. Wallowa Lake Tramway
23. Wallowa Lake
24. Chandler's Bed, Bread & Trail Inn
25. Valley Bronze Foundry
26. Eagle Cap Wilderness Pack Station & High Country Outfitters
27. Hat Point
28. Nee-Me-Poo Trail

Northeastern Oregon

Cowboy and Ranch Country

A region of wheat farms and vast cattle ranches, the farthest corner, in the high Wallowa Mountains and Eagle Cap Wilderness, was also once home to Chief Joseph and the Nez Percé Indians. Long before reaching Hermiston, Echo, and Stanfield via I-84 from the Columbia Gorge, you'll begin to see cowboy hats on the heads of guys and gals in cars and pickups that pass. You most likely won't see new lizard-skin cowboy boots on their feet, however, because well-worn leather ones are the norm here. Extremely well-worn. As in Southeastern Oregon, travelers find themselves usually above 3,000 feet in elevation, even above 4,000 and 5,000 feet, and, at one viewpoint, a whopping 6,982 feet above sea level.

For a close-up encounter with the not-too-distant past, pause in Pendleton to trek back in time to one of the city's unusual historical places, the ◆**Pendleton Underground.** You'll walk through a section of the underground where scores of Chinese laborers lived during the early days of this Wild West town. Because of the negative feelings against those of Asian backgrounds, the men rarely came above these dimly lit caverns except to work on the construction of the railroad; even their own businesses and services were located in the underground tunnels. The guided tour starts from the renovated Shamrock Cardroom, 37 SW Emigrant Street, formerly one of the wild-and-woolly honky-tonks that flourished in the early 1900s. Tours run at intervals between 9:30 A.M. and 4:00 P.M., and reservations are recommended; call (541) 276-0730.

Once each year the underground **Comes to Life** with local folks dressing the part and reenacting colorful scenes of a hundred years ago in the underground—the Shamrock Cardroom, Hop Sing's Laundry, Empire Ice Cream Parlor, the Empire Meat Market, the Prohibition Card Room, and, upstairs in the nearby old hotel, the Cozy Rooms Bordello. For the current schedule call (541) 276-0730 or check with the Pendleton Visitors' Center, 501 South Main Street, Pendleton 97801; (541) 276-7411. History buffs can also ask for information about the ◆**Living Heritage Tours**, which are narrated by a hometown lover of history, Patrick Temple. You'll hear colorful tales from the past, see some Oregon Trail wagon ruts, and learn about a nearby town once inhabited entirely by train robbers. Call (541) 278–2446 for reservations.

Folks have wrapped up in Pendleton blankets for more than eighty years, and you can watch them being woven during tours offered at the ◆ **Pendleton Woolen Mill,** 1307 SE Court Place. You can also visit the mill store where robes, shawls, and blankets are for sale. Tours are offered Monday through Friday, 9:00 and 11:00 A.M. and 1:30 and 3:00 P.M. Call (541) 276–6911 for more information.

◆ **The Inn on Main Bed & Breakfast,** a restored 1905 Colonial Revival structure located at 704 South Main Street, offers three spacious guest rooms on the second floor and comfortable common areas on the first. For current information and reservations call (541) 278–1743. If the inn is filled, ask about **Swift Station Inn Bed & Breakfast,** 602 SE Byers, another turn-of-the-century home that has been refurbished (541–276–3739). One of the busy tourist times happens in mid-September when the town bulges with rodeo cowboys, cowgirls, townfolk, visitors, and Native Americans all attending the annual rip-snortin' **Pendleton Round-Up.**

For eateries try **Cimmiyotti's** on Main Street, **Crabby's Underground Saloon & Dance Hall** on First Street, or **Raphael's** on Fourth Street. Further information can be obtained from the the Pendleton–Umatilla County Visitors' Information Center, 25 SE Dorion Street, Pendleton 97801. The telephone number is (541) 276–7411 or (800) 547–8911.

To experience a taste of real ranch life, head north on Highway 37 along the Umatilla River. At ◆ **Baker's Bar M Ranch** you can visit as folks have done since 1938 when the Baker family first opened the old stagecoach stop to city slickers. You can pitch in with ranch chores if you wish, or you can watch and learn from the three generations of Bakers who tend this 2,500-acre spread. By midweek most tenderfoots are ready to ride horseback to an overnight camp-out in a high mountain meadow. Can't spare a whole week? Well, not to worry, weekend visits can be arranged during spring and fall. Write or call Bar M Ranch, 58840 Bar M Lane, Adams 97810; (541) 566–3381.

Although the four seasons come and go in the nearby Walla

Walla Valley, the ❖ **Frazier Farmstead Museum and Gardens,** at the south end of Milton-Freewater, seems preserved in time, resembling a slice of small-town America at the turn of the century. The six-acre farmstead, with its large, white, circa 1892 house, gardens, and outbuildings, is located near downtown Walla Walla. William Samuel Frazier and his wife, Rachel Paulina, first bought a 320-acre land claim here, near the Walla Walla River, and built a cabin in 1868.

The family, including seven children, left Texas in the early spring of 1867 in three wagons and arrived in the valley at the base of the Blue Mountains in late autumn of that year. A plain pine secretary desk transported in one of the wagons is one of the prized pieces you can see in the house. When the farmstead was willed to the Milton-Freewater Area Foundation in 1978, to be maintained as a museum, volunteers from the local historical society cataloged more than 700 items and memorabilia, including vintage farm equipment, old photographs, heirloom linens, and family letters from the Civil War.

Working as hard in the beautiful flower and vegetable garden as in the house, the curator and volunteers plant annuals, herbs, and perennials early each spring. Harvested in late summer and fall, the lush flowers and plants provide bouquets, herbs, and dried flowers sold at the annual **Frazier Farmstead Festival,** held on the first Saturday of October. If you're fortunate enough to be in the area that weekend, you can watch demonstrations of old pioneer crafts and skills, munch an authentic farm-country lunch, and buy homemade preserves, herbal vinegars, and voluminous bouquets. The Frazier Farmstead Museum, located at 1403 Chestnut Street in Milton-Freewater (541–938–4636 or 541–938–3480), is open April through December; visitors are welcome Thursday through Saturday from 11:00 A.M. to 4:00 P.M. and Sunday from 1:00 to 4:00 P.M.

It's time to head into the heart of northeast Oregon's ranch country, driving south via Highway 395 past **McKay Creek National Wildlife Refuge,** past **Battle Mountain State Park** (where you can camp at a brisk 4,300-foot elevation), and toward Ukiah, Lehman Springs, and the Umatilla National Forest. Speaking of hot water, ❖ **Lehman Hot Springs** has warmed travelers, including Native American families, year-round for hundreds of years. If you'd like to swim or float a spell, detour at

Ukiah and access the historic resort via Highway 244 (about an hour south of Pendleton). Bubbling from the ground at temperatures of 140–157° F , the waters are cooled to around 88–92° F in the large pool and to 100–106° F in the adjacent small pools. Facilities include RV spaces and primitive campsites. For further information call or write P.O. Box 263, Ukiah 97880; (541) 427-3015.

Highway 395 connects with Highway 26 at Mt. Vernon and turning east you'll reach another historic cattle town, John Day. *Note:* Stay alert, you may need to halt for a short spell anywhere along this route when herds are being moved from one grazing area to another.

Highway 26 meanders into the **John Day Valley,** where vast cattle ranches spread to the east and where yellow pine is logged in the Malheur National Forest to the south and north. Native peoples roamed for thousands of years in this region, hunting in the same mountains and fishing the rivers and streams. Many features in the area were named for John Day, the Virginia pioneer, explorer, and trapper who in 1812 traveled through the area with the Overland Expedition of the Pacific Fur Company, on his way to the mouth of the Columbia River and the new fur-trading settlement of Astoria. Throughout this region also live mule deer, Rocky Mountain elk, antelope, mountain sheep, and many species of upland game.

At the ❖**Grant County Museum & Oxbow Trade Co.** in nearby Canyon City (you're at an elevation of 3,197 feet here), you'll see an old jail from a nearby ghost town—Greenhorn, located just northeast of John Day—and a cabin that reportedly once belonged to poet Joaquin Miller. In its heyday Canyon City bulged with more than 10,000 miners and gold prospectors; gold was discovered here in 1862 by several miners who were on their way to the goldfields in Idaho. The placers of Whiskey Gulch, Canyon Creek, and other nearby streams produced several million dollars' worth of the gold stuff before the turn of the century. The historical museum, located at 101 South Canyon Boulevard–Highway 395, is open June through September from 9:30 A.M. to 4:30 P.M., Monday through Saturday, and from 1:00 to 5:00 P.M. on Sunday. Call (541) 575–0666 for further information.

If you'd like to find out what it's really like to be a cowboy or a cowgirl and sample the rigors of ranch life, consider making reservations at ❖**Ponderosa Cattle Company and Guest**

Ranch. Located south of Canyon City via Highway 395, the 120,000-acre spread runs up to 4,000 head of cattle and has done so for more than one hundred years. It's one of the largest ranches in the state. New owners Izzy and Nancy Oren, and their capable staff, welcome guests ages eighteen and over to assist with herding cattle, sorting and branding calves, and checking fences in the Silvies Valley. You'll learn how it feels to spend a full day in the saddle, and you'll most likely get dirt in your boots and calluses on your hands. After a day on the trail you can relax in the 7,000-square-foot log lodge and eat meals family-style when the chow bell rings. And you'll sleep in a rustic cabin with all the comforts of home. For further information about the Cowboy Program, May to October, contact the ranch staff at (541) 542–2403 or toll-free at (800) 331–1012. The address is P.O. Box 190, Seneca 97873.

If you decide to continue east on Highway 26 from John Day, stop by the Grant County Visitors' Center, 281 West Main Street, John Day 97845, to pick up current maps and brochures about the area. Ask about the **Strawberry Mountain Scenic Route** and about the **Kam Wah Chung Museum.** (This was the home of a Chinese herbal doctor who served Chinese immigrants who worked in the gold mines at the turn of the century.) The visitors' center phone number is (541) 575–0547 or toll-free (800) 769–5664. You'll find friendly service at either **The Grubsteak Restaurant** (541–575–2714) or **Motherlode Restaurant** (541–575–1970), both located on Main Street in John Day.

A few miles east, in the small community of Prairie City, Linda and Bill Harrington welcome northeastern Oregon travelers to their bed and breakfast, ◆**Strawberry Mountain Inn.** "We're here at the gateway to the marvelous Strawberry Mountain Wilderness," says Linda. Guests can sit on the wide deck and drink in the mountain views or explore the area with day hikes, horseback rides, or mountain bike excursions. The yellow clapboard and brick vintage home offers comfortable guest rooms, cozy parlors, and bay windows, and Linda offers her guests delicious breakfasts of, for example, deep-dish apple cinnamon pancakes and fresh apple juice from the orchard. For further information and reservations, contact the Harringtons at HCR 77 #940, Prairie City 97869 or call (800) 545–6913.

While you're in the area, be sure to plan a visit to the

◆ **DeWitt Depot Museum.** This historic railroad depot contains memorabilia from Grant County's pioneer days. The depot was the end of the line when the Sumpter Valley Railway was built from Baker City to Prairie City in 1890 and in 1910. It served as the economic lifeline for logging companies, mining outfits, and families for some fifty years before this section of the rail line was finally closed. Rail buffs and volunteers are in the process of reclaiming a section of the rail line in the Sumpter area, closer to Baker City. For further information and current hours, contact the DeWitt Depot Museum staff at (541) 820–3598 and the Malheur National Forest Headquarters, 139 NE Dayton Street, John Day 97845; (541) 575–1731.

Highway 26 winds north and east to Austin Junction, climbs across a 5,000-foot pass toward Unity, and then descends some 50 miles to connect with the Vale-Ontario-Nyssa communities on the Oregon–Idaho border. If you take this route, consider detouring at Unity and either camping at **Unity Lake State Park,** or traveling on to Hereford to spend the night at quaint ◆ **Fort Reading Bed & Breakfast.** "We're a working cattle ranch in the Burnt River Valley," says innkeeper-rancher Barbara Hawes. After a pleasant stay, including waist-bulging breakfasts, from here you could access Baker City via Highway 245 connecting with Highway 7 near Sumpter. Call or write the Hawes family for more information, HCR 86, Box 140, Hereford 97837; (541) 446–3478 or (800) 573–4285.

If time allows, before continuing to Baker City, detour at Sumpter for a nostalgic train ride on the ◆ **Sumpter Valley Narrow Gauge Railroad.** Board the train at the Sumpter Valley Railroad Park; then ride behind puffing, wood-burning 1914 Heisler steam locomotive, *Stumpdodger,* through the forested valley etched with dredge tailings. The old train once transported gold ore and logs from the hard-rock mountain mines and pine-dotted Sumpter Valley. During the hour-long ride, watch for geese, heron, beaver, deer, and coyotes—and an occasional raid by "honest-to-goodness train robbers." The train runs weekends through the summer and into September.

A live ghost town, Sumpter is home to about 140 residents, three restaurants, two stores, and a restored circa 1900 church and offers visitors a summer celebration, a winter snowmobile festival, and more than 200 miles of cross-country ski trails.

While eating at the **Sumpter Nugget,** at **Borello's,** or at the **Elkhorn Saloon and Cafe,** you'll most likely encounter one of those old prospectors and hear a yarn or two about the 1800s gold rush days and how the town was destroyed by fire in 1917.

To explore the historic Sumpter area on your own, get a copy of the **Elkhorn National Forest Scenic Byway** map, which is packed with helpful information and photographs. This self-guided summertime drive takes you along the 100-mile Sumpter Valley loop, where you can see old mines, abandoned mine shafts, and even a ghost town or two. If you're a ghost-town buff, visit the remains of two towns along the route, **Bourne** and **Granite.** Such characters as Skedaddle Smith, One-eyed Dick, and '49 Jimmie reportedly lived in Granite in the old days.

Call innkeeper Joy Myers at ◈**Sumpter Bed and Breakfast** (541–894–2229) and plan to stay overnight at her rustic four-guest-room inn that dates back to the turn of the century. This way you can fully immerse yourself in gold mining history and, perhaps, even spot the "ghost locomotive," a phantom of old logging and mining days that folks occasionally say they spy hiding along the Middle Fork of the John Day River. Other ghost towns in the area include Greenhorn, Susanville, and Whitney.

You can obtain a copy of the Elkhorn National Forest Scenic Byway map from the Baker Ranger District, Route 1, Box 1, Baker City 97814, or call Wallowa-Whitman National Forest headquarters in Baker City at (541) 523–6391. Further information about Sumpter, the *Stumpdodger* train schedule, and the restoration of the Sumpter Dredge can be obtained from the Baker County Visitors' Information Center, 490 Campbell Street, Baker City 97814; call (541) 523–3356 or (800) 523–1235.

OREGON TRAIL COUNTRY

The settlement of Baker City grew up around a mill built in the 1860s by J. W. Virtue to process ore brought from those first hard-rock gold mines. By 1890 the town had grown to nearly 6,700, larger than any city in the eastern section of the state, and a fledgling timber industry had been started by David Eccles, who also was founder of the Sumpter Valley Railroad. When mining declined after World War I, loggers, cattle herders, and ranchers replaced those colorful miners and gold prospectors.

The **Baker City Historic District** includes about sixty-four early buildings, some constructed from volcanic tuff and stone. Also worth a visit is the **Historical Cemetery,** located near the high school. For both attractions pick up the self-guided walking-tour map at the visitors' center on Campbell Street. And plan a visit, too, to the U.S. National Bank, at 2000 Main Street, where you'll see a whopping, 80.4-ounce gold nugget that was found in the area during the early gold rush days.

To sleep in sumptuous splendor, consider the newly renovated and refurbished 1889 ◆ **Geiser Grand Hotel** located nearby at 1996 Main Street, Baker 97814. Guests choose from thirty suites and guest rooms and enjoy the hotel's historic restaurant and lounge, meeting and private dining rooms, and, perhaps the loveliest, the splendid oval mahogany Tea Court with skylight, all polished and new again. Contact the hotel staff at (541) 523–1889.

Located just a few blocks north of the visitors' center, at the corner of Campbell and Grove Streets, is the ◆ **Oregon Trail Regional Museum,** featuring a collection of pioneer artifacts gathered from the Old Oregon Trail. Often such prized posses-sions as trunks, furniture, china, silver, and glassware were left along the trail in order to lighten the wagons for the starving and exhausted oxen or horses who pulled them. The kids will enjoy the historic gold mining exhibits, an impressive gem and mineral col-lection, and regional Native American baskets, arrowheads, tools, and clothing. Be sure to look for the vintage freight wagon, the old school bus, the large sleigh, and a number of vintage autos and trucks, all stored in a cavernous space to the rear of the build-ing. Each one has a story to tell. The museum is open daily from 10:00 A.M. to 4:00 P.M. but is closed during winter months; its phone number is (541) 523–9308.

For cozy lodgings in the Baker City area consider **A' Demain Bed & Breakfast** located at 1790 Fourth Street (541–523–2509); **York's Bed & Breakfast** at 2650 Main Street (541–523–5360); or **Grant House Bed & Breakfast** at 2424 Third Street (541–523–6685). The pleasantly funky **Front Street Coffee Co. & Cafe,** located at 1840 Main Street (541–523–7536), offers espresso, gourmet sandwiches, large salads, and Mexican dishes. It's open Monday through Saturday from 7:00 A.M. to 4:00 P.M.

From Baker City detour about 5 miles east on Highway 86 to

Flagstaff Summit to visit the impressive and new ❖**National Historic Oregon Trail Interpretive Center.** This panoramic site overlooks miles of the original wagon trail ruts that have, over the last 150 years since the 1840s and 1850s, receded gently into the sagebrush- and bitterbrush-littered landscape. Now the ruts are just dim outlines, reminders of the pioneer past, and eyes squint to follow the old trail across the wide desert toward the Blue Mountains, a low, snow-dusted range that hovers on the far northwestern horizon.

In the main gallery of the 23,000-square-foot center, more than 300 photographs, drawings, paintings, and maps depict the toil, sweat, and hardships of the 2,000-mile journey from Independence, Missouri, to Fort Vancouver, Oregon City, and the lush Willamette Valley located south of the Portland area.

For brochures, maps, and other information, contact the Bureau of Land Management, P.O. Box 987, Baker City 97814. The telephone number is (541) 523–1843. Many volunteers assist the Oregon Trail Center staff, and you, too, can get involved in bringing history alive at Flagstaff Hill. The Interpretive Center is open May 1 through September 30 from 9:00 A.M. to 6:00 P.M. daily and October 1 through April 30 to 4:00 P.M. daily. *Note:* Bring wide-brimmed hats and water if you want to walk the nature trails here—summers are hot and dry with temperatures often 90–100° F.

HELLS CANYON AND THE HIGH WALLOWAS

While the Oregon Trail left the Snake River at Farewell Bend, south of Baker City toward Ontario, and continued northwest into Baker Valley and over the Blue Mountains toward The Dalles, the ancient river headed directly north, chiseling and sculpting **Hells Canyon**—a spectacular, 6,000-foot-deep fissure between high craggy mountains. To experience this awesome chunk of geography that separates Oregon and Idaho and is the deepest river gorge in the world, head east to Halfway via Highway 86 from Flagstaff Summit.

Included in this vast region are the 108,000-acre **Hells Canyon Wilderness,** the 662,000-acre **Hells Canyon National Recreation Area,** and the **Wild and Scenic Snake River Corridor.** Visit the canyon during spring or early autumn, when native shrubs, trees, and flowers are at their best; summers are quite hot and dry. If possible take one of the float or jet-boat trips on the river or, if you're in good shape, a guided backpack or horseback trip into the wilderness areas. For helpful information contact the Eagle Cap Ranger District, Wallowa-Whitman National Forest, Enterprise 97828; (541) 426–4978.

If you're interested in fall hunting in the region, contact the Oregon Hunter's Association, Baker County Chapter, at (541) 523–6561. Try lovely Hewitt Park and the 50-mile Brownlee Reservoir for picnicking, fishing, and camping on the waters of the Snake River behind Brownlee Dam, just south of Halfway.

You might want to refill your picnic basket and cooler in Halfway and take the narrow road that winds from Oxbow Dam along a 23-mile scenic stretch of the Snake River down to Hells Canyon Dam spillway and one of the jet-boat launch areas. There is a portable rest room here and a visitors' information trailer, but no other services. In late spring you'll see masses of yellow lupine, yellow and gold daisies, and pink wild roses blooming among crevices in craggy basalt bluffs and outcroppings that hover over the narrow roadway. It's well worth the 46-mile round-trip to experience this primitive but accessible section of the ✦ **Hells Canyon National Recreation Area.** You could enjoy your picnic at the boat-launch site, or return to **Hells Canyon Park,** located about halfway back to Highway 86. The park offers picnic areas, comfortable grassy places to sit, and a boat launch, all next to the river. Overnight campsites are available at Copperfield Park, located on this scenic drive about 17 miles from Halfway. Further information can be obtained from Hells Canyon National Recreation Area, 88401 Highway 82, Enterprise 97828 (541–426–4978); from the Wallowa-Whitman National Forest headquarters in Baker City (541–523–1205); and from the Hells Canyon Visitors' Information Center, South Main Street, P.O. Box 841, Halfway 97834 (541–742–5722). Ask, too, about comfortable bed-and-breakfast inns in the Halfway area— **Clear Creek Farm** (541–742–2238) and **The Birch Leaf Farm** (541–742–2990).

Heading north from Baker City toward LaGrande, take old Highway 30 instead of I–84 and detour at Haines to eat at one of the best and most well-known restaurants in the northeastern section of the state, ✦ **Haines Steak House.** Owners Steve and Gail Hart remodeled the old structure several years ago after a fire, filling it once again with western cowboy memorabilia and offering the old-fashioned hospitality so typical of this region. After the salad bar you'll work your way through a bowl of hearty soup, western-style baked beans, and a delicious charcoal-grilled steak fresh off the rangelands. The restaurant, open for dinner Wednesday through Monday, is on Old Highway 30 in Haines, about 10 miles north of Baker City; the phone number is (541) 856–3639.

If you pass through this region of the Beaver State in mid-spring, say, late May, continue from Haines on Highway 237, ignoring I–84 for a while longer, and drive slowly through the small community of Union. Here pause to feast your eyes on a number of enormous lilac trees in full, glorious bloom. Many of the original cuttings were brought across the Oregon Trail in the 1840s, "starts" from beloved plants growing at former homes and homesteads back East. Also look for patches of wild iris that bloom profusely in pastures and fields between North Powder and Union.

And, located in the rustic ◆**Union County Museum,** 333 South Main Street, a structure built in 1881, you can visit the new home of the extensive ◆**Cowboy Heritage Collection.** Besides showing the evolution of the cowboy myth, from nineteenth-century dime novels to 1940s B movies, you'll see boots, spurs, saddles, and hand-braided ropes galore. The exhibit also spotlights early Texas trail drives, railhead towns such as Abilene and Dodge City, and flinty-eyed frontier marshals. The exhibit is open Monday through Saturday 10:00 A.M. to 5:00 P.M. Call the museum curator for further information at (541) 562–6003.

You could decide to stay over in LaGrande, just a few miles northwest of Union via Highway 203, a good-size town with many restaurants, shops, and services. If you do, call innkeepers Marjorie and Pat McClure at ◆**Stang Manor Inn.** In this spacious Georgian Colonial mansion, built in the 1920s by an early lumber baron, you can rest in elegant comfort surrounded by lovely grounds in which are growing several large lilac trees and a collection of old roses. The McClures are continuing the bed-and-breakfast tradition begun by Steve and Gail Hart, who initiated the restoration of the 10,000-square-foot mansion in the late 1980s. For information and reservations contact the innkeepers at 1612 Walnut Street, LaGrande 97850. The telephone number is (541) 963–2400.

Next, drive from LaGrande into Enterprise and Joseph to treat yourself to a ride on the ◆**Wallowa Lake Tramway.** Snuggling with three other mountain lovers in a small, open-air gondola, you'll ascend safely in fifteen minutes to the top of 8,200-foot Mt. Howard for some of the most breathtaking views in the entire region. More than a mile below, Wallowa Lake shimmers in the afternoon sun, reaching into the **Eagle Cap Wilderness** and mirroring eight other snowcapped peaks. To the east lie the rugged canyons of the Imnaha and Snake Rivers. As one soaks in the alpine vastness of it all, it's easy to understand why Chief Joseph and his Nez Percé tribe fought to remain in this beautiful area in the mid-1800s when the first white settlers began to encroach on their historic territory. At the top of the tramway are short trails for hiking and a snack shop, **Summit Deli & Alpine Patio,** for obtaining cold drinks or cups of hot coffee before you head back down the mountain. Call ahead for the current schedule, (541) 432–5331, although the tram is generally open daily from June through August and part-time in May and September.

Access the Enterprise-Joseph area from LaGrande, via I–84 from Haines, heading north on Highway 82. You'll travel about 65 miles to Enterprise, 6 miles farther to Joseph, and another 6 miles to ◆**Wallowa Lake** and the tramway. The Wallowa Lake area opens for the summer season on Memorial Day weekend; winter visits offer miles of cross-country ski trails through a snowy wonderland.

If the notion of packing your tent and camping beneath tall alpine fir at the edge of a mountain lake sounds inviting, consider making a reservation at the Wallowa State Park campground; call (800) 452–5687, the state reservation number. Be sure to call sometime in midspring, before all the spaces are taken, because everyone else likes to go off the beaten path here as well. For reservations at **Wallowa Lake Lodge,** perched at the south end of the lake since 1923 and recently renovated, contact the staff at Route 1, Box 320, Joseph 97846; (541) 432–9821. In the refurbished dining room you can sit at a table overlooking the lake and enjoy delicious entrees from farms, fields, and streams throughout the Northwest. The lodge and restaurant are open from May 1 until the snow flies, around November 1, though plans are underway to operate year-round.

Wallowa Lake Tramway

For a pleasant overnight bed-and-breakfast experience, call the friendly innkeepers at ❖ **Chandler's Bed, Bread & Trail Inn** in the small community of Joseph. The hosts, Jim and Ethel Chandler, offer five lovely guest rooms, scrumptious breakfasts, and lots of helpful information about what to see and do in the Wallowa Lake area. The inn's telephone number is (543) 432–9765.

One such excursion is a visit to the ❖ **Valley Bronze Foundry,** which offers tours year-round, although schedules may vary. On the two-hour tour, you'll get to see the labor-intensive bronze-making process, including the "lost wax process," a production method the business has used since it began operation with a handful of workers in 1982. Many elegant bronze sculptures are on display, some of which are destined for places as far away as Berlin, Germany. For further details phone the staff at (541) 432–7551. Additional information about the area can be obtained from the Joseph Visitors' Information Center, P.O. Box 13, Joseph 97846. The telephone number is (541) 432–1015.

Further information about the area can be obtained from the Wallowa County Visitors Information Center, 107 SW First Street, P.O. Box 427, Enterprise 97828; (541) 426–4622. For maps and information about camping and hiking in the Wallowa Mountains and Eagle Cap Wilderness, contact the Wallowa-Whitman National Forest headquarters, P.O. Box 907, Baker 97814; (541) 523–6391.

If you'd like to see this spectacular mountain wilderness area from atop a trusty horse, there are experienced guides and outfitters to contact: ❖ **Eagle Cap Wilderness Pack Station & High Country Outfitters,** 59761 Wallowa Lake Highway, Joseph 97846 (800–681–6222)—ask about short or long rides, including overnight pack trips, and ask about Minam Lodge located in the heart of the Eagle Cap Wilderness (accessible by horseback or small airplane); during winter months **Wing Ridge Ski Tours** leads experienced skiiers on hut-to-hut ski tours in the snowy Wallowa Mountains—for information call (541) 426–4322.

To explore on your own, during summer months, and with a sturdy four-wheel drive vehicle, ask about the condition of the gravel road up to ❖ **Hat Point,** elevation 6,982 feet, with its showstopping views of the Snake River and its canyon, elevation 1,276 feet, and Idaho's Seven Devils Mountains, over 9,000 feet in elevation. The spectacular viewpoint is accessed about 25 miles from Imnaha (restaurant, limited groceries, seasonal motel, and no gasoline), which is located about 50 miles northeast of Joseph via Highway 350 and skirting Little Sheep Creek. To experience an historical section of the Nez Percé country, ask for directions to ◆ **Nee-Me-Poo Trail** (meaning "route to freedom"), located about 15 miles north of Imnaha (the last 10 miles are best negotiated with high-clearance vehicles, no vehicles pulling trailers). Here you can walk in the footsteps of Chief Joseph and his people. Chief Joseph, in 1879, said, "The earth is the mother of all people, and all people should have equal rights upon it . . . let me be a free man . . . free to travel . . ."

PORTLAND AND ENVIRONS

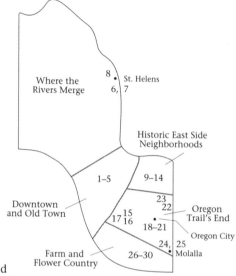

1. RiverPlace
2. Sculling on the Willamette River
3. Forest Park and Hoyt Arboretum
4. Heron Haus Bed and Breakfast Inn and Nob Hill Neighborhood
5. Heathman Hotel
6. Sauvie Island Wildlife Refuge
7. James Bybee House and Agricultural Museum
8. Columbia View Park
9. Historic Sellwood Neighborhood
10. Crystal Springs Rhododendron Garden
11. Hawthorne Neighborhood
12. Grand Central Bakery
13. Clinkerbrick House Bed and Breakfast
14. Northeast Broadway Neighborhood
15. Willamette Falls Locks
16. Stern-wheelers
17. Swift Shore Chalet Bed & Breakfast
18. End of the Oregon Trail Interpretive Center
19. Oregon City Municipal Elevator
20. McLoughlin House
21. Fellows House Restaurant and Inn
22. German Methodist Church and Baker Cabin
23. Tallina's Garden
24. Philip Foster National Historic Farm
25. Pacific Northwest Live Steamers
26. Aurora National Historic District
27. The Inn at Aurora
28. St. Josef's Winery
29. Swan Island Dahlias
30. Canby Depot Museum and Clackamas County Fair

PORTLAND AND ENVIRONS

DOWNTOWN AND OLD TOWN

In the late 1840s Portland was a small clump of log cabins on the banks of the Willamette River, where riverboats laden with people and supplies scuttled back and forth between Fort Vancouver and Oregon City, some 20 miles upriver. Early settlers chopped down stands of tall Douglas fir along the riverbanks to make room for those first small cabins, and the place was called The Clearing. Later the tree stumps were whitewashed to prevent folks from stumbling over them after dark, and the nickname Stumptown emerged.

During the 1850s and 1860s, steamboats appeared, and Stumptown emerged a full-fledged town with a new name decided by the toss of a coin. Now, a century and a half later, the greater Portland area is a large region containing three of the most populated counties in the state—Multnomah, Washington, and Clackamas—and offering visitors a variety of mountains and rivers, vineyards and wineries, museums and historic sites, and contemporary homes and vintage farms as well as theaters, zoos, festivals, gardens, unique shops, eateries, bed and breakfast inns, and hostelries.

The city proper and its far-flung environs are now situated on both sides of the broad **Willamette River,** stretching east toward Mt. Hood, west into the Tualatin Hills toward the Tualatin Valley and Coast Range, and south toward Lake Oswego, West Linn, and historic Oregon City. The Willamette flows into the mighty Columbia River just a few miles northwest of the downtown area. The whitewashed stumps long gone, today's visitor will find broad avenues and fountains, parks and lovely public gardens, and, of course, nearly a dozen bridges spanning the Willamette to connect the east and west sides of town.

One of the best ways to get acquainted with the Beaver State's largest city is to take a walking tour of the Historic Old Town area, where Stumptown began. First, stop by the Greater Portland Visitors' Information Center at 26 SW Salmon Street, just across from **Waterfront Park,** for helpful brochures and maps. Then slip into your walking shoes and head across the street to the paved esplanade along the Willamette River.

Incidentally, travelers who like to walk can call the local **Volkssport Hotline,** (503) 243–4725, to get the current schedule of walks with this hale and hearty group. It's an international group of volksmarchers—walking aficionados—that began in Germany, then came to the United States. For further information call the American Volkssport Association at (800) 830–WALK; if you have Internet access, you can visit the local web site at http://www.teleport.com/~walking.

For a shoreside view of the river, first while away an hour or so at ◆ **RiverPlace,** located on the west riverbank near the heart of the downtown area. It contains condominiums and offices, restaurants—one of them floating right on the water—and delis, gift shops and boutiques, the European-style **RiverPlace Hotel** (503–228–3233), and a large boat marina. There are comfortable benches for sitting and watching myriad activities, both on the water and ashore. On blue-sky days, lunching at one of the round tables outdoors is a pleasant option.

On almost any day you can see energetic members of the Portland Rowing Club ◆ **sculling on the river** in sleek shells that hold from two to four rowers; one of the best times to watch, though, is at 5:00 A.M., when some of the most devoted rowers scull across the river's early morning, glasslike surface. When the group formed in 1879, it was called the Portland Rowing Association; by 1891, the North Pacific Association of Amateur Oarsmen had been established by active rowing clubs in Portland and as far away as Vancouver, British Columbia, and Coeur d'Alene, Idaho.

World War II brought an end to rowing in Portland for about thirty years, until the early 1970s, when a group of former college oarsmen organized a group called Station L, composed of master oarsmen and college-club crews from both Reed College and Lewis and Clark College. Given the former dusty, leaking boathouse and empty racks, the sport in Portland has come far— the spiffy new racing shells have found not only a permanent home on the new docks at RiverPlace but many ardent participants and enthusiastic spectators as well.

Two women's crews from the Portland Rowing Club won national championships in Seattle in 1986, and rowers now congregate from all over the Northwest to compete in the annual Portland Regatta in mid-April. At this event, both men and women vie for the racing cups and there are competitions for juniors as well.

You can watch the races from RiverPlace Marina or from the grassy sloping lawn at **Tom McCall Waterfront Park,** just next to the RiverPlace Hotel. Following the races there's usually a water-ski extravaganza that features barefoot waterskiing, ski jumping, human pyramids, swivel-ski ballets, and adagio doubles. All in all, the goings-on make for a fun day on the historic Willamette River, where Stumptown began. If you'd like to explore learning to row the sleek racing shells yourself, stop for information at the Rowing Shop, near the marina shops and delis.

To continue your walking tour, head north from RiverPlace and Waterfront Park on the esplanade along the seawall. During Portland's annual **Rose Festival,** held the first three weeks in June, the seawall is filled with ships of all sizes and lengths, heralding from U.S. Navy and Coast Guard as well as Canadian ports, and many can be toured during the festival. At SW Ankeny and First Avenues, stop to see the **Skidmore Fountain,** one of the city's first public fountains. It was donated by a local druggist "for the benefit of the horses, men, and dogs of Portland." **New Market Theatre,** at 50 SW Second Street, is now full of specialty shops but was built in 1872 as both a market and a theater—sopranos sang arias on the second floor while merchants sold cabbages on the first. And at the north end of the Central Fire Station is a small museum devoted to fire fighting and containing vintage fire engines; find it just across from Ankeny Park and the Skidmore Fountain.

At the **Architectural Preservation Gallery,** on NE Second and Couch Streets, you can see changing exhibits of historic building fragments, paintings, and old photographs; you can also visit the **Portland Police Museum,** housed in the same site. The **Pioneer Courthouse,** at SW Fifth and Yamhill, was built in 1869, making it the oldest public building in the Pacific Northwest. Just across the street from the courthouse, detour through **Pioneer Square,** an enormous, block-wide square almost in the heart of the city; colorful outdoor events are held here throughout the year.

The **Park Blocks,** constructed on land set aside in 1852 for a city park, stretch from SW Salmon Street south, and slightly uphill to the **Oregon Historical Center,** the **Portland Art**

Museum, and the campus of **Portland State University.** Here you'll find shady places to walk, rest, and watch the pigeons, and you may well encounter roving musicians or street performers from such local theater groups as Artists Repertory, New Rose, Storefront, and Firehouse, along with the ever-present college students, museum-goers, and people watchers.

The **Oregon Historical Center,** at 1230 SW Park Avenue, comprises a fine museum of changing exhibits, a historical research library, a gift shop, and a bookstore. The center is open Monday through Saturday from 10:00 A.M. to 4:45 P.M.; its phone number is (503) 222–1741.

Located directly across Park Blocks from the Historical Center, the **Art Museum** contains an excellent permanent exhibit of Northwest Coast Indian art and artifacts; museum and gallery lovers can also inquire here about the numerous small galleries sprinkled throughout the downtown area. If you're in the area in late fall, when the tall, leafy trees in the Park Blocks are ablaze with bright yellow, orange, and red autumn hues, consider attending one of the **Wednesday Evening Jazz Concerts** held in the indoor sculpture court at the Art Museum; the concert program starts around the third week in October. The museum is open Tuesday through Thursday from 11:00 A.M. to 7:00 P.M., Friday from 11:00 A.M. to 9:30 P.M., and Saturday and Sunday from noon to 5:00 P.M. For more information call the museum at (503) 226–2811.

For an impromptu snack in the Park Blocks, pick up picnic fixings at **Metro on Broadway,** near Broadway and Salmon Street, just a couple of blocks south of Pioneer Square, or at the **Heathman Bakery and Deli** (503–227–5700), on Ninth and Salmon Streets. Should you walk through the lower downtown area on a weekend, stop by the colorful **Saturday Market,** situated under the west end of the Burnside Bridge, just north of the Skidmore Fountain between SW First Avenue and SW Ankeny Street. Here you can stroll through a variety of booths that offer a handsome array of Oregon and Pacific Northwest goods, from pottery, wood, and leather to jewelry, candles, and handwoven items. Jugglers and musicians entertain, and from open-air food stands you can choose tasty, ready-to-eat meat and veggie items.

If you're ready to leave the bustle of downtown and enjoy a lazy afternoon in the outdoors, visit cool, shady ◆**Forest Park,** one of the largest urban parks in the United States. All 4,700 acres of the park begin just a few blocks from downtown, off West Burnside Street and adjacent to **Washington Park International Rose Test Gardens** and the gorgeous **Japanese Garden.** The easy Wildwood Trail can be accessed either near the Japanese Garden or from the **World Forestry Center,** near the **Portland Metropolitan Zoo,** just west of Washington Park.

Along 10 miles of trails in nearby ◆ **Hoyt Arboretum,** you can try your hand at identifying Douglas fir, Jeffrey pine, broad-leaved maple, hemlock, red cedar, and grand fir, as well as cherry, ash, madrona, and Indian plum. Spectacular in the spring are native wildflowers, including trillium and buttercups. More than 110 different species of birds and more than 50 species of animals have been identified in Forest Park and the arboretum.

Pick up trail maps and informational literature at **Tree House,** located at 4000 SW Fairview Boulevard (503–823–3655). Ask about guided tours through Forest Park and the 175-acre arboretum, which contains some 600 species of trees from all over the world. Information about other guided tours, nature walks, and interesting day trips in the area can also be obtained from the staff at the Portland Parks and Recreation office, 1120 SW Fifth Avenue, Suite 1302 (503–823–2223) and from the Metro Regional Parks and Greenspaces Department, 600 Northeast Grand Avenue, Portland 97232; (503) 797–1850.

And, to experience another nearby city forest, this one in southwest Portland near Lewis & Clark College, in splendid second-growth Douglas fir, call the friendly park staff and volunteers at **Tryon Creek State Park,** (503) 636–9886. Ask about hiking and bicycle trails and about current nature programs.

After a busy day of exploring, you can arrange an overnight stay at one of the many comfortable inns or small hotels in the city. ◆ **Heron Haus Bed and Breakfast Inn** is located in the northwest hills near Washington Park. Its entire back side layered with a lush growth of ivy, the elegant Tudor-style mansion looks very much like one that belongs on a sorority or fraternity row. On the second and third floors are six spacious guest rooms with comfortable sitting spaces, cozy pillows, a plethora of books and magazines, and private baths. One suite features a romantic whirlpool spa, where you can relax in bubbly comfort and see twinkling city lights far below. A light continental breakfast is served in the fireplace dining room, or, on sunny mornings, perhaps in the enclosed sun porch overlooking the swimming pool, the city, and Mount Hood to the east.

The inn is also close to Washington Park Rose gardens, the Japanese Garden, and the historic ◆ **Nob Hill Neighborhood,** an assortment of interesting northwest Portland shops, boutiques, and eateries that range along Twenty-first and Twenty-third Avenues just north of Burnside Street. For information and reservations contact innkeeper Julie Keppeler at Heron Haus, 2545 NW Westover Road, Portland 97210. The telephone number is (503) 274–1846.

One of the most charming hostelries right in the heart of the downtown area, just up Broadway from Pioneer Square, is the ◆ **Heathman Hotel.** It's also conveniently located next door to the **Arlene Schnitzer Concert Hall,** the **Performing Arts Center,** and the South Park Blocks. Making its debut in the jazzy 1920s, the Heathman served Portlanders and travelers for nearly fifty years before it began showing its age.

When you find this classy gem, all polished and new again, you'll discover one of the traditions that road-weary travelers especially appreciate: a genuinely friendly and helpful staff. Enjoy afternoon tea in the grand Tea Court, looking just as it did in 1927, including its paneling of polished eucalyptus, or try a cold beverage, along with late-afternoon hors d'oeuvres, in the nearby marble and mirrored bar or in the intimate mezzanine lounge.

Then settle into leather armchairs in the hotel's elegantly casual restaurant. Here guests can sample the chef's award-winning Northwest cuisine—including freshly cooked entrees from the ocean, farms, and fields—during each of the four seasons. The guest rooms and suites are comfortable nests decorated in warm earth tones, accented with soft English chintzes covering rattan sofas, armchairs, and queen-size beds. Green plants add a fresh, outdoorsy touch. For additional information and reservations, contact the staff at the Heathman Hotel, SW Broadway at Salmon Street, Portland 97205; (503) 241–4100.

Music and theater lovers can also check out summertime offerings, some outdoors, for the following: **Tigard Hot Air Balloon Festival,** mid-June (503–245–5220); **Your Zoo and All That Jazz,** in July and August (503–226–1561); and the fabulous **Mount Hood Festival of Jazz,** during the first weekend of

August (503–666–3810). When you get to town, pick up a copy of *Willamette Week* for current listings of stage, theater, gallery, and film offerings, as well as bistro and restaurant listings and reviews.

For current information write or call the Portland Oregon Visitors' Association, 26 SW Salmon Street, Portland 97204; (503) 222–2223 or (800) 345–3214 (or browse the web site at http://www.pova.com/).

WHERE THE RIVERS MERGE

For another pleasant excursion head north and west of downtown via Twenty-third Avenue to access Highway 30, and then drive about 10 miles to **Sauvie Island,** a pastoral area lying along the confluence of the Willamette River from the south and the Columbia River from the east. The small island was settled in the late 1840s, and at one time some forty dairy farms were scattered about it. The southern half now contains lush strawberry and raspberry fields, fruit orchards, and vegetable farms; many Sauvie Island farmers offer their homegrown fruit and produce in open-air stands all summer and into early autumn.

After crossing the Sauvie Island Bridge onto this flat, oblong island that is loved by weekend bicyclers, enjoy meandering along the quiet roads that nearly encircle the terrain. Take a detour to **Oak Island** for some serious bird-watching, canoe on tiny Sturgeon Lake or quiet Multnomah Channel, or bring your bicycle and pedal around the quiet byways. The northern half of the island—where Oak Island and Sturgeon Lake are located— remains a native wetlands area, the ◆**Sauvie Island Wildlife Refuge.** Hundreds of birds migrating along the busy Pacific Flyway make pit stops here twice each year to rest and refuel.

Meriwether Lewis and William Clark also passed near this area on their trek to the Northwest during the early 1800s. On November 3, 1805, Clark, while camped along the Columbia River and feeling somewhat disgruntled, wrote in his journal that the party couldn't sleep "for the noise kept up during the whole of the night by the swans, Geese, white & Grey Brant, Ducks, & c on a small Sand Island. . . . They were imensely numerous, and their noise horid."

With the aid of binoculars, you'll probably spot Canada geese, snow geese, white-fronted geese, assorted ducks, and smaller birds and wildlife. Without binoculars, however, you'll often see many larger birds, such as marsh and red-tailed hawks, vultures, tundra swans, sandhill cranes, and blue herons. During winter a population of about thirty bald eagles roosts in an old-growth forest some miles away, leisurely commuting to Sauvie Island at sunrise to spend the day.

Because something like 500,000 acres of U.S. "wetlands"—a composite description for ponds, lakes, and sloughs and their adjacent grasslands and meadows loved by waterfowl, other birds, and wildlife—are being drained and filled each year, the numbers of birds using the Pacific Flyway has changed dramatically since the days of the Lewis and Clark expedition. For helpful information about efforts to conserve wetlands in the Portland area, including a schedule of bird-watching treks to Sauvie Island and other nearby wildlife habitats, contact the education director, or Mike Houck, an urban naturalist, at the **Portland Audubon Society,** 5151 NW Cornell Road, Portland 97210; (503) 292–6855). Better yet, stop by the society's visitors' center on your way from downtown Portland, via Lovejoy Street (head west), for maps and bird-watching lists before continuing out to Sauvie Island. The headquarters of the Sauvie Island Wildlife Refuge can be reached at (503) 621–3488. The refuge office is open Monday through Friday, 8:00 A.M. to 5:00 P.M. (but closed noon to 1:00 P.M.).

While you're exploring Sauvie Island, stop at the ✦**James Bybee House and Agricultural Museum,** circa 1850, at Howell Territorial Park. In the pioneer orchard you can inspect 115 varieties of apple trees; in the restored farmhouse you can see vintage furnishings and, on the second floor, a wonderful children's room; and in the side yard you can have a picnic amid the collection of old, scented roses. Be sure, too, to poke into the huge barn to see pioneer farm equipment, sacks of grain, and old-time wagons. The pungent aroma of hay and grain always reminds me of visiting a grandparent's farm in the country.

Reaching the farmstead is simple: After crossing narrow Multnomah Channel on the Sauvie Island Bridge from Highway 30, follow the signs to 13801 NW Howell Park Road and turn down the lane to the large parking area. The Bybee House is open June through Labor Day, Wednesday through Sunday, from noon to 5:00 P.M.; a schedule of annual events can be obtained from the Oregon Historical Society, 1230 SW Park Avenue, Portland 97205. The Wintering-In festival takes place on the last Saturday in September and offers freshly pressed cider, demonstrations of pioneer handicrafts, and a sale of old photographs as well as games for children, live music, and tours of the Bybee House.

You could also stay the night on the island by arranging quarters at **Sauvie Island Bed & Breakfast.** Perched on the

James Bybee House and Agricultural Museum

bank of the Columbia River and with views of four of those ice-cream-cone mountain peaks in the Cascades, you can enjoy vegetables from island gardens plus a delicious country breakfast served by innkeepers Marie and A. J. Colasurdo. For information and reservations the address and telephone are 26504 NW Reeder Road, Portland 97231; (503) 621–3216. Incidentally, for a copy of the latest *Oregon Bed & Breakfast Directory*, a statewide listing of small inns, write to the publishers at P.O. Box 1283, Grants Pass 97526, or call (800) 841–5448.

If time allows continue west out Highway 30 about 12 miles farther, toward St. Helens, to enjoy a panoramic view from the historic waterfront area of this circa 1844 city. Find ◆**Columbia View Park** just next door to the courthouse; then post yourself at the old-fashioned gazebo or the brick viewing platform and watch the powerboats, sailboats, and barges on the river. One of the Beaver State's oldest cities, St. Helens is located at the confluence of the Columbia River and the Multnomah Channel on the Oregon side. The Lewis River and Bachelor Island Slough are to the north on the Washington side.

At **Bayport Marina** on Scappoose Bay, just south of Columbia View Park, you'll find boat-launch and picnic facilities. The **St. Helens Sailing Club** holds weekly sailboat races here from April through August, and on the Fourth of July a stunning display of fireworks explodes over offshore Sand Island. For more information about annual events and historic inns in the area, contact the St. Helens-Scappoose Visitors' Center, 1934 Columbia Boulevard, St. Helens 97051; (503) 397–0685.

HISTORIC EAST SIDE NEIGHBORHOODS

Enjoy visiting a bevy of secondhand stores and antiques shops in ◆**Historic Sellwood Neighborhood,** via Macadam Avenue and Sellwood Bridge, located just south of the downtown and old town areas. This old neighborhood, with its small homes and tidy lawns, skirts the Willamette River's east bank near the Sellwood Bridge and **Oaks Park.** Amble along SE Thirteenth Avenue, stopping for lunch or tea and dessert at one of the many delis or small restaurants in the area, or take a picnic down to the new park along the river, just north of the bridge, or to Westmoreland Park, where you can watch youngsters and oldsters sail their boats on the large pond. You'll find comfortable benches for sitting and enjoying the view all along the west side of the pond. Access **Westmoreland Park** just off Bybee Boulevard near Twentieth Avenue.

From Westmoreland Park continue east on Bybee Boulevard where you'll pass **Eastmoreland Public Golf Course** and circle around to SE Woodward Street and Twenty-eighth Avenue (along the way notice the vintage homes of Eastmoreland shaded by enormous old trees). Detour onto Twenty-eighth Avenue for a block or so to find the entrance to lovely ◆**Crystal Springs Rhododendron Garden.** Spend an hour or so walking through this special place where you'll marvel at fifty-year-old rhododendrons; walk a boardwalk across the lake with its plethora of ducks, waterbirds, and songbirds; and watch golfers across the water playing the "front nine." The seven-acre garden is open daily and is managed by the City of Portland.

Wish you had brought a picnic lunch to eat at one of the benches along Crystal Springs Lake? Well, stop first at **Otto's Sausage Kitchen and Meat Market,** just up the hill past Reed College, at 4138 SE Woodstock, to collect sandwiches, salads, chips, imported cheeses, imported and domestic ales, muffins, cookies, coffee, and lattes. Otto's has been making great sausages since 1929. Open Monday through Saturday from 9:30 A.M. to 6:30 P.M.

Then wend your way over to the ◆**Hawthorne Neighborhood** by turning north onto Thirty-ninth Avenue at Woodstock Boulevard. On Hawthorne Boulevard, between Fortieth and Twentieth Avenues, you'll find a restored area of interesting shops, delis, restaurants, and boutiques. Stop by **Dragonfly Gardens,** near Twenty-second, for a good selection of plants and garden-related goodies; snoop through the **Hawthorne Coffee Merchant,** near Thirty-fifth Avenue, for gourmet coffees, teas, and candies; or have lunch at **Pastaworks** or at **Tabor Hill Cafe,** both, near Thirty-sixth Avenue. For a real treat stop in at ◆**Grand Central Bakery** for outstanding cinnamon rolls, scones, and espresso as well as the rustic Italian breads for which the bakery has become famous: thick, crusted, free form, and very chewy, made by slow-rise and long-fermentation processes. Among the greatest hits are the Como loaf, rustic baguette, Sole Mio, sour white round, and rosemary roll. Find the bakery at 2230 SE Hawthorne Boulevard, (503) 232–0575.

Continue east on Hawthorne Boulevard and drive up 600-foot **Mt. Tabor** for a view of the city from atop one of Portland's extinct volcanic cinder cones. For the best view wind up to the top, where you'll be sheltered beneath towering Douglas fir, their long branches swaying in the gentle breezes like graceful ballerinas. Below are the city's water reservoirs, which hold water from the Bull Run watershed area located in the Cascade foothills about 30 miles east of Portland. Picnic tables are located in shaded or sunny spots here and there, and you can hike around the park for views of snowcapped Mt. Hood, also to the east.

You can also discover comfortable places to spend the night on the east side of town. One of the coziest, a 1908 Dutch Colonial faced with clinker bricks, is tucked into a side street just north of the **Lloyd Center** shops and ice arena. Here Peggie and Bob Irvine welcome travelers to the ◆**Clinkerbrick House Bed and Breakfast,** where, amid Peggie's collections—including antiques, quilts, and strawberries—guests find three spacious suites on the second floor that offer quiet havens after a busy day of seeing the city; an example is the lovely Garden Room, with its wicker chaise longue and canopied queen-size bed, a cozy room that gets the morning sun. You can also use the common room on the second floor, which has books and magazines, a color television, a microwave oven, and a small refrigerator stocked with complimentary soft drinks.

Peggie's gourmet breakfasts are the kind you'll write home about—you might be served Eggs Bravato with salsa, sour cream, and avocado; Ricotta Pancakes with fresh blueberries and warm blueberry syrup; and fresh seasonal fruits, Apricot Breakfast Roll, Oregon Plum Cobbler Cake, and cinnamon rolls. For further information and reservations, contact the Irvines at 2311 NE Schuyler Street, Portland 97212; (503) 281–2533. Children are welcome.

Work off your breakfast by browsing the trendy ◆**Northeast Broadway Neighborhood**—dozens of great shops, delis, and galleries range from NE Tenth to NE Twentieth avenues. You may even want to linger another day in the area.

Should the Clinkerbrick House be booked up when you call, ask about **Georgian House B&B** (503–281–2250); **Portland Guest House** (503–282–1402); **John Palmer House B&B** (503–284–5893); and **The Lion & the Rose Victorian B&B**

(503–287–9245), other fine bed-and-breakfast inns located in this area. Also nearby are the Memorial Coliseum, the **Rose Garden,** and the **Convention Center,** where numerous sports and other public events are held throughout the year.

OREGON TRAIL'S END

Those blue-sky afternoons often beckon young and old alike to the **Willamette River,** just as they did when those first pioneers arrived and settled near the base of the falls at Oregon City. In the late 1800s the Willamette River was the "main street" for life in the Willamette Valley: People traveled by riverboats and stern-wheelers, produce and supplies were shipped in and out by steamboats, and Oregon's principal cities started as river towns and steamboat landings. No fewer than seven major cities are located along the river, and more than half the people in Oregon live within 10 miles of the Willamette; in fact more than sixty percent of all Oregonians live within the Willamette River Basin.

One of the best ways to cool off and see this historic area from a different perspective is to take a boat ride upriver about 18 miles, south toward Lake Oswego, West Linn, Milwaukie, Gladstone, and Oregon City. The boat proceeds south from downtown Portland, first maneuvering under the **Ross Island Bridge,** and then continues upriver past tiny Ross Island toward the Sellwood area. Sunlight sparkles from the moving water, and the city skyline recedes in midafternoon's golden light. The air smells fresh and clean.

Cruising upriver at a comfortable speed, the boat may pass a flotilla of small sailboats engaged in a race. White sails catch the wind, and sunlight turns them brightly translucent. Tinkly music from the **Oaks Park** merry-go-round wafts across the water as the boat passes under the **Sellwood Bridge,** continuing south toward the small communities along both banks of the river and the Willamette Falls at Oregon City.

A profusion of greenery passes by—cool canopies of trees, shrubbery, and mosses clinging to basaltic ledges and rocky walls here and there on both east and west banks of the river. The boat cruises past waterside homes; a small pontoon plane crouches at its dockside resting place; water-skiers glide past on wide skis; and great blue herons—Portland's official bird—catch the wind overhead, often in the company of seagulls who have flown in from the coast some 80 miles west.

At **Clackamette Park,** near Gladstone and Oregon City, peer over the railing to see where the smaller Clackamas River quietly enters the Willamette. The boat passes beneath the I–205 and old Oregon City bridges, toward the falls.

The boat maneuvers around to the entrance to ✦ **Willamette Falls Locks,** the early settlers' solution to the water problem of navigating the river at this point. Someone jumps onto the dock and yanks the rope, which, in turn, activates a light and horn alerting the lock tender. If there's no tugboat coming through the locks from upriver, your boat will be next in line.

The giant wooden doors soon open wide, and the boat moves into the first of the four watery chambers. The lock master waves from the small station, keeping track of the gates and traffic on a television monitor while relaying instructions to a second lock tender in the upper station. It takes about thirty minutes to reach the upper Willamette River channel above the falls with the help of the historic locks. Constructed in 1872 by Chinese laborers, these locks have operated since 1873. In 1974 the project was placed on the National Register of Historic Places, and in 1991 the American Society of Civil Engineers, Oregon Section, designated the locks a national civil engineering landmark. *Note:* Midweek, after 5:00 P.M., is the best time to enter the locks without waiting; such delays can run thirty or forty minutes on a busy summer weekend.

Its passengers warmed by the late-afternoon sun, the boat then cruises upriver a couple of miles before returning through the locks to the lower channel and heading downriver, past Clackamette Park and waterside homes. A great blue heron balances long, spindly legs on a rock outcropping, and the city reappears, a surreal image of thick vertical lines on the sunset horizon.

✦ **Stern-wheelers** resurrected from yesteryear are once again cruising up both the Willamette and the Columbia Rivers. To join one of the cruises on either river, check with the stern-wheeler *Columbia Gorge,* which makes frequent trips. The office is located at 1200 NW Front Street, Suite 110, in Portland; the telephone number is (503) 223–3928. For smaller charter boats inquire at the visitors' center in downtown Portland, (503) 222–2223.

If you would like to visit the Willamette Falls Locks and arranging a boat ride isn't feasible, you can drive from downtown Portland south via Macadam Avenue and Highway 43 through Lake Oswego to West Linn. Drive under the I–205 bridge, continue to the redbrick building housing West Linn City Hall and Police Department, and look for the sign—just before crossing the old Oregon City bridge—that says WILLAMETTE FALLS LOCKS AND ARMY CORPS OF ENGINEERS. Don't give up—it's well worth the effort to find this out-of-the-way gem. Park nearby and follow the paved walk and series of concrete stairs that lead down to the public viewing area.

Just for fun, spend a couple of hours on land watching tugboats, barges, pleasure boats, and perhaps a party of canoes pass through the four lock chambers. The lock tenders are a congenial lot and are usually pleased to answer questions about the historic locks; there is a large grassy area with shade trees, picnic tables, and sunny spots. The public rest rooms are wheelchair-accessible. A small Historical Museum on the grounds offers detailed information and wide-angle photographs of the construction of the four-lock chambers; it is open daily from 8:00 A.M. to 5:00 P.M. For additional information contact the Lockmaster, Willamette Falls Locks, U.S. Army Corps of Engineers, West Linn 97068. The telephone number is (503) 656–3381.

To visit the tiny community of Willamette, the most historic part of West Linn, head west on the frontage road, Willamette Falls Drive, winding above the locks and the Willamette River for a couple of miles. Here you'll find a couple of antiques shops, several eateries, a large city park along the river (great spot for a picnic), and, a bit farther, just off Swift Shore Drive, the elegant ❖ **Swift Shore Chalet Bed & Breakfast** perched on a bluff overlooking the Tualatin River (this small river empties into the larger Willamette River near the City Park). On the guest room level are cozy havens in which to hole up and a spacious common area decorated western-style; it's warmed by a woodstove on chilly mornings. From the expansive deck you'll look down on lovely terraced grounds that beckon one outdoors—pause on the charming bridge and look at pond life, sit in the willow swing, meditate in the quaint garden house, and enjoy a plethora of perennials, annuals, flowering trees, fragrant shrubs, and native grasses. This inspirational garden was created by owners Nancy and Horace

Duke . . . "we love sharing our special haven with travelers," they smile. Breakfast is an equally elegant affair. For further information and reservations write or call the Dukes at 1190 Swift Shore Circle, West Linn 97068; (503) 650–3853.

Just east, after you've crossed the Willamette River from West Linn via the old **Highway 99 Oregon City Bridge,** you'll find historic Oregon City, which boasts the distinction of being the first incorporated city west of the Rocky Mountains. In the winter of 1829–30, however, there were just three log houses here, and in the following spring, the first vegetables—potatoes—were planted. Apparently the local Native Americans resented this infringement on their territory and reportedly burned the houses. A flour mill and a sawmill, constructed near the falls in 1832 by the British Hudson's Bay Company, made use of the first waterpower in the territory.

The emigration over the Oregon Trail in 1844 added several hundred folks to Oregon City's population. The provisional government body, formed in 1843 at Champoeg, located on the banks of the Willamette River south and west a few miles, chose Oregon City as its seat; the first provisional legislature assembled here in June 1844, at the Rose Farm.

By 1846 Oregon City contained some seventy houses and about 500 citizens. In January 1848 Joe Meek carried the request of the provisional legislature for territorial status to President James K. Polk in Washington, D.C. Meek returned in March 1849 with the newly appointed territorial governor, Joseph Lane. Oregon City was made the territorial capital and remained so until 1852, when the seat of government was moved to Salem, some 50 miles south, in the heart of the Willamette Valley.

To begin your tour stop first at the ◆ **End of the Oregon Trail Interpretive Center,** located near Washington and Abernethy Streets—you can't miss the three gigantic pioneer wagons with their white canvas tops! You'll take a guided tour that illustrates and explains the rigorous, 2,000-mile journey from Independence, Missouri, to Oregon City—the land route across the prairies, mountains, and deserts to The Dalles, including the float on crudely made barges down the swift and dangerous Columbia River. Later, the alternate Barlow Trail route was forged over Mt. Hood. Of the 300,000 immigrants who undertook this formidable trek, some 30,000 died on the way and were buried along the trail. The interpretive center is open daily from 9:00 A.M. to 5:00 P.M. Call (503) 657–9336 for more information.

The 150th anniversary of the Oregon Trail migration was celebrated in 1993. For a complete list of events planned for other historic celebrations and local festivals, write to the Oregon City Visitors' Center at 1795 Washington Street, Oregon City 97045 (503–656–1619) or to the Clackamas County Historical Society, 211 Tumwater Street (P.O. Box 294), Oregon City 97045; (503) 655–5574.

Next, pick up the *Historic Walking Tour* brochure and map, park on Main Street near the courthouse, and walk a few blocks to the ◆**Oregon City Municipal Elevator,** accessing it via the lower entrance, on Railroad Avenue at Seventh Street. You'll enjoy the thirty-second vertical ride up the face of the 90-foot basalt cliff—the city is built on two levels. The elevator—one of only four municipal elevators in the world—replaced the old Indian trails and pioneer paths that originally led from river's edge to the top of the basalt bluff.

The first elevator, which took three minutes to travel up and down, was powered by water. It was constructed in 1915— much to the chagrin of citizen Sara Chase, who objected to its location in front of her Victorian mansion. Not only did Sara never use the municipal elevator, but she had a heavy wrought-iron fence erected so that "none of those elevator people" could trespass on her property. On the interior wall of the observation area atop the elevator, you can see an artist's painting of the Chase mansion.

Walk south a few blocks along the upper **Promenade** (it's also wheelchair-accessible) for a spectacular view of Willamette Falls. Imagine what the area must have been like before the settlers arrived, before power lines and buildings, before bridges and freeways and automobiles. Actually, the first long-distance transmission of electricity in the United States happened here—from Oregon City to Portland—in 1888.

The early Native American families fished for salmon along the forested riverbanks amid stands of Douglas fir, the roar of the falls ever present. The falls cascade some 42 feet over several basaltic ledges in the middle of the wide river. You can sit at any of the public benches along the Promenade, basking in the late-afternoon sun while imagining a bit of Oregon history.

McLoughlin House

Continuing a few blocks north and east, visit the historic
◆**McLoughlin House,** at 713 Center Street, which was the
home of Dr. John McLoughlin, a dominant figure in not only
the Hudson's Bay Company but also the early development of
the region. Appointed chief factor, or superintendent of trade, of
the British company in 1824, the tall, white-haired, cane-
carrying man ruled over the entire Columbia country before the
Oregon Trail migration began in 1843.

Under orders from the Hudson's Bay Company, McLoughlin
established the first settlement at Oregon City and, later, moved
here from **Fort Vancouver,** across the Columbia River, when he
resigned from the company in 1845. Incidentally, reconstructed
Fort Vancouver and its splendid reclaimed British-style vegetable, herb, and flower gardens are well worth a visit. The stockade, including living history programs in the kitchen quarters,
baking quarters, general store, blacksmith shop, and main house
are provided by National Park Service staff and volunteers. **Fort
Vancouver National Historic Site** is located just across the
Columbia River from Portland, at 612 East Reserve Street, Vancouver, WA 98661; (360) 696–7655 or (800) 832–3599, open

daily. Further information and directions can be obtained from the McLoughlin House staff. Born in the Canadian province of Quebec, Dr. McLoughlin became a U.S. citizen in 1851 and spent his later years operating his store, gristmill, and sawmills near the base of Willamette Falls at Oregon City.

McLoughlin's house, a large clapboard-style building with simple, dignified lines, was saved from demolition and moved from its original location along the Willamette River near the falls up to the top of the bluff and placed in what is now McLoughlin Park at Seventh and Center Streets. On the lovely grounds are large rhododendrons, clumps of azaleas, and old roses, and to the rear of the house sits a moss-covered fountain, shaded by tall Douglas firs and trailing ivy. For information about the annual Candlelight Holiday Tour and the August Family Festival, contact the staff at McLoughlin House, 713 Center Street, Oregon City 97045; (503) 656–5146. The house is open Tuesday through Saturday from 10:00 A.M. to 4:00 P.M. and Sunday from 1:00 to 4:00 P.M., except on holidays and during the month of January.

For a tasty treat, stop at the ◆ **Fellows House Restaurant and Inn** for lunch in a restored, circa 1867 Gothic Revival structure, painted a cheerful peach with white trim and surrounded by a lovely flower garden. It's located on McLoughlin Boulevard—old Highway 99E—in the **Canemah Historic District,** just beyond the **Clackamas County Historical Society Center,** both just south of the Oregon City Municipal Elevator. Refurbished by Tom and Mary DeHaven in 1989, the Fellows House also offers travelers four comfortable bed-and-breakfast guest rooms. The second-level balcony, across the front of the inn, offers splendid views of the Willamette River and falls. Captain Fellows, who built the house, was a shipbuilder, a ship engineer, and a stern-wheeler captain on the river during those early years when it served as the region's "main street."

Guests are served the Captain's Special Breakfast in one of the two dining areas on the main level; for lunch, with tables open to the public, Tom creates specialty sandwiches like the Canemah, with Dungeness crabmeat, melted cheddar, avocado, onion, tomato, lettuce, and the inn's special sauce.

For information and reservations contact the DeHavens at the Fellows House, 416 South McLoughlin Boulevard, Oregon City

97045; (503) 656–2089. The inn's restaurant is open Monday through Friday from 11:00 A.M. to 3:00 P.M.

You can also stay overnight in another historic house, **Captain Ainsworth House Bed and Breakfast,** restored by Claire and Tom Met to its mid-1800s elegance. For information and reservations call (503) 655–5172.

Another rural loop from Oregon City offers a ramble into the eastern section of Clackamas County, reaching into the foothills of the Cascade Mountains. Take the Park Place exit from I–205 and turn left at the first light, toward Park Place. Settle into the slow lane and wind along Clackamas River Drive toward Carver. Rather than crossing the river here just yet, continue east on Springwater Road; then just beyond the boat-ramp entrance, turn right for about a quarter-mile to the ◈ **German Methodist Church** and the ◈ **Baker Cabin.**

The small church, built around 1895, sits like a tidy little dowager under tall firs surrounded by well-kept grounds. Walk the gravel drive to the far end of the grassy area to inspect the Baker Cabin, which dates to 1856; notice the old grapevine, with its enormous main trunk, which must have been planted around the same time as the cabin was built. The logs were hand-hewn into square-shaped timbers that deftly interlock at the four corners. Tiny ferns and wildflowers grow from crevices in the old rock fireplace chimney at the west end of the cabin. For information about the annual Pioneer Bazaar and other events open to the public, contact the Baker Cabin Historical Society, P.O. Box 741, Oregon City 97045; (503) 631–8274. The cabin and church are located at the corner of Hattan and Gronlund Roads.

Now backtrack to the Carver bridge, cross the Clackamas River and angle to your left onto Highway 224 to feast your eyes on one woman's spectacular flower garden, ◈ **Tallina's Garden,** located at 15790 SE Highway 224. Usually the first thing visitors notice is the large lath dome and extensive pergola atop a small knoll just south of the main house. Built to replicate a similar one seen in a French garden, this forms an impressive backdrop for Tallina George's lavish rose garden, growing in terraced beds just below. The intimate knot-garden design was copied from the Barnsley House garden of Gloucestershire, England. You'll also find several intimate "garden rooms" filled with luscious roses, annuals, perennials, and vegetables, too. A gazebo is covered with roses as well. At last count this lover of gardens had planted more than a thousand rose varieties that now climb up posts, sprawl over walls, and line walkways. Although it is a private garden, Tallina George welcomes visitors to park in the large parking area and stroll through her beautiful creation. She asks that children always be supervised by adults. You may also enjoy visiting the large white barn that houses her fabric-and-lace business.

From Tallina's you can head farther off the beaten path by taking Highway 224 back toward the Clackamas River but heading, this time, east about 15 miles toward Estacada.

For history buffs, your next stop is the ✪ **Philip Foster National Historic Farm** located just off Highway 224 at 29912 SE Highway 211, Eagle Creek. Offering living-history programs during the year, this site offers a nostalgic look at the 1840s, when Philip and Mary Foster ran a general store, restaurant, and resting place for Oregon Trail pioneers on the final lap of their trek to the West. You'll see Mary's lilac tree blooming in the front yard; it was planted in 1843, having survived the arduous journey "around the horn" from Calais, Maine. Mary, bless her heart, cooked meals for some 10,000 emigrants over those early trail years. And she raised nine children and tended the orchards and gardens as well. In mid-August at the farm, you can sample one of Mary's meals: beef and potatoes, biscuits and cole slaw, cobbler and coffee. For further information and a schedule of events, call the Jacknife-Zion-Horseheaven Historical Society, (503) 637–6324 or (503) 630–5051.

In the small community of Estacada look for **Harmony Bakery,** tucked away at SW Second and Wade Streets. Here you can join a diverse group of local folks who meet to drink coffee, eat freshly made bagels, and, of course, have a good-morning or afternoon chat about the weather and the state of the world's economic affairs. A bagel with cream cheese to go is still just 50 cents, or you could order the omelet with spicy hash-brown potatoes, vegetarian fare, or more traditional sandwiches and burgers. The restaurant is open daily from 7:00 A.M. to 3:00 P.M.

From Estacada continue south another 15 miles or so via Highway 211 to Molalla to discover ✪ **Pacific Northwest Live Steamers,** a miniature railroad park set in the Cascade foothills of eastern Clackamas County. Congenial volunteer engineers, members of the Pacific Northwest Live Steamers Club, run miniature trains on some 6,000 feet of track from noon to 5:00 P.M. on Sundays, May through October. There's a shady picnic area nearby in the park.

Riding with the kids in one of the small open-air cars behind your "Sunday engineer" is reminiscent of one's childhood days, dreaming of choo-choo trains, clanging bells, and whistle blasts. Two long toots signal "start" or "release brakes"; a long and a short mean "warning"; three shorts when a train is stopped designate "back up"; and one long whistle indicates the train is approaching a station. The miniature engine huffs and puffs steam from a tiny smokestack, just like its full-size original counterpart: the sleek steam locomotive that replaced horse-drawn wagons as well as the Pony Express and helped to settle the west.

In recent decades these mechanical marvels have all but disappeared, especially the steam locomotives, although many full-size models are also being restored and put back into service for nostalgic weekend trips; examples are the **Mt. Hood Railroad** in Hood River (541–386–3556); the **Sumpter Valley Railroad** in Sumpter, near Baker City (541–894–2362); and the **Oregon Coastline Express** in Tillamook (503–842–7525). Pacific Northwest Live Steamers miniature railroad park is located at 31083 South Shady Dell Drive in Molalla; call (503) 829–6866 for more information. To access the park from Highway 211, drive into Molalla and turn south at the Y-Grocery for about ½ mile, then west onto Feyrer Park Road to Shady Dell Park.

Farm and Flower Country

From Molalla complete your rural loop back to the Portland area by heading west on Highway 211 to Woodburn and turning north on old Highway 99E through Hubbard to Aurora, Canby, and back to Oregon City. Old Highway 99, which divides into two sections, 99E and 99W, as it winds through Willamette Valley towns, was the first paved north-south route (it followed sections of the early stagecoach route) linking all cities and towns along the Willamette River and south into the Umpqua and Rogue River valleys. From my childhood in the 1940s, I remember trips on Highway 99 that took seven "long" hours of driving from Grants Pass, in southern Oregon, to Portland.

Although travelers can now whiz up and down sleek I–5, covering the same distance in about four and a half hours, once in a while it's nice to get off the freeway and ramble along sections of Old Highway 99 and its rural tributaries. It's a nostalgic trek into yesterday for native Oregonians, one generously shared with visitors.

Pull off Highway 99E in Aurora to visit the ✦ **Aurora National Historic District** and the **Old Aurora Colony Museum,** which inhabits a large, refurbished ox barn. The colony's history began in the Harmony Colony in Pennsylvania, from which William Keil, a German tailor, physician, and preacher, and his followers emigrated to found the town of Bethel, Missouri, near the start of the Oregon Trail.

Some of the historic landmarks have vanished over the years, but many of the buildings remain, including the ox barn that houses the museum, a small log cabin, a washhouse, a machine shed, an assortment of farm machinery, and a lovely miniature garden, the **Emma Wakefield Herb Garden.** The colony was well known for its fine cooking and music; its brass band entertained at community festivities and events. In the museum you'll see many of the brass instruments, including the *schellenbaum,* a rare bell tree.

The museum has an excellent collection of historic quilts made by various women of the community, and many of these quilts are displayed throughout the year. Further information about other annual events, such as the **Spinner's Festival,** can be obtained from the Old Aurora Colony Museum, Second and Liberty Streets, Aurora 97002; (503) 678–5754. The museum complex is open Tuesday through Saturday from 10:00 A.M. to 4:00 P.M. and is closed during January.

For a pleasant overnight stay in this historic community, try ✦ **The Inn at Aurora,** located just half a block from the museum complex at 15109 NE Second Street, Aurora 97002. A sparkling new structure built by the Heininge family, the inn reflects the peaceful simplicity of the Old Aurora Colony. Light from both wide windows and from sliding glass deck doors spills into the spacious morning room–open kitchen where Elizabeth prepares and serves her guests a delicious breakfast; on chilly mornings the gas "woodstove" burns cheerily at the far end of the room. Ask about guest rooms, including The Master Suite, which offers a deluxe spa tub, kingsize bed, gas woodstove, and balcony views of the historic district. Call (503) 678–1932 for information and reservations.

As you head north toward Canby from Aurora, you can take another side ramble by turning east onto Barlow Road and proceeding about 4 miles to ◆ **St. Josef's Winery.** Owners Lilli and Josef Fleischmann decided to trade the bakery business for wine making more than ten years ago. In 1983, their first year as vintners, St. Josef's Cabernet won the Consumer's Choice award at a festival in Spokane, Washington.

Join the congenial crowd here at the annual **Grape Stomping Festival,** held the first weekend of October, or take a picnic along during the spring and summer months and sit under enormous redwood trees at one of the tables on the grounds. In the tasting room you can sample Oregon Rieslings, gewürztraminers, and several varieties of zinfandel, as well as the most recent pinot noirs. Located at 28836 South Barlow Road, St. Josef's Winery is open daily from noon to 5:00 P.M., and the tables usually remain outdoors until cool weather begins, around the end of October. Call (503) 651–3190 for more information.

As you head back toward Canby on Barlow Road to Highway 99E, notice the large fields of tulips and other bulbs that bloom during mid-April. In these far southern reaches of Clackamas County, the rich alluvial soils from ancient rivers support more than a hundred nurseries, where growers raise everything from annuals and perennials to ornamentals and fruit stock. You can also see, just west of Aurora, acres and acres of lush green turf grass, which is cut into strips and rolled into compact bundles destined for someone's new lawn.

Most of the nurseries are the wholesale variety, shipping to destinations throughout the United States, but a few are open to the public. Near Canby, just a few miles west of the downtown area at 995 NW Twenty-second Avenue, visit ◆ **Swan Island Dahlias** and wander through some forty-three acres of the gorgeous perennials that bloom in late summer, beginning in August and lasting until the first frost, sometime in mid- to late October.

This large nursery has been operated by the Gitts family since the 1950s, and dahlias have been part of the Canby area since the late 1940s. The farm features more than 250 varieties, with blooms ranging from 12 or more inches in diameter to those of tiny pompons, at less than 2 inches across. The voluptuous flowers are reported to

141

have originated in Mexico. Walk through the labeled rows to find selections like Gay Princess, Cuddles, Sassy, Cameo, Matchmaker, and First Love—visitors can even select and purchase a take-along bouquet.

From Canby access Swan Island Dahlias from Ivy Street to Second Street, then Holly Street to Twenty-second Street. During the farm's indoor Dahlia Show, usually held the first or second weekend of September, you can watch professional designers fashion the vibrant blooms into creative arrangements. If you miss that event, you can still stroll through the blooming fields, beginning in August, Monday through Friday from 9:00 A.M. to dusk. Call (503) 266–7711 for further information.

If the kids or the grandkids are along, consider stopping at the nearby **Flower Farmer and Phoenix & Holly Railroad** located at 2412 North Holly Street, Canby 97013. Train rides to the farm's Pumpkin Patch in October are a special treat. The open market stand is loaded with the freshest seasonal varieties of corn, beans, tomatoes, peaches, and the like; the indoor gift shop offers a fine selection of dried flowers and fresh flowers from the fields. Open May through November from 10:00 A.M. to 6:00 P.M. Call (503) 266–3581.

To delve into more history about the area, stop at the ◆**Canby Depot Museum** at the north edge of town. The museum, maintained by the Canby Area Historical Society, is housed in the oldest railroad station owned by the C&C Railroad. The restored building is just off Highway 99E at the Fairgrounds exit and is open weekdays from 10:00 A.M. to 4:00 P.M. and Saturday and Sunday from 1:00 to 4:00 P.M. Also, be sure to poke into the charming restored caboose located a few steps from the museum's entry door. Call (503) 266–9421 for more information. To inquire about the old-fashioned ◆**Clackamas County Fair,** one of the best late-summertime events in the area, contact the Canby Visitors' Center at 266 NW First Street, Canby 97013; (503) 266–4600.

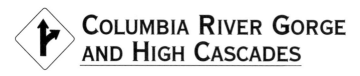

COLUMBIA RIVER GORGE AND HIGH CASCADES

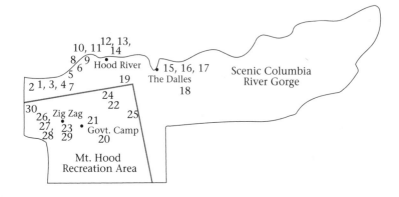

10, 11 12, 13, 14
8 9 Hood River
6
5
2 1, 3, 4 7   19   15, 16, 17   Scenic Columbia
24   The Dalles   River Gorge
22   18
30
26, Zig Zag   25
27, 21
28 23 Govt. Camp
29 20

Mt. Hood
Recreation Area

1. Columbia River
   Scenic Highway
2. Black Rabbit Restaurant and
   McMenamin's Edgefield
3. Women's Forum Park and
   Chanticleer Point
4. Crown Point Visitors' Center
   and Vista House
5. Multnomah Falls
6. Elowah Falls–McCord Creek
7. Gorge Hiking Weekend
8. Bonneville Dam
9. Port of Cascade Locks
   Marine Park
10. Bridge of the Gods
11. Columbia Gorge Interpretive
    Center
12. Hood River Boat Basin
    and Marina Park
13. Mt. Hood Railroad
14. Hood River Hotel
15. Fort Dalles Historical
    Museum
16. Sorosis Park

17. Williams House Bed and
    Breakfast Inn
18. Balch Hotel and Dufur
    Threshing Bee
19. River Bend Farm and Country
    Store
20. Summit Meadows and
    Trillium Lake
21. Falcon's Crest Inn
22. Mt. Hood and Timberline
    Lodge
23. Salmon River National
    Recreation Trail
24. Silcox Hut
25. Five Mile Butte Fire Lookout
    and Valley View Cabin
26. Heart of the Mountain Gifts
    and Treasures
27. Don Guidos Restaurant
28. Old Welches Bed and
    Breakfast Inn
29. Zig Zag Inn
30. Mt. Hood Coffee Roaster and
    Merchantile

COLUMBIA RIVER GORGE AND HIGH CASCADES

SCENIC COLUMBIA RIVER GORGE

Although much of the original winding highway, clinging along-side the Columbia River Gorge since 1915, has deteriorated or become part of streamlined I–84, visitors can enjoy two good-size segments of the historic ◆ **Columbia River Scenic Highway** east of Portland between Troutdale and The Dalles.

Before heading east into the Columbia Gorge, particularly if you've not eaten, consider stopping in Troutdale to find the ◆ **Black Rabbit Restaurant** in the main lodge at ◆ **McMenamins Edgefield.** It is located at 2126 SW Halsey Street, just south of I–84 at the Wood Village exit. For dinner you might order such Northwest fare as salmon with hazelnut butter or clams steamed in ale. If time allows, you'll enjoy touring the twenty-five-acre complex that, in the early 1900s, housed the fully self-contained Multnomah County Poor Farm. Now completely restored, including an herb garden and small vineyard, the complex includes bed-and-breakfast lodging, meeting rooms, a winery and wine-cellar pub, an outdoor barbecue and picnic area, and, in the old power station, a brew pub and theater for showing vintage movies. The Black Rabbit Restaurant offers breakfast, lunch, and dinner daily. The telephone number is (800) 669–8610.

Railroad buffs can plan to stop and browse a nice collection of memorabilia at the **Troutdale Rail Depot Museum** located at 473 East Columbia River Highway, Troutdale 97060; (503) 665–0423. Originally built in 1882, the depot was one of the earliest stations along the Columbia River route. It's open June through October, Saturday and Sunday, 1:00 to 4:00 P.M.

Punctuated with a dozen or more cascading waterfalls and enough hiking trails to keep outdoor buffs busy for weeks, the eighty-two-year-old Scenic Highway offers a low-stress, relaxed alternative to busy I–84. To access the first section of the old highway, detour from the freeway at the Lewis and Clark State Park exit east of McMenamin's Edgefield and Troutdale, just across the Sandy River.

The Scenic Highway parallels the east bank of the Sandy River and loops several miles south then angles east through a sun-filtered canopy of big-leaf maples and Douglas fir, climbing gradually to the small community of Corbett. Just east of Corbett, pull into the ◆ **Women's Forum Park,** at ◆ **Chanticleer Point,** for one of the best panoramas of the Columbia River Gorge and the wide Columbia River, which separates Oregon and Washington.

The view is almost too vast to absorb. You'll see the massive stone **Vista House** perched atop **Crown Point** just a couple of miles distant; the silver ribbon of river shimmering some 750 feet below; then 800-foot **Beacon Rock,** a volcanic monolith about 25 miles upstream on the Washington side of the river; and the Union Pacific railroad tracks and I–84, narrow ribbons paralleling the mighty river.

Samuel Hill, a Washingtonian and a lover of roads, inspired the building of the Scenic Highway. Combining forces with Samuel Lancaster, the consulting engineer, and Portland businessmen Simon Benson and John Yeon, Hill not only envisioned the economic and tourist potential of such a road but appreciated the aesthetic and natural beauty of the gorge as well. The highway's rapid completion date was prodded by Portland's desire to lure the state's turn-of-the-century motorists as well as travelers en route to the 1915 Panama Pacific Exhibition in California.

In the design of this first major highway in the Northwest, Lancaster incorporated graceful stone bridges, viaducts, stone walls, tunnels, and stone benches. He had been inspired by a trip to Europe with Sam Hill for the purpose of studying the historic Roman roads there. Alongside the Columbia River the ancient trail of deer, native peoples, and those first fur trappers was replaced with the functional yet beautiful highway that clung so closely to the gorge's lush moss, fern-covered, and tree-laden outcroppings. It is said that more than one early historian referred to the Scenic Highway as one of "poetry and drama."

Stop at the ◆ **Crown Point Visitors' Center** at ◆ **Vista House** for more camera clicking and history recollecting; the impressive stone structure was dedicated in 1918 as a monument to the early pioneers and early settlers of Oregon. (Notice the eight carved panels that line the dome's interior.) Those interested in helping with the historic building's upkeep and continuing restoration may write or call **Friends of Vista House,** P.O.

145

Box 204, Corbett 97019; (503) 695–2230. Passing Shepperd's Dell, continue on to **Wahkeena Falls** (*Wahkeena* is an Indian word for "most beautiful"), where you'll find more parking and a large picnic area. Wahkeena tumbles and cascades in a series of frothy falls; dainty wildflowers bloom around rocks and in mossy crevices.

◆**Multnomah Falls,** just east of Latourell and Wahkeena Falls, is the most spectacular in the Columbia River Gorge, cascading in a long drop of 620 feet from the basaltic gorge rim. It's one of the highest waterfalls in the United States. If time allows, walk the easy trail to the upper bridge for a close encounter with the cascading water, accompanied by its swishing roar and cool mist.

An easy, though somewhat steep, trail continues from the bridge up to the rim for a top-of-the-falls, panoramic view of the world below. It's well worth the 2⁹⁄₁₀-mile round-trip trek, especially midweek, when you'll encounter fewer tourists. Take along some water or another beverage, and keep an eye out for poison oak, which lurks here and there along the trail's edge; the leaves look like a miniature oak leaf, and almost everyone is allergic to every part of the plant.

At the base of the falls, linger to visit rustic **Multnomah Falls Lodge,** also constructed in 1914–15, where breakfast, lunch, and dinner are served in a lovely atrium dining room; there are also a snack bar and a gift shop. Call (503) 695–2376 for dinner or Sunday brunch reservations.

East of Multnomah Falls, and still on the historic Scenic Highway section, is **Oneonta Gorge.** Oneonta Creek bubbles through the narrowest of high, mossy chasms here, and those who don't mind getting their feet wet can walk up the shallow creek to the cascading falls. Hikers are asked to be cautious of large boulders, however, which can dislodge and cause injury. Just east a trail at **Horsetail Falls** leads behind the upper falls, crossing Oneonta Creek right before the water plunges over the rim in a frothy ribbon.

For helpful trail maps and hiking information, contact the Columbia River Gorge Ranger Station, 31520 SE Woodard Road, Troutdale 97060; (503) 695–2276. The ranger station is open year-round, Monday through Friday, from 8:00 A.M. to 4:30 P.M. You can also find maps at Crown Point (503–695–2240) and at Multnomah Falls Lodge.

If your visit coincides with the busy summer crush of traffic on the narrow Scenic Highway and you want to get away from the crowds, continue east toward **Ainsworth State Park.** Instead of pulling onto I–84 at this point, stay to the right on the frontage road that parallels the freeway, and continue just a half-mile or so to a large parking area and the ◆ **Elowah Falls–McCord Creek** trailhead. Bask in the sun on large rounded rocks at the lower falls—take a left at the trail's first fork—or relax in sun-filtered shade on large rocks at the upper falls. Both hikes are easy—fewer than 2 miles in length—and the views of the falls and gorge are spectacular, particularly on the upper falls route. These quiet, peaceful walks are far removed from the crowds and allow a focused interlude with the incredibly beautiful gorge habitat.

If time permits, don't miss this trek into history, geology, and plant life that numerous wildlife and conservation groups are working to protect. From the Native Plant Societies of Oregon and Washington to local chapters of the Audubon Society, the Sierra Club, and the Nature Conservancy, as well as the Friends of the Columbia River Gorge, the U.S. Forest Service, the Mazamas, the Trails Club of Oregon, the American Alpine Club, and the Historic Preservation League, thousands of folks are dedicated to the task of preserving the fragile and irreplaceable as well as historical habitats within the Columbia River Gorge. For current information contact the Columbia River Gorge Visitors' Association, P.O. Box 2047, Corbett 97019; (800) 98–GORGE. Also ask to be sent a brochure about the annual ◆ **Gorge Hiking Weekend,** which offers group hikes of various lengths and terrain in the western section of the gorge in mid-June.

Connect with I–84 near McCord Creek, continuing east toward Bonneville Dam and Cascade Locks. First detour to see ◆ **Bonneville Dam,** the first hydroelectric dam constructed on the Columbia River. Built in 1937 and dedicated by President Franklin Roosevelt, the dam offers underwater views of salmon and steelhead as they swim up the fish ladders to reach the upper section of the river. There are locks for use by riverboats, a children's playground, and large shallow pools for seeing the enormous Columbia River sturgeon. These light gray, leathery-looking fish reach lengths of 5 feet and longer.

Just east of the dam, exit at Cascade Locks for a good assortment of hamburgers, soups, salads, and desserts at the **Char-**

burger Restaurant and enjoy a view of the Columbia River as well. In a cottonwood-shaded park along the river, just a few blocks from the restaurant, the ◆ **Port of Cascade Locks Marine Park** has a small historical museum, situated in one of the original lock masters' houses, that offers an extensive photo and artifact collection. It's open daily, afternoons, June through September 1; (503) 374–8619. On the grounds you can also take a look at the first steam engine used on Northwest railroads. During summer the 145-foot stern-wheeler *Columbia Gorge* takes visitors up and down the river boarding from the Marine Park dock. The larger stern-wheeler, 230-foot, four-deck *Queen of the West,* offers two- to seven-day cruises out of Portland. For current information and reservations call (541) 374–8427 or, in Portland, (503) 223–3928.

In 1875 army engineers recommended building a canal to circumvent the dangerous rapids at both Cascade City and The Dalles; the work was completed in 1896. Before then passengers and cargo were unloaded and moved overland to a safer point on the river, at which location they were reloaded on a different steamboat for the continuing journey. Later, bridges connected the two sides of the Columbia River at Cascade Locks, Hood River, The Dalles, and Umatilla.

If time allows, cross the historic ◆ **Bridge of the Gods** from Cascade Locks to the Washington side of the river, turning west on Highway 14 for a few miles to **Beacon Rock.** A steep, safe trail with steps here and there leads to the top of this volcanic remnant. On a bright sunny day, you can sit rather comfortably on large flat rocks atop the monolith to enjoy great views of the gorge upriver to the east and downriver to the west.

When you return east on Highway 14, continue a couple of miles beyond the bridge toward Stevenson, turning north in just a quarter mile or so to visit **Skamania Lodge.** It overlooks the gorge to the east, on the Washington side of the Columbia River. The rustic Cascadian-style lodge (with its enormous fireplace lobby-lounge) offers overnight accommodations, an 18-hole golf course, tennis courts, walking and horseback-riding trails, a gift shop, an indoor swimming pool, and a natural-rock outdoor whirlpool spa. A lovely restaurant and lounge both take advantage of all that marvelous scenery. For information and reservations call (800) 221–7117. And don't miss a visit to the

◆ **Columbia Gorge Interpretive Center** located just below the lodge. It also commands a grand view of the river and gorge toward the east. Inside you'll see the replica of an enormous Indian fishwheel and a gigantic old Corliss steam engine, once used in logging, that still actually works. The interpretive center and its splendid collection of artifacts and reference materials is open daily. For a schedule of current special programs call or write the staff at P.O. Box 396, Stevenson WA 98648; (509) 427–8211.

Return to the Oregon side and I–84 via Bridge of the Gods, heading east again. Detour at Hood River, about 8 miles east of Cascade Locks, and wind down to the ◆ **Hood River Boat Basin and Marina Park** to watch dozens of men and women ply the Columbia's rough waters on sailboards that sport sails of bright rainbow colors. This particularly windy stretch of the river between Cascade Locks, Hood River, The Dalles, and Rufus has become, within the past several years, a mecca for the intrepid sailboarders. With their oblong boards firmly attached atop cars and vans, these enthusiasts return like flocks of migrating birds, beginning in April and remaining through September.

In mid-July the **Gorge Games** feature adrenalin-pumping competition in lively outdoor events—from windsurfing, paragliding, kayaking, and kite-skiing to snowboarding, mountain biking, and rock climbing. For entry information (for hardy daredevils and those in top physical condition), for spectator information, or a schedule of events call (541) 386–7774 or check with the Hood River Visitors' Center. Stop at the well-stocked center, located near the marina, for current maps and local tourist information, or write ahead to the center's mailing address: Port Marina Park, Hood River 97031; (541) 386–2000. Helpful information and brochures can also be obtained from the Columbia River Gorge National Scenic Area, Wacoma Center, 902 Wasco Avenue, Hood River 97031; (541) 386–2333.

For a glimpse into Hood River's interesting past, plan to visit the **Hood River County Historical Museum**—also located near Port Marina Park—where exhibits of Native American culture, pioneer history, lumbering, and fruit-growing memorabilia are displayed. The museum is open April through October, Wednesday through Saturday from 10:00 A.M. to 4:00 P.M. and Sunday from noon to 4:00 P.M. Call (541) 386–6772 for additional information.

Sailboarding on the Hood River

Speaking of fruit, if travels bring you to the area in early spring, plan to take in the annual **Hood River Valley Blossom Festival** during the third weekend of April, when thousands of pear, apple, and cherry trees are in glorious bloom in the Hood River Valley. Local tours through the orchards, along with arts-and-crafts fairs, quilt sales, antiques sales, and open houses at fruit-packing establishments, wineries, and fire departments, are among the eclectic round of activities that take place throughout the weekend.

One of the best offerings is a nostalgic train ride on the ❖**Mt. Hood Railroad**'s Fruit Blossom Special, which winds through the flowering orchards to Parkdale and Odell. The old railroad, which began in 1906 as a passenger and freight line, was resurrected in 1987, when a group of enterprising Hood River–area citizens purchased it from the Union Pacific Railroad. Several circa 1910–26 Pullman coaches have been restored and are pulled by two General Motors/EMD GP-9 locomotives built in the 1950s. For current information contact the Mt. Hood Railroad, 110 Railroad Avenue, Hood River 97031; (541) 386–3556.

For overnight accommodations check with the friendly folks at the refurbished ❖**Hood River Hotel,** located in the uptown area near the railroad depot. After a year of intensive renovation in the early 1990s (the empty old hotel was purchased by Canadian sailboarder Pasquale Barone), the four-story redbrick structure has reopened its doors to Columbia River Gorge travelers. Forest-green carpeting with touches of coral replaces old checkerboard tiles, and graceful, Queen Anne–style furniture upholstered in soft teal, green, and cream replaces the prim, overstuffed mohair chairs and settees of 1913. The hotel was built as an annex to the circa 1890 Mt. Hood Hotel, which was razed in 1920. Now awakened from its slumber, the light-filled old dowager today offers an Old World European charm and twenty-six lovely guest rooms.

Breakfast, lunch, and dinner are available in the hotel restaurant, Pasquale's Ristorante, open daily from 7:00 A.M. to 10:00 P.M.; guests are served a continental breakfast. For further information and reservations, contact the Hood River Hotel, 102 Oak Street, Hood River 97031; (541) 386–1900. For current information about comfortable bed-and-breakfast inns in the aea, contact the visitors' center, (800) 336–3530.

If you decide to detour from Hood River south toward Parkdale and the Mt. Hood Recreation Area, the **Coffee Spot,** located at 12 Oak Street, is a good place to stop for made-to-order deli sandwiches, salads, soups, and special desserts. The restaurant is open daily except Sunday.

Also welcoming travelers are **Sweet Dreams Bakery & Dream Wakers Espresso** at 509 Cascade Street, Suite B (541–386–6083); **6th Street Bistro & Loft** at 509 Cascade Street (541–386–5737); and **Pastabilities Italian Deli** at 106 Oak Street (541–386–1903).

If, as many Oregonians do, you love live local theater, call for the current play schedule at the **Hood River Performing Arts Theatre,** 105 Fourth Street, (541) 386–4147. Recently the group presented an all-time favorite, *Blithe Spirit.*

You might now head into the eastern section of the Columbia River Gorge to attend a second, equally popular spring festival that takes place just 21 miles east of Hood River, in The Dalles. The **Northwest Cherry Festival** is celebrated during the third week of April, from Monday through Saturday, and culminates with the Festival Parade on Saturday morning at 11:00 A.M. Equestrian units, Native Americans, local marching bands, and colorful clowns wind through the historic downtown area.

Another good spot for watching those intriguing sailboarders, along with a bevy of ducks and geese, is **The Dalles Boat Basin Beach,** where there is protected onshore wind most of the time, a minimal river current, and no barge traffic. In the mid-1840s this portion of the Columbia River Gorge, at The Dalles, was the end of the arduous, 2,000-mile trail for those first Oregon-bound pioneers. At this location the families and their heavy wagons were loaded aboard makeshift barges and floated down the swift river some 80 miles to Fort Vancouver, near the confluence of the Columbia and Willamette Rivers.

Over the years the power-generating dams built on the Columbia River gradually obliterated both the historic rapids and the ancient fishing grounds of native peoples. An example is the famous Celilo Falls, which were near the site of **The Dalles Dam.** For centuries the Indians fished from rocky basalt ledges on this stretch of the river, and later they fished from spindly wooden "scaffolding" affairs near the falls, catching the large salmon with long-poled nets.

For information about visiting the dam contact The Dalles Area

Visitors' Center, 901 East Second Street, The Dalles 97058; (541) 296–6616. Also inquire about other interesting festivals, such as the **Celilo Wyam Salmon Feast** in early April, the **Tygh Valley All Indian Rodeo** in mid-May, the Fort Dalles Rodeo in mid-July, the historic **Dufur Threshing Bee** in early August, the Gorge Cities Windsurfing Blowout in mid-August, and the **Wasco County Fair** at the end of August.

To better understand the historical significance of this area, visit the ◆ **Fort Dalles Historical Museum,** at Sixteenth and Garrison, set in the only remaining building, the Surgeons Quarters, at 1857 Fort Dalles. The charming Carpenter Gothic structure is listed on the National Register of Historic Places, and the museum is open March through October, daily. Call (541) 296–4547 for information about winter hours.

Ask, too, about the self-guided walking or driving tour of historic homes and buildings and for directions to lovely ◆ **Sorosis Park,** located above the city and offering a magnificent viewing spot and a rose garden at the top of the bluff. From the viewing area notice the large bend in the Columbia River. By the point where the river reaches The Dalles, the Douglas fir–clothed western section of the gorge has changed to another elevation, above 2,000 feet, to the sunny eastern high desert. Now the rounded, hunched hills are sparsely clad, and in nearby canyons, sagebrush and bitterbrush bloom splashes of yellow in the spring and early summer. Rolling wheat country extends east and north of The Dalles up into Wasco, Moro, and Grass Valley, and thousands of cherry trees blossom in nearby orchards as well. Other sweeping vistas of the river and distant hills can be enjoyed from **Rowena Plateau,** located about midway on a short section of Scenic Highway 30 between Hood River and The Dalles, accessed from I–84 at the first Mosier exit.

You can stop at **Dobre Deli,** located downtown at 308 East Fourth Street, for sandwiches, freshly made salads and soups, and desserts; at **Holstein's Coffee Co.,** 811 East Third (541–298–2326) for cinnamon rolls, espresso, and lattes; and at **Cousins Restaurant & Saloon,** 2116 West Sixth Street (541–298–2771) for down–home cookin'. Diners are greeted with a friendly, "Hi, cousin," from waiters dressed in black slacks, white shirts, and black vests. The bar stools in the cafe section are fashioned of stainless steel milk cans with round seats covered in black vinyl; the Formica table tops are of whimsical black-and-white cowhide patterns. You'll also hear the distinct "mooo-ing" of cows when you enter and leave the restaurant. Great fun for the kids, too.

Then call ahead to see if innkeepers Don and Barbara Williams have guest rooms available at the historic ◆ **Williams House Bed and Breakfast Inn,** located at 608 West Sixth Street, The Dalles 97058. The Victorian mansion, with its extensive gingerbread trim and elegant cupolas, was constructed by a local judge in 1899, fifty-six years after the first families trekked across the dusty Oregon Trail from Independence, Missouri. The home has been in the Williams family since 1926. The well-kept grounds are especially lovely in the spring. For information and reservations contact the innkeepers at (541) 296–2889.

Short excursions on the near Washington side of the Columbia River include the impressive European-style **Maryhill Museum,** east on Highway 14, where you can see an extensive collection of vintage chess sets, a sampling of Rodin sketches and sculptures, and a splendid restored collection of French designer mannequins (miniatures) dating back to postwar 1945; call (509) 773–3733 for current hours and exhibits. Nature lovers can continue to the small community of **Bickleton** to see hundreds of blue-and-white birdhouses along fence posts that house colonies of the endangered mountain bluebird. If thirst overcomes, you could stop at the vintage **Bluebird Tavern,** 121 Market Street, reported to be the oldest such establishment in the state.

From The Dalles take another pleasant side trip into history, the rural past, by heading south on Highway 197 just 13 miles to the tiny farming community of **Dufur.** You're definitely in the slow lane now. Gently rolling wheat fields, the color of golden honey, extend for miles and miles in all four directions. Several tall grain elevators punctuate the wide blue skyline. You see Mt. Hood's snowy peak to the west. There is no freeway noise, just quantities of fresh, clean air and friendly smiles from local residents. You ease into the rhythm of the farmland, and you aren't bothered by the fact that there is only one place to stay overnight in Dufur, the ◆ **Balch Hotel.** You don't mind that your room has neither television nor telephone.

Pat and Howard Green bought Charley Balch's circa 1907 rundown, brick hotel in 1986 and spent several years bringing it, and twenty-one guest rooms, back to life. In the early 1900s wealthy stockmen, loggers and rough farmhands, and women in long, black dresses walked through the doors of the hostelry that was an elegant showpiece where the Great Southern Railroad line once ended. Lodging is offered most weekends and you'll get a delicious continental breakfast; there are two restaurants within walking distance. For information and reservations contact Balch Hotel staff at P.O. Box 5, Dufur 97021, or call (541) 467–2277. Ask, too, about the annual ◆ **Dufur Threshing Bee.**

From Dufur you could continue about 30 miles south on Highway 97 through Tygh Valley to Maupin and the **Deschutes River Recreation Area.** In addition to many campgrounds and places to fish, you could bed down in rustic comfort at **The CJ Lodge,** on the banks of the Deschutes. The owners specialize in one- to three-day rafting trips (with gourmet meals) on this popular stretch of the river. For current information write or call The CJ Lodge, P.O. Box 130, Maupin 97037; (541) 395–2404. Additional information about the area can be obtained from the Maupin Visitors' Center, located in a small log structure at the edge of town, 502 Deschutes Avenue, Maupin 97037; (541) 395–2613.

MT. HOOD RECREATION AREA

Mt. Hood, an imposing, snow-covered, andesite volcano rising some 11,235 feet from the forested Cascades, easily dominates the skyline to the south of Hood River and is always seen on clear days from Portland, 50 miles to the west. Newcomers, as well as those of us who have lived in Portland and in the Columbia River Gorge area most of our lives, all naturally claim the mountain as our personal property.

One of the most scenic routes to the mountain is accessed from Hood River at the exit near Port Marina Park. Along Highway 35 you'll encounter the venerable, snowcapped peak around many bends while winding up through the Hood River Valley's lush orchards. When driving through the area in the fall, detour at **Sappington Orchards** or at ◆ **River Bend Farm and Country Store** to sample fresh apple cider and purchase homemade applesauce and gift packages of delicious apples and pears. The orchards are located at 3187 Highway 35, about 6 miles from

Hood River; visitors are welcome to stop in daily from September 15 to December 15.

River Bend Farm is situated a few miles west, to Odell, then north on Odell Highway to Tucker Road. A popular nosh-and-shop, the organic farm is located at 2363 Tucker Road, Hood River 97031; (541) 386–8766 It's open daily April through December. From corn relish and spiced peaches to huckleberry preserves and apple cider, you'll feel that you've stepped back in time a number of years. If you wish, ask about the sheepshearing and spinning demonstrations that take place each fall.

Legend passed down by native peoples says that Mt. Hood was at one time a mighty volcano known as Wy'east, a great chief turned into a mountain, spouting flame and hurling boulders skyward in anger. The first recorded white people, members of the British Royal Navy, saw the mountain in 1792 from their vessel while sailing on the Columbia River. A British naval officer named it Hood, after his admiral. The earliest whites to trek over the slopes of Mt. Hood were most likely French fur trappers, in about 1818; botanist David Douglas, in 1833; and a few other hardy souls who followed the main deer and Indian trails connecting the east and west sides of the mountain.

For a good bit of history and a helpful map of the first emigrant road across the Cascades along those ancient Indian trails, pick up a copy of *The Barlow Road,* available from the Mt. Hood National Forest Office, 2955 NW Division Street, Gresham 97030 (503–666–0700); or stop at the Hood River Ranger Station at 6780 Highway 35 near Parkdale; the phone number is (541) 352–6002 .

The **Barlow Road,** opened in 1845, completed the Oregon Trail as a land route from Independence, Missouri, to the Willamette Valley. This alternate land route to Oregon City on the Willamette River became a major entry into western Oregon for those who wanted to avoid the dangers or costs of floating down the Columbia River from The Dalles to Fort Vancouver.

Samuel K. Barlow, his family, and others literally chopped the crude wagon trail through the thick evergreen forest on the southeast and southwest flanks of Mt. Hood to a location between Government Camp and Rhododendron. Following roughly the same route, Highway 35 winds past family-oriented **Cooper Spur Ski Area** (541–352–6037) and intersects with Highway 26 just south of the busy **Mt. Hood Meadows Ski**

Area (541–337–2222), turning west about 6 miles to historic Government Camp. (You can also head east at this point, toward Kah-Nee-Ta Resort and central Oregon.)

As you make your way to Government Camp, stop and take a look at the remnants of the Barlow Trail and ◈**Summit Meadows,** which is where the immigrants camped, near ◈**Trillium Lake.** The Forest Service access road, from Highway 26, is just opposite the **Snow Bunny Ski Area**—a great place for families with small children—a few miles west of the Highway 35 junction. Near the large meadow are a small pioneer cemetery and the site of one of the early tollhouses, Summit House. See if you can find the many pioneer names scratched into the surface of nearby boulders—perhaps to notify the next contingent of immigrants scheduled to arrive.

At this site once stood Perry Vicker's log cabin, barn, lodge, and shingled tepee. Vickers also built, across the north edge of the meadows, a corduroy road—a type of early road constructed by laying small tree trunks side by side. Such roads became familiar surfaces for horse-drawn wagons and, later, for the first automobiles. Needless to say, traveling in those early days was a distinct challenge and more often than not included moving branches, or even fallen trees, off the roadway in order to continue the journey.

Hike or drive down to Trillium Lake for a picnic and stay in one of the nearby campgrounds: one right on the lake and the other, **Still Creek Campground,** along the creek just north of the pioneer graves and Summit Meadows. During July and August you'll probably find delicious huckleberries along Still Creek; during winter you'll want to clamp on cross-country skis and trek across the snowy meadow and onto the same roads all the way around the picturesque frozen lake. This is a lovely, and easy, trek not to be missed, especially on a crisp blue-sky day.

In historic Government Camp sleep snug and warm at ◈**Falcon's Crest Inn,** at an elevation of 4,000 feet and imagine what sleeping outdoors in a covered wagon might have been like. Good-natured innkeepers Bob and Melody Johnson pamper guests with special treats, the sort those emigrants probably never experienced at Perry Vickers's tollgate cabin just up the road at Summit Meadows. Try evening aperitifs and appetizers served in the comfortable Great Room, warmed by an enormous woodstove; then a supper, if you wish, a prix fixe affair; and finally a morning tray, set just outside your door, of steaming-hot coffee and freshly baked muffins, often with both orange and cranberry butters. Breakfast at the dining table, with its ample window views, may consist of waffles with a strawberry compote, a special mushroom quiche, or a cheesy omelet, along with fresh seasonal fruits, juices, and coffee or herbal teas.

During winter guests can ski at the nearby **Ski Bowl**; sleigh rides can sometimes be arranged, and you can enjoy the inn's holiday decor. (Doesn't everyone have seven lighted and decorated Christmas trees?) During summer go hiking on nearby trails into wilderness areas or alpine meadows filled with white bear grass, red-orange Indian paintbrush, blue lupine, pale pink native rhododendrons, white and pink foxglove, red elderberry, and many other native plants, depending on the season. For the particulars and for reservations, contact Bob and Melody Johnson at Falcon's Crest Inn, P.O. Box 185, Government Camp 97028; (503) 272–3403.

In the early 1900s pioneer guide Oliver Yocum built a hotel at Government Camp, and it survived until 1933, when a fire destroyed it. Within ten years after the Barlows' pioneering route over the shoulder of ◆**Mt. Hood,** the mountain became a much-sought-after landmark, instead of a formidable nuisance, and for more than a century and a half it has drawn city dwellers to its slopes year-round.

As early as 1890 skiers and climbers flocked to the snowy slopes of Mt. Hood. And in those days their journey was substantial, involving several days' travel to get from Portland to the mountain. Until a graded road was constructed to Government Camp in the 1920s, the last day's trek during winter months was via snowshoes from Rhododendron. In 1924 the first hotel at timberline was built by the Forest Service, near the present Timberline Lodge. Serving as emergency shelter during summer and winter, the original lodge was about 8 by 16 feet, with several additional tents nearby. Mountain lovers brought their own blankets, rented a mattress, and got a meal.

Today, however, you can sleep in more luxurious comfort at this 6,000-foot level by checking in at one of the state's oldest mountain inns, ◆**Timberline Lodge,** located just 6 miles up the mountain from Government Camp. Construction of the lodge was approved in 1935 by President Franklin Roosevelt as a project of the Works Progress Administration during the Great Depression. A contingent of more than 250 Northwest artisans—carpenters, stonemasons, woodcarvers, metalworkers, painters, weavers, and furniture makers—created in two years a magnificent lodge that looks like the rough-hewn castle of a legendary Norse mountain king.

The lodge was dedicated by President Roosevelt in September 1937 and officially opened to the public in February 1938. Fires crackled in the massive fireplaces—hexagonal, 14 feet in diameter, constructed with 400 tons of native stone, and rising 92 feet in the peak, six fire pits in all—as a parade of some 150 guests registered for the opening weekend. Today you can hear FDR's voice crackling from a vintage recording—a portion of his dedication speech—as you walk through the **Rachel Griffen Historic Exhibition Center** on the refurbished main-entry level.

Just imagine, however, in the not-too-distant past, us skiers grouped about those massive entry-level fireplaces drying our ski socks and munching sack lunches before heading back to the snowy slopes. Nowadays skiers use the new **Wy'east Day Lodge,** just across the upper parking area, and this practice does, of course, greatly protect the original lodge, which often logs more than a million visitors each year.

Most of the fifty-nine guest rooms are one of a kind, with carved headboards, patchwork quilts, and hooked rugs. Everything was made by hand—some of the original curtains, from dying old army uniforms and blankets. The original fabrics and weavings, along with the Native American, pioneer, native wildflower, and animal motifs, have all been restored and repaired through the painstaking efforts of the **Friends of Timberline.** Above the second-floor lounge and restaurant is a quaint, hexagonal balcony with small alcoves, some with benches and desks offering a place to write letters or read. To the north, floor-to-ceiling windows frame spectacular Mt. Hood.

For information about year-round activities and events, and for reservations, contact the staff at Timberline Lodge, Government Camp 97028; (503) 231-7979. The person who initiated the fine restoration of Timberline Lodge is longtime mountain lover Richard Kohnstamm.

In the early 1940s the state highway commission decided

upon a great experiment: to keep the section of narrow road between Welches and Government Camp open throughout the entire winter. Winter sports enthusiasts were exhilarated. They flocked to the mountain, and the pilgrimage to Mt. Hood has never ceased. For information about alpine and Nordic skiing areas, as well as the names of expert instructors and mountain-climbing guides, contact the **Mt. Hood Area Visitors' Center,** 65000 East Highway 26, Welches 97067; (503) 622–4822. *Note:* Do not entertain the notion of climbing Mt. Hood—or any other mountain in the high Cascades—without expert guidance, preparation, and assistance.

If you visit the **Mt. Hood Recreation Area** from July through September—summer on the mountain—use your copy of *The Barlow Road,* which has a clearly marked map, along with a copy of the Mt. Hood National Forest map, and explore to your heart's content on well-marked Forest Service roads. Both maps can be obtained at the Zig Zag Ranger Station, just below Toll Gate Campground and Rhododendron, 70220 East Highway 26, Zig Zag 97049; (503) 622–3191.

While you're there, ask for current information about summer and fall day hikes in the area. In the nearby **Salmon Huckleberry Wilderness** is the easily accessed **✦Salmon River National Recreation Trail.** The Salmon River Gorge, with its many waterfalls, is a picturesque area of volcanic plugs, pinnacles, and forested cliffs. The trail lies several hundred feet above the river, except for the lower 2½-mile section.

Ask for directions to the **Hidden Lake Trail,** located just 6 miles east of the Zig Zag Ranger Station. In early to mid-June you'll find the lakeside section of the trail punctuated with masses of pale pink blooms from the stately native rhododendrons.

In addition, the 2-mile **Mountaineer Trail,** located higher on the mountain, is an especially good hike for families. Passable from August through October, this trail is found on the east side of **Timberline Lodge** and climbs through gnarled alpine fir beyond the timberline to **✦Silcox Hut,** at the 7,000-foot level. You could also arrange to stay overnight at Silcox Hut, which offers dormitory-style lodging for small groups. For information call Timberline Lodge at (503) 231–7979. You'll have splendid panoramic views of Mt. Jefferson, Three Sisters, and Broken Top to the south and east and, on a clear day, of the Coast Range some 85 miles to the west. The trail, though steep in some places, is easy to navigate during summer months and takes about two hours round-trip.

If you're more than a bit adventurous and a rugged outdoors type of person in good physical condition, consider camping a couple of days at ❖ **Five Mile Butte Fire Lookout,** located west of Dufur at the 4,600-foot elevation level in the **Mt. Hood National Forest.** In a 14-foot-square rustic cabin-shelter atop a 30-foot wood tower, campers have the ultimate room with a view—a stunning 360-degree panorama of Cascade mountain peaks, alpine and Douglas fir forests, and the rolling wheat fields of central and eastern Oregon. Lots of stairs? Yes, but the view is worth it! The lookout is available from November through May; campers need to bring in their own water and be prepared for snow and very cold weather. For current information and regulations, contact the Barlow Ranger Station, P.O. Box 67, Dufur 97021; (541) 467–2291. Ask, too, about ❖ **Valley View Cabin** in the nearby Badger Creek Wilderness. It's at a lower elevation and open year-round.

If you decide to take a snack or a picnic along on your mountain hikes, stop at **The Honey Bear Express** (503–622–5726) in Welches before leaving the Zig Zag area and heading east, climbing toward Laurel Hill, Government Camp, or Timberline. Hearty sandwiches, delicious homemade soups, and marvelous cinnamon rolls, together with a selection of imported beers and regional wines, are available here Monday through Saturday. Located in the minimall next to the Thriftway Grocery, the Deli also serves breakfast and lunch.

For lovely handmade gifts and willow furniture along with note cards, candles, and casual sportswear, stop and browse through the many treasures offered by Susie Welch at ❖ **Heart of the Mountain Gifts and Treasures.** Her charming gift shop is located at 67898 East Highway 26 in Welches, (503) 622–3451. Susie usually has gourmet coffees and teas to try as well, and she offers personalized gift wrapping, too. Hours are noon to 5:00 P.M. on Sundays and 10:00 A.M. to 6:00 P.M. all other days except Tuesdays, when the shop is closed.

For a delicious supper pull over at ❖ **Don Guidos Restaurant** in Rhododendron, just a few miles down the mountain from Government Camp. Owners Doug and Anne Kinne have renovated the interior of the old Log Lodge, long known to skiers and mountain dwellers. Notice the walls of large polished logs with their original horsehair chinking. The place has a warm, inviting atmosphere, and the Kinnes especially welcome families. They and their friendly staff (Don does much of the gourmet cooking) serve Italian-style entrees such as eggplant Renee, seafood cannelloni, chicken piccata, and veal Marsala. Call ahead for current hours and dinner reservations at (503) 622–5141.

Since bedding down at lower elevations may be just as appealing as sleeping in the clouds, consider ◆**Old Welches Bed and Breakfast Inn,** located just below Zig Zag on Welches Road—turn south at the stoplight—just across from the old front 9 of the original Bowman's Resort (now a classy resort, with the golf course expanded to 36 holes). Judi Mondun and her family have restored Jennie Welch's home, and Judy especially welcomes bed-and-breakfast travelers who appreciate a sense of history.

Sunlight fills the old home, which, during the 1890s, was an inn that welcomed early Portlanders who came to the mountain during summer to camp, fish, and pick gallons of juicy blackberries and huckleberries. For reservations contact innkeeper Judi Mondun, 26401 East Welches Road, Welches 97067; (503) 622–3754.

Nearby, the innkeepers at **Doublegate Inn Bed & Breakfast** also welcome travelers who trek to the mountain year-round. Charlene and Gary Poston have created a cozy inn with three lovely guest rooms on the second floor, one overlooking the bubbling Salmon River. Breakfast is a hearty affair, served in the main floor dining area. For further information and reservations call or write the Postons at 26711 East Welches Road, Welches 97067; (503) 622–4859.

For a romantic gourmet dinner, try the splendid **Rendezvous Grill and Tap Room,** located in Welches just off Highway 26; call (503) 622–6837 for reservations. For an informal ski lodge atmosphere, a bit more rustic, try the well-worn but well-loved ◆**Zig Zag Inn** located just east of Welches and near the Zig Zag Ranger Station; call (503) 622–4779 to check out the current specials. And, to take home a bit of the mountain, stop by and select a pound of freshly roasted coffee beans from ◆**Mt. Hood Coffee Roaster and Merchantile** located nearby at 64235 East Brightwood Loop Road, Brightwood 97011. Special blends include WyEast, Wemme, Brightwood, and Zig Zag; call (503) 622–5153 for further information and current hours.

Summer visitors can take in **Sandy Mountain Days,** held in the community of Sandy, just down the mountain from Welches and Brightwood, toward Gresham and Portland. Highlighting the mid-July festival are, in addition to a carnival and parade, the international Bed Race finals, a wine fair and feast, the annual **Black Powder Shoot,** and a gathering of about 150 Northwest artists and craftspersons who display, demonstrate, and sell their wares in shady **Meining Memorial Park.**

While visiting Meining Memorial Park, stroll through the lovely garden designed for the blind; it contains a variety of scented herbs and an assortment of perennials and annuals of different textures.

For additional information and a helpful brochure about the festival and the park, write to the Sandy Visitors' Center, P.O. Box 536, Sandy 97055, or call (503) 668–4006.

THE WILLAMETTE VALLEY

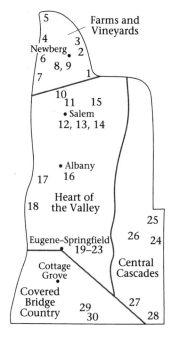

1. Champoeg State Park
2. Helvetia Tavern
3. Draft-Horse Plowing Exhibition
4. Ballad Town U.S.A.
5. Trolley Park Museum
6. Flying M Ranch
7. Lafayette Schoolhouse Antiques Mall
8. Springbrook Hazelnut Farm Bed and Breakfast
9. Rex Hill Winery
10. Wheatland Ferry
11. Pacific Northwest Truck Museum and Great Oregon Steamup
12. Mission Mill Village
13. Bush House and Deepwood Estate Gardens
14. Marquee House Bed and Breakfast
15. Mt. Angel Abbey
16. Albany Historic Districts
17. Avery Park and Rose Gardens
18. William L. Finley National Wildlife Refuge

19. Euphoria Chocolate Company
20. Starbuck's Coffee House
21. Canoeing on the Millrace
22. Campbell House
23. Dorris Ranch
24. McKenzie Pass Scenic Drive and Dee Wright Observatory
25. Belknap Springs Lodge
26. McKenzie River Driftboats
27. Salt Creek Falls
28. Odell Lake Lodge
29. Red Bridge
30. June Mountain Trail

THE WILLAMETTE VALLEY

FARMS AND VINEYARDS

Eons old, with rivers meandering through and bisecting its green hills and rich alluvial soils, the Willamette Valley was surely a welcome sight to the weary pioneers fresh off the Oregon Trail. Out of those abundant soils grew many farms in the 1840s and 1850s and, much later, the hundreds of orchards, nurseries, and vineyards that continue to thrive in this moist and mild zone between the high Cascade and lower Coast Range mountains and the Pacific Ocean.

This gentle region, now scattered with cities, towns, hamlets, and inviting side roads that skirt I–5 and old Highways 99E and 99W, was also home to the Calapooya Indians. For thousands of years they roamed throughout the broad valley, digging tiny bulbs of the purple camas in early spring, picking juicy blackberries in late summer, and hunting deer and fishing its rivers and streams nearly year-round. If you visit in mid-May, you'll see waves of purple camas blooming along roadsides in meadows throughout the valley.

To get acquainted with this large region, which lies like an enormous green carpet between the mountains and the ocean, first head south from Portland on I–5 past Wilsonville to ◆ **Champoeg State Park.** This 567-acre park preserves the historic site of the May 2, 1843, meeting at which valley settlers, by a narrow vote, established the first organized territorial government in the Northwest. George Abernethy was elected the territory's first governor. Champoeg was later an important stagecoach stop, trading post, and port for steamboats plying the upper and lower sections of the Willamette River—until the late 1880s, when the small settlement, like many others along the banks of the river, was destroyed by flood.

In July and August you can take in an annual outdoor drama at the park, *Champoeg: The Story of Old Oregon,* depicting the region's history. The historic meeting at Champoeg climaxes the drama's first act; the second act includes bits about the Oregon Trail and the political struggle between the United States and Great Britain for control of the territory. Troubled relations between Indian

166

tribes and settlers, the Whitman Massacre, and the constitutional debates leading to statehood are also dramatized. For current information call the park staff at (503) 633–8170.

The Champoeg Visitors' Center exhibit area is open year-round, and the park offers picnicking, biking, hiking, and camping, including several yurts. For campground reservations call (800) 452–5687.

Before continuing south toward the state capital, meander over to **Newberg, McMinnville,** and **Forest Grove** to see where many of the old orchards were planted, where new fields of wine grapes are taking root, and where fine old homes are living new lives as tasting rooms or bed-and-breakfast inns. Hundreds of acres are planted with premium wine grapes, and scores of small wineries process the fruit into more than 100,000 gallons of vinifera wines and into thousands of gallons of premium fruit and berry wines. With helpful maps, strike out on your own to visit many wineries and tasting rooms.

To plan a self-guided tour, pick up the handy map at the Washington County Visitors' Association, 5075 SW Griffith Drive, Suite 120, Beaverton 97005; (503) 644–5555 or (800) 537–3149. The locations of these wineries and vineyards range from Beaverton and Newberg out to Hillsboro and Forest Grove. Ask, too, for a copy of the annual *Discover Oregon Wineries,* containing detailed maps for visiting vineyards throughout the state.

If you head out toward the Hillsboro area from Portland or Beaverton via Highway 26 (the Sunset Highway), plan to stop at the ◆**Helvetia Tavern,** on Helvetia Road just beyond where the road dips under the railroad trestle, about 2 miles north of the highway. Your reward for finding this local gem will be hamburgers the size of dinner plates and fresh-cooked french fries—with skins left on—piled all around. Watch the folks play pool, or join in yourself. And notice the interesting collection of hats hanging from the walls and rafters. The tavern is open for lunch and dinner every day; its phone number is (503) 647–5286. *Note:* The gentle back roads in this area are fine for bicycling, as well; ask about bike maps at the Washington County Visitors' Association.

If the notion of gargantuan burgers sounds too much for lunch, backtrack on the Sunset Highway a couple of miles and exit at Cornelius Pass for a lunch or dinner stop at the historic 1866 Imbrie Farmstead. It's been transformed into a restaurant and microbrewery, the **Cornelius Pass Roadhouse.** At the exit head south just a short distance to the restored, two-story Victorian, with its large front porch and balcony. The roadhouse is open for lunch and dinner every day, from 11:00 A.M. to 10:00 P.M.

Farms are a way of life in the Willamette Valley, where the passing of the four seasons signals familiar chores having to do with plowing, planting, growing, and harvesting. One group of dedicated draft plowmen, members of the Oregon Draft Horse Breeders Association, continue efforts to improve the five major draft-horse breeds still used for plowing in many areas of the United States. Each spring they, along with the Washington County Historical Society and local service organizations, sponsor the annual ◆ **Draft-Horse Plowing Exhibition.**

At the historical society's center, on the Rock Creek Campus of Portland Community College, you can watch some twenty teams of draft horses (and draft mules) in three-horse teams, each with one plow, demonstrate disk harrowing and plowing. All major breeds of the gentle giants are represented, including Belgian, Clydesdale, Percheron, Suffolk, and Shire. Sets of carefully maintained harnesses used 150 years ago and brought to the territory over the Oregon Trail are used with several of the teams.

Park the car and ride horse-drawn hay wagons to the re-created 1889 farmstead exhibition area, where both you and the kids can watch demonstrations of blacksmithing, harnessing, shoeing, and wheelwrighting, as well as plowing. Bring a picnic lunch or purchase fried chicken, barbecued beef, hamburgers, desserts, and beverages at the farmstead village. The exhibition is held the third Saturday in May, from 10:00 A.M. to 4:00 P.M., near the Washington County Historical Museum on the college campus at 17705 NW Springville Road, just north of the Sunset Highway turning off Highway 26 at the 185th Avenue exit; call (503) 645–5353 for further information.

Next throw a corkscrew into the picnic basket and head west on Highway 8 from Hillsboro to Forest Grove. Incidentally, Forest Grove is known as ◆ **Ballad Town U.S.A.,** where championship barbershop quartets raise melodious voices in old-fashioned harmony each year in mid-March. Friendly volunteers, and contestants, too, often dress in Gay Nineties garb. The tickets disappear like hotcakes, and so for current information, you'll want early to contact the Forest Grove Visitors' Information Center, 2417 Pacific Avenue,

Forest Grove 97116; (503) 357–3006. In addition, pick up another helpful map for self-guided trips to more Washington and Yamhill Counties vineyards from the Yamhill County Wineries Association, P.O. Box 871, McMinnville 97128; (503) 434–5814.

Keep in mind that the back roads into vineyards and wineries are often narrow, lack shoulders, and sometimes change from paved to gravel in the hinterlands. Both farm equipment and straying cows can be encountered along the way, and locals tend to drive somewhat faster than visitors. Look for places to pull off the road completely, and then walk back to viewing areas. Sturdy walking shoes and umbrellas are also helpful to have along in case of dusty roads or showers.

Just west of Forest Grove, at the 38-mile post on Highway 6, climb into an old-time trolley for a ride into ◆ **Trolley Park Museum** to see a collection of trolleys, double-deckers, and interurbans that have been restored by the **Oregon Electric Railway Historical Society.** Access Highway 6 from Forest Grove via Highway 8, turning toward Tillamook at the junction. The park is located at 61550 NW Agaard Road, Timber, and is open to visitors from May through October on weekends and holidays. Call (503) 357–3574 for more information.

While rambling through the rolling Yamhill County area, and if time allows, plan dinner and western-style dancing at the ◆ **Flying M Ranch,** located in the Coast Range foothills near Trask Mountain, just west of the historic community of Yamhill. Rebuilt after a disastrous fire by owners Bryce and Barbara Mitchell, the 17,000-square-foot main lodge is constructed of enormous logs, many of them from the ranch property. In the dining area relax at polished hand-hewn tables and chairs grouped around the large stone fireplace that survived the fire. In the lounge sit by large windows and spy deer as they cross the North Yamhill River, bubbling below; or belly up to the 30-foot-long bar, constructed from a Douglas fir trunk that, when felled, was 36 inches across. The hand-carved bar weighs about six tons.

Bryce is a logger, and Barbara manages the inn—the ranch has a motel-bunkhouse offering overnight accommodations—and both Mitchells love horses; more than fifty head graze in the lower pastures. Overnight trail rides, complete with hearty meals cooked outdoors, are featured during summer months. If you're a small-aircraft enthusiast, you could fly in for lunch or dinner, using the ranch's 2,200-foot grass airstrip; fuel is available at the Newberg and McMinnville airports.

The restaurant is open for breakfast, lunch, and dinner Monday through Thursday from 8:00 A.M. to 8:00 P.M. and Friday through Sunday from 8:00 A.M. to 10:00 P.M. (except December 24–25). The ranch is 10 miles west of Yamhill; follow the FLYING M signs to 23029 NW Flying M Road. The facilities also include campsites for tents and recreational vehicles along the river, as well as several cabins with kitchens. For reservations and more information, call (503) 662–3222.

From Yamhill take Highway 47 south to Highway 99W and detour west to McMinnville, the largest community in the Tualatin Valley.

Lovers of antiques can easily find the nearby community of Lafayette and poke through eight classrooms filled with treasures and memorabilia of all kinds, sizes, and shapes at the ◆ **Lafayette Schoolhouse Antiques Mall.** Housed in the circa 1910 school building at 748 Third Street (Highway 99W), the mall is billed as the state's "largest permanent antique show," a place where some ninety entrepreneurs display their wares—from porcelain, china, glassware, and pottery to dolls, linens, vintage clothing, and furniture. The mall is open every day from 10:00 A.M. to 5:00 P.M.; the phone number is (503) 864–2720.

Also located nearby, the monks at **Trappist Abbey** offer for sale their delicious ginger date nut cake and two kinds of mouthwatering biscotti. For current hours call (800) 294–0105 or write to Trappist Abbey, P.O. Box 97, Lafayette 97127.

If you'd like to stay overnight near the antiques and wine country, there are a number of fine bed-and-breakfast inns to choose from in the McMinnville-Newberg area, among them ◆ **Springbrook Hazelnut Farm**—ask about the romantic Carriage House (503–538–4606); **The Partridge Farm**—with exotic game birds and gardens of perennials and vegetables (503–538–2050); or **Wine Country Farm**—with five varieties of growing grapes and Arabian horses (503–864–3446).

Just next door to Springbrook Hazelnut Farm Bed & Breakfast, folks can drop in for tasting locally produced wines at ◆ **Rex Hill Winery.** While in the tasting room you can also have a gander at the winery's inner sanctum where the bubbly stuff is carefully created and aged. The garden grounds are lovely, filled with annuals and perennials that bloom in bright profusion from early spring through late fall. For a current schedule of musical and wine events, including a Winemaker's Dinner, contact the Tasting Room staff at (503) 538–0666.

For dining, amenable choices are **Red Hills Cafe,** for fine Provincial dishes, 976 Highway 99W, Dundee (503–538–8224); **Tina's,** for Northwest and French cuisine, 760 Highway 99W, Dundee (503–538–8880); **Nick's Italian Cafe,** for northern Italian entrees, 521 East Third Street, McMinnville (503–434–4471); **Sir Hinkleman's,** for good soups and salads, 729 East Third Street, McMinnville (503–472–1309); and **Cornerstone Coffee,** for espresso and lattes, 403 East Third Street, McMinnville (503–472–6622).

For further information about Yamhill County's fabulous wine country, contact the Newberg Visitors' Center, 114 North Washington Street, Newberg 97132 (503–538–2014); and the McMinnville Visitors' Information Center, 417 North Adams Street, McMinnville 97128 (503–472–6196). Ask, too, about the many farms and nurseries open to visitors and about the current schedule of plays offered by the **Gallery Players of Oregon** (or call the group at 503–472–2227).

THE HEART OF THE VALLEY

Head toward the state capital by backtracking about 4 miles to Highway 221, turning south through Dayton into the heart of the Willamette Valley, and crossing the Willamette River on the ◆ **Wheatland Ferry,** one of the last three ferries operating on this historic river. These old-fashioned contrivances are really just cable-operated barges. The ride is short, but you're treated to views upriver and downriver while lumbering across, and the kids will love it. Moreover, the price is right—about $1.00 for an auto. The two others in operation are the **Canby Ferry,** found just north and east of Canby, off Highway 99E, and the **Buena Vista Ferry,** located about halfway between Salem and Albany, near the confluence of the Willamette and Santiam Rivers. The usual hours are from 6:00 A.M. to 9:00 P.M. daily. Passengers on bicycles or on foot can usually ride free of charge.

In the early days of the territory, when competition for trade along the Willamette was keen, various boat landings and trading-post sites in the valley sprang up on the banks of the

Wheatland Ferry

river but were often washed away, as Champoeg was, by peri-
odic floods. Just Albany and Corvallis have survived as good-
sized river towns. Before heading in that direction, though,
detour at Brooks for a look-see at a well-preserved collection of
vintage tractors and various types of farm equipment at the ◈
Pacific Northwest Truck Museum. In August you can take
in the lively ◈ **Great Oregon Steamup** here, with the fun of
seeing these enormous mechanical wonders fired up and running. There's even a small 1938 Oregon microbrew truck and a
small steam-driven sawmill that gets fired up and running during
the annual event. Food and beverage booths, too, of course. For
further information call the museum at (503) 393–2424. Visit
June through September on Saturdays and Sundays, 10:00 A.M. to
4:30 P.M.

In **Salem,** pause for a walk through the lovely grounds of the state capitol. In early spring, dogwood, azaleas, and rhododendrons bloom about the well-manicured lawns that surround a large fountain. The setting also offers, from atop the capitol dome, a panoramic view of the city and the broad valley where the Calapooya Indians once lived. Inside the rotunda notice the large, colorful murals depicting historic scenes of the territory and Oregon's beginnings. There's a small visitors' center here where you can pick up local information.

Nearby at 1313 Mission Street, stroll through ❖ **Mission Mill Village,** which houses small shops, boutiques, and eateries, as well as the historic **Thomas Kay Woolen Mill,** in operation from 1889 to 1962. The restored mill now contains the Marion County Historical Society collections, and its displays show the process of changing fleece into fabric; the mill is open Tuesday through Saturday from 10:00 A.M. to 4:30 P.M. Don't miss the great gift shop on the ground level for a good selection of books and historic memorabilia. You can also join in a tour of the woolen mill and the array of historic houses at the village. Be sure to visit the circa 1841 **Jason Lee House,** the oldest remaining frame house in the Northwest and the structure that served as the territory's earliest Methodist mission. See, too, the **Pioneer Herb and Dye Garden's** accumulation of old-fashioned herbs and rare dye plants; the garden is located behind the Methodist Parsonage.

The woolen mill drew its power from **Mill Creek,** where there are shady places to feed the ducks and reflect upon the not-so-distant past. For further information contact the Mission Mill Museum Association, 1313 Mill Street SE, Salem 97301; (503) 585-7012. The Salem Visitors' Center (503-581-4235) is also located here at the village; the large parking area is a good place to leave your car or recreational vehicle while exploring the nearby historic areas by foot.

Just four blocks south, from Twelfth to Sixth along Mission Street, flower lovers flock to see the marvelous gardens at ❖ **Bush House** and ❖ **Deepwood Estate Gardens.** At Bush House—an 1878, Italianate-style mansion built by Asahel Bush, a prominent politician and newspaperman—and at **Bush Pasture Park,** you can see and sniff a fine collection of old roses that bloom all summer. The extensive grounds offer grassy areas for picnicking and for playing with the kids; there's also a small play-

173

ground area near the well-stocked gift shop and art center, **Bush Barn.** Notice, too, the lovely wisteria vine that climbs on the front porch of Bush House; the old vine is draped with a profusion of pale lavender blossoms in mid to late May. It's a real showstopper. Bush House is open for tours Tuesday through Sunday, noon to 5:00 P.M. during spring and summer months and from 2:00 to 5:00 P.M. during winter months. To check ahead in case hours have changed, and for more information, call (503) 363–4714.

At Deepwood the 1894 Queen Anne mansion is surrounded by perennial, cottage-style, and formal gardens, and you can also browse through the adjacent greenhouse, filled with lush tropical palms, ferns, orchids, and begonias. Deepwood Estate is open May through September on Sunday and Monday and on Wednesday through Friday from noon to 4:30 P.M. (Saturdays are reserved for private weddings); call (503) 363–1825 for further information.

For a comfortable overnight stay, consider ◆**Marquee House Bed and Breakfast,** an impressive Mt. Vernon Colonial–style house located bankside, on Mill Creek, just a few blocks from Deepwood Estate and the Bush House rose gardens. Innkeeper Rickie Hart offers five guest rooms decorated with collectibles and memorabilia to represent these famous old movies: *Auntie Mame, Blazing Saddles, Pillow Talk, Christmas in Connecticut,* and *Topper.* Breakfast, a hearty affair, is served in the sunny dining room or on the veranda, which overlooks the creek. You are invited to watch the evening movie and munch popcorn with other guests. For further information and reservations, contact Rickie Hart, 333 Wyatt Court NE, Salem 97301. The inn's phone number is (503) 391–0837. For eateries in the area, ask about **McGrath's Fish House, The Olive Garden, Union Oyster Bar, Tudor Rose Tea Room,** and **Morton's Bistro.**

In addition to visiting Oregon's state capital, consider making another detour, this one from I–5 east to **Silver Creek Falls State Park** and ◆**Mt. Angel Abbey.** Located in the foothills of the Cascade Mountains, the park contains fourteen waterfalls interlaced with a maze of inviting trails in the cool forest—an especially good option on those occasional ninety-degree days in late summer. In autumn a colorful Oktoberfest is held near Mt. Angel.

The lovely abbey is situated on a hill the Indians called

Tapalamaho, meaning "a place for communion with the Great Spirit." Swiss Benedictines established the monastery in 1883 and renamed the hill Mt. Angel. In addition to the monastery, the four-year seminary, a fine library (which is open to the public), and a museum, the abbey offers modest rooms and meals for folks who may have overdosed on work or simply have had too much civilization. The abbey also houses the **Russian Center Museum,** with its assortment of materials about the Russian Old Believers, who maintain a small community in the nearby French Prairie area. The abbey's library has an extensive Civil War and Swiss collection as well. For information about how to retreat to this lovely place, contact the staff at Mt. Angel Abbey, St. Benedict 97373 (503–845–3030).

Information about the annual **Oktoberfest** celebration, held in mid-September, can be obtained from the Silverton Visitors' Information Center, located in old Silverton depot at 421 South Water Street (503–873–5615). Silverton is about 14 miles northeast of Salem, via Highway 213. The abbey is located just 5 miles north of Silverton, and Silver Falls State Park lies about 15 miles south, on gently winding Highway 214. From the park head west back to I–5, via Highways 214 and 22.

You can also head east into the high Cascades on Highway 22, going across 4,817-foot **Santiam Pass** and reaching central Oregon at Sisters, near the headwaters of the Metolius River. Santiam Pass, flanked by Mt. Washington and Mt. Jefferson, emerged as the main wagon route into the Willamette Valley from the high desert and rangeland areas; it was scouted up the South Santiam River by Andrew Wiley in 1859. Highway 20 from Albany roughly follows the old wagon route, connecting with Highway 22 near **Hoodoo Ski Area** at the top of the pass.

From Highway 22 wind west and south of Salem to Albany. Back in 1845, two enterprising Scots, Walter and Thomas Monteith, bought the Albany town site along the Willamette River, just 15 miles south of Independence, for $400 and a horse. Each of the three ❖ **Albany Historic Districts** offers fine examples of early-nineteenth-century architecture. If possible, do the walking tour—you can park your car near the Visitors' Gazebo on Eighth Street. Some 350 homes—from Georgian Revival, Colonial Revival, and Federal to Classic, Stick, Gothic, and Italianate—have been restored and given status on the National

Register of Historic Places. Next to Astoria on the north coast, Albany has one of the most impressive collections of such vintage structures in the state.

You'll see all styles, except, perhaps, the more flamboyant Steamboat Gothic so well known in the southern United States. Folks can also contact the State Historic Preservation Office for more information about all kinds of vintage structures open to the public at various times throughout the year—from restored homes and historic churches to vintage department stores, carriage and stable companies, and early theaters. These structures are located throughout the entire state. For current schedules call the Historic Preservation Office staff in Salem at (503) 378–6508.

Before beginning the walking tour, linger at the gazebo to see old photos of Albany's beginnings and to enjoy a small garden graced by scented lavender, bright snapdragons, pale clematis, deep purple heliotrope, and double hollyhocks. For helpful maps and information about the historic districts and the annual **Victorian House Garden Tours,** contact the Albany Visitors' Information Center, 300 Second Avenue SW (P.O. Box 965), Albany 97321. The telephone numbers are (541) 928–0911 or (800) 526–2256.

For a pleasant drive into the countryside, ask about the self-guided map to ten covered bridges in the surrounding area. At **Larwood Bridge,** circa 1939, crossing Crabtree Creek off Fish Hatchery Road, just east of Albany, enjoy a shady park near the swimming hole, along with the nostalgia of an old waterwheel that has been restored just downstream.

Visit one of the most recently renovated covered bridges just 14 miles west of Albany, in **Corvallis,** near the campus of Oregon State University. The bridge spans **Oak Creek** near Thirty-fifth Street and is now part of a popular bicycle and jogging path that meanders from here to nearby **Philomath.** The bridge, dismantled and mothballed in 1988, originally spanned the Long Tom River at Irish Bend, a tiny community near Monroe, just south of Corvallis. Local bridge buffs and an army of volunteers worked several weekends to reposition the old covered bridge and give it a new roof and fresh coats of white paint. Everyone turned out for the dedication in November 1989, including the OSU president, the Corvallis mayor, and all those hearty volunteers. For additional information about the area, contact the Corvallis Visitors' Information Center, 420 NW Second Avenue, Corvallis 97330; (541) 757–1544.

For a pleasant midsummer afternoon outdoors, get directions at the Visitors' Center to ❖ **Avery Park and Rose Gardens** located at Sixteenth Street and Allen Lane. Here you can sit amid a fine stand of towering redwoods near the extensive rose gardens while the kids somersault and play Frisbee on the enormous lawn. The roses bloom all summer and into fall.

Resuming the trail of the Calapooya Indians, continue south on old Highway 99W from Corvallis, past weathered barns, broad fields, and knolls dotted with oak, to the ❖ **William L. Finley National Wildlife Refuge.** Except for a few stragglers, the whole population of dusky Canada geese winters in the wide Willamette Valley and along the lower Columbia River, feeding on such winter grasses as ryegrass and fescue, as well as on the cereal grains and corn that are planted in fields near the refuge just for their use. Two additional refuges are located just north of Corvallis—**Ankeny Refuge** and **Baskett Slough Refuge.**

The 5,325-acre Finley Refuge was named for the early naturalist who persuaded President Theodore Roosevelt to create the first national wildlife refuges. Along the self-guided **Woodpecker Loop Trail,** open year-round, visitors can also see wood ducks, hooded mergansers (summer nesters), and ruffed grouse, as well as ring-necked pheasants, California and mountain quail, mourning doves, and black-tailed deer. Further information is available at the office of the refuge complex, 26208 Finley Refuge Road, Corvallis 97333; (541) 757–7236.

From the wildlife refuge continue south on Highway 99W through Monroe and Junction City into the southernmost portion of the Willamette Valley, which includes Oregon's second-largest metropolitan area, **Eugene-Springfield.** This region also contains portions of three national forests—Siuslaw, Willamette, and Umpqua—as well as four high Cascades wilderness areas—French Pete, Three Sisters, Diamond Peak, and Mt. Washington.

Eugene, home of the University of Oregon, offers not only miles of jogging and bike paths but, especially for chocoholics, the ❖ **Euphoria Chocolate Company.** Hiding inside dark and light chocolate truffles the size of golf balls are tempting morsels of *ganache* or crème Parisienne, a rich creamy center that may be laced with amaretto, peppermint schnapps, pecan, toasted almond, or Grand Marnier, or try solid chocolate, milk chocolate, or coffee royal chocolate. You may also find owner Bob Bury there. Bob represents the third generation of chocolate makers, and his version is from an old family recipe handed down by his grandmother. If you can't eat the whole confection at one sitting, store the truffles in your cooler; they need to be refrigerated. The Euphoria Chocolate Company can be found in a small house-turned-store at 6 West Seventeenth Street, just off Willamette Street a few blocks south of the downtown area; the phone number is (541) 343–9223.

Then, too, you could make a pit stop at ❖ **Starbuck's Coffee House,** nearby at West Eighteenth near Willamette Street, for a steaming cup of the coffee of the day, foamy lattes, and pungent espresso as well as delicious scones, muffins, and cookies. Actually, you can find the now familiar green-and-white Starbuck's sign in major cities and towns throughout Oregon and Washington (where the regional espresso mania began).

Of course you could always jog or bicycle off the extra calories on the area's network of trails and paths, but ❖ **canoeing on the Millrace** might offer a more inviting, less strenuous alternative. Constructed in 1851 by Hilyard Shaw to generate power for the flour mills, woolen mills, and sawmills lining its banks, the narrow stream bubbles up from a pipe that diverts water from the nearby Willamette River; the Millrace then flows through the blackberry vines and ambles behind a number of motels and eateries just across Franklin Boulevard from the University of Oregon campus. For many decades it's been the site of college pranks and canoe fêtes—often occurring under a full moon. When the water iced over during winter, everyone skated on it, and by the end of the 1920s—when the mills switched to electricity—the Millrace had become the recreational hub of the city.

In the days of the canoe fêtes, around 1915, barges and even empty oil drums were transformed into everything from water lilies to seashells. Colored lights were strung along the water, and bleachers were set up along the shore. The boys would swim alongside the floats, while the girls held court on top. Although such fêtes on the Millrace are a tradition of the past, you can still enjoy paddling a canoe along its lazy, 2-mile-long, backyard journey to Ferry Street, where the water rejoins the Willamette River. Park close to Franklin Boulevard and near the bridge that crosses over to the **Alton Baker**

Park nature trails, and enjoy sitting in the sun or picnicking on the grassy banks in the company of friendly quacking ducks that will eagerly chase after your bread scraps. For current information about renting canoes, call the Canoe Shack (located near the bridge) at (541) 346–4386, River Runner's Supply at (541) 343–6883, or contact the city's Outdoor Recreation Office at River House (541–687–5329).

For classy overnight accommodations consider ◆ **Campbell House,** a city inn located on the east side of Skinner's Butte at 252 Pearl Street, Eugene 97401. Originally constructed in 1892, the structure has been fully restored as an elegant thirteen-room inn. We're talking deluxe here—four-poster beds, fireplaces, whirlpool tubs, telephones, TVs with VCRs, private baths, and sumptuous breakfasts. For current rates and reservations call innkeeper Myra Plant at (541) 343–1119 or (800) 264-2519.

Other comfortable bed and breakfast accommodations in Eugene include **Pookie's Bed 'n' Breakfast** on College Hill, 2013 Charnelton Street, (541) 343–0383; **MaryEllen's Guest House** at 1583 Fircrest, (541) 342–7375; **Kjaer's House in the Woods** at 814 Lorane Highway, (541) 343–3234; and **Coyote Creek Bed & Breakfast** at 83032 Territorial Road, (541) 343–8605.

If you want to sleep a bit farther from city lights, consider heading out to Junction City via Old Highway 99W and bedding down at Irma and Don Mode's **Black Bart Bed and Breakfast** located at 94125 Love Lake Road, Junction City 97448. Black Bart isn't a nefarious outlaw relative; rather, he's a famous National Grand Champion mammoth donkey who loves to have his ears scratched and who often takes guests for a ride in the Modes' antique shay, an open two-wheeled carriage.

Nearby are antiques shops and golf courses, as well as wineries, dairies, and museums to tour and visit. For further information and reservations, call Black Bart's folks at (541) 998–1904.

A leisurely and pleasant drive from Junction City, especially with a well-filled picnic basket, loops west along pastoral Highway 36, across Bear Creek, along Long Tom River, around **Triangle Lake,** through Deadwood and Swisshome to Mapleton and the tidewaters at the mouth of the Siuslaw River at Florence, and then back to Eugene on Highway 126, through Walton, Elmira, and Veneta. Linger at Triangle Lake for your picnic or stop along the way and pick out a river-worn rock to sit on. While listening to the singing of the streams and rivers, relax into nature's setting and feel the warmth of the afternoon sun—maybe even take a snooze. Along the way are several waysides and picnic areas, some with boat landings, but no campgrounds on this particular route.

You could, however, arrange to stay overnight in a lovely log house by calling **McGillivray's Log Home Bed & Breakfast** located at 88680 Evers Road, Elmira 97437. Innkeeper Evelyn McGillivray often cooks breakfast for her guests on a wonderful old wood-burning cookstove in the kitchen-dining area. The walls in the kitchen area are of logs called "blue and buggy pine." For reservations and directions (the inn is about 14 miles west of Eugene), call (541) 935–3564.

In the shadowy coolness of groves of mature filbert (hazelnut) trees planted by pioneer farmer George Dorris in 1903, you and the kids will also enjoy visiting the historic ❖**Dorris Ranch** in nearby Springfield. Listed on the National Register of Historic Places, the ranch still produces a good-sized crop of the small, round hazelnuts each fall. Actually, farmer Dorris would probably be surprised to learn that less than a hundred years after he planted those first trees, the Willamette Valley produces nearly 98 percent of the world's commercial hazelnuts.

The **living-history program** here offers workshops in tree maintenance, old orchard restoration, and nature photography, along with guided walks of the ranch. Meet at the barn for tours, which take place year-round; call (541) 726–4325 for additional information and to arrange for a large-group tour.

CENTRAL CASCADES

If you pass through the Eugene-Springfield area during September or October, consider taking a walking tour of the **University of Oregon** campus before heading into the mountains.The outing provides a pleasant visual overdose of autumn hues clustered on a wide variety of well-established native and non-native tree species, and you'll find plenty of places to park in and around the campus just off Franklin Boulevard.

Then head about 70 miles farther on the trail of glorious autumn foliage by continuing east from Springfield via Highway 126, to access the ❖**McKenzie Pass Scenic Drive.** After driving through the tiny communities of Vida, Blue River, and McKenzie Bridge—each hugs the banks of the McKenzie River like a dedicated trout angler—turn onto Highway 242, just east of the McKenzie Ranger Station, for one of the best displays of fall colors in the region.

That characteristic nip in the air signals the return of another season in the Northwest woods, and autumn declares its arrival with leaves turned bright crimson, vibrant orange, and vivid yellow. On the quiet winding road that loops and twists about 20 miles to the top of McKenzie Pass, soft breezes whisper through dark green Douglas fir and stir the strikingly colored leaves of big leaf maple, vine maple, alder, and mountain ash.

You're in the **Willamette National Forest** now—the largest of eighteen forests within Oregon and Washington and one of the largest in the United States. The original incentive for finding a route across the Cascades in this area was the discovery of gold in Idaho more than a century ago. In 1862 Captain Felix Scott and a couple of colleagues, John Cogswell and John Templeman Craig, formed a party at Eugene to deliver supplies to the Idaho mining area. Under the auspices of his firm, the **McKenzie Salt Springs and Deschutes Wagon Road Company,** John Craig collected tolls at McKenzie Bridge until 1891. He lived nearby for many years and is buried at the summit.

Sometime around 1810 an automobile chugged over the summit, probably with extra fuel, water, and a supply of axes and saws to remove limbs and trees that seemed always to plague early travelers on the rutted, bumpy gravel and dirt roads. You will reach the top of 5,325-foot McKenzie Pass with relative ease, however, and can detour into the parking area to walk stone steps up to the ◆ **Dee Wright Observatory.** From this towerlike stone structure, constructed in the early 1930s by the Civilian Conservation Corps, you can peer through eleven narrow windows, each focused on a particular mountain peak; the peak's name and distance from the viewpoint are carved into the stone.

To the southeast are Belknap Crater, Mt. Washington, the North and Middle Sister, and Mt. Scott; Mt. Jefferson and Mt. Hood hover over lesser peaks to the north. If time allows, walk the 2-mile trail—it's part of the Pacific Crest National Scenic Trail—up **Little Belknap Crater** to see fissures, lava tunnels, and spatter cones. Like Lava Cast Forest near Bend, it's an intriguing, close-up encounter with those massive lava fields of the high central Cascades, which cover thousands of acres with at least three layers of the rough black stuff.

Although the volcanoes are quiet now, geologists believe the fires deep inside Oregon's Cascade crest are just napping and may someday erupt again, as did Mt. Saint Helens to the north, in Washington, in May 1980. The McKenzie Ranger Station just east of McKenzie Bridge will have current weather and road information for the area; maps of the nearby **McKenzie River National Recreation Trail,** which is especially suited to beginning hikers and families with young children; and directions to nearby Forest Service campgrounds. Located on Highway 126, the ranger station is open from 8:00 A.M. to 4:30 P.M. on weekdays; its phone number is (541) 822–3381. *Note:* Highway 242 is closed by snow during winter months; Highway 126 remains open across Santiam Pass to Sisters and Central Oregon.

You can also call the folks at ❖**Belknap Springs Lodge** to reserve a room in their historic, refurbished lodge on the banks of the McKenzie River a couple of miles from the ranger station. A few small cabins—bring your own bedding—and camping/recreational vehicle spaces are also available, all within walking distance of the hot mineral springs swimming pool. You can also walk to a picturesque section of the McKenzie River Recreation Trail from the upper campground and enjoy a short walk within earshot of the bubbling river.

The many mineral springs in the area were long known to Indian peoples, who believed they held restorative and healing powers. Trails led to secret places where the Indians stopped regularly to take baths in the warm waters. Belknap Hot Springs, discovered by R. S. Belknap around 1869, was a longtime favorite of families living in the valley.

The lodge was built just across the river from the mineral springs, and by 1910 a daily motor stage from Eugene had been established—the trip on the original dirt and gravel road took a whole day. During the season of 1890, some 700 lodge guests were registered, at a cost of $15.00 per week; one could tent camp at a weekly rate of $1.50.

On your visit you'll notice billows of steam rising from the hot springs on the far side of the McKenzie River; the 130-degree mineral water is piped across the lodge and pool. The mineral water is cooled to a temperature of about 102 degrees in the swimming pool and is perfect for soaking one's weary bones at the end of a day of hiking and exploring the area. For further information and reservations, contact the staff at Belknap Springs Lodge, McKenzie Bridge 97413; (541) 822–3512.

Playing hide-and-seek with Highway 126, the snow-fed **McKenzie River** has long been known by lovers of fishing. According to lively accounts from old newspapers of the early 1900s, "wet flies were disdained by the swiftly traveling denizens of the rapids and many misses suffered before anglers acquired the knack of handling the rod properly . . . whether trout bite or not, there are times when a fisherman must stop fishing and tell fish stories." For current regulations and angler's licenses, stop at one of the local grocery stores in **Vida, Leaburg, Blue River,** or McKenzie Bridge. You can also contact the Oregon Department of Fish and Wildlife for helpful maps, brochures, and current regulations: 2501 SW First Avenue, Portland 97207; (503) 229–5403.

For information about guided river fishing in the well-known ◈ **McKenzie River Driftboats,** as well as about guided rafting trips, contact the Eugene-Springfield Visitors' Center, 115 West Eighth Street, Eugene 97440 (541–484–5307 or 800–452–3670 in Oregon and 800–547–5445 outside Oregon).

A final detour into this valley section of the high Cascades is accessed via Highway 58, just south of Eugene and winding up to the community of **Oakridge.** Along the way notice the Southern Pacific Railroad tracks, a historic transportation link to the upper Willamette area that has operated since 1912. In the early 1930s as many as five passenger trains passed through Oakridge each day, with stops at Fields, McCredie Springs, Cascade Summit, and Crescent Lake on the east side of the pass. Rotary snowplows, mounted on the trains, kept the Cascade line open during the winter, and the train crews stopped at a cook house at the summit for hot meals.

In good weather a popular excursion in those early days was to get off the train at Diamond Creek, hike down a trail to ◈ **Salt Creek Falls,** enjoy a picnic beneath tall firs, and then take the next train back home. Travelers can do the same using an automobile. The falls are located about 8 miles up Highway 58 east of Oakridge, and there you can also hike a short trail to this spectacular, frothy ribbon, which cascades some 286 feet down into a small canyon. These are the second-highest falls in the state; two other lovely falls, **Sahalie** and **Koosah,** can be visited in the McKenzie Bridge area, just above the ranger station, off Highway 126.

Next continue on Highway 58 east to the 5,128-foot summit, **Willamette Pass,** to see one of the state's oldest ski areas. Of course the original rope tow built by Roy Temple and fellow ski enthusiasts from Oakridge in the 1940s is now gone, but in its place rises a chair lift that carries a new crop of skiers nearly a mile to the top of 6,666-foot Eagle Peak. Roy and his wife, Edna, ran the original ski area for a number of years and lived at Cascade Summit, at the west end of nearby Odell Lake. Edna remembers making and serving chili, hot dogs, cupcakes, and coffee from the ski shack, with a roaring bonfire out in front. You can enjoy seeing memorabilia about Oakridge and the ski area at the **Oakridge Pioneer Museum,** located at 76433 Pine Street, Oakridge 97463. The museum is open on Saturday from 1:00 to 4:00 P.M. and by appointment. Call (541) 782–3904 or (541) 782–2402 for further information.

For an overnight stay just east of the summit, at an elevation of 4,800 feet, check with owners John and Janet Milandin at ◆**Odell Lake Lodge,** located at the sunny southeast corner of the lake. There is moorage space at the marina, and motorboats, canoes, rowboats, and small sailboats are available to rent by the hour or day. In summer and fall anglers fish for Kokanee salmon, Mackinaw lake trout, and native rainbow trout on the 5-mile-long, 300-foot-deep lake; during winter cross-country skiers and snow bunnies flock to the area from the valley.

The small restaurant in the lodge is open daily, year-round, and serves all three meals. For further information and reservations, contact the Milandins at Odell Lake Lodge, P.O. Box 72, Crescent Lake 97425; (541) 433–2540.

COVERED BRIDGE COUNTRY

Continuing south on I–5 from the Eugene-Springfield area, exit at **Cottage Grove** and, bearing to the east past the Village Green Inn on Row River Road, stop at the Forest Service Ranger Station to pick up maps and information about covered bridges and historic mining areas. From Row River Road, take back roads past vintage covered bridges into the **Bohemia Mine** area, enjoying the rural countryside along the way.

With a radiator full of water and good brakes, adventurous travelers can negotiate the narrow, winding gravel road to **Fairview**

Peak and **Musick Mine,** at the top of 5,933-foot Bohemia Mountain. On a clear day Mt. Shasta can be seen to the south, the gossipy Three Sisters Mountains to the north, and the Coast Range to the west. Along the 70-mile loop drive are other places to stop as well.

Although some 400 miners once called the Calapooya Mountains in this area home, now gentle breezes rattle broken, rusted hinges and scuttle through a fallen-down cookhouse or blacksmith shop or remnants of an old hotel or store. The mines flourished from 1890 until 1910, with some activity after World War I, but most of the mines have given way to wind, rain, snow, and time. In the old days it took six to eight horses from eight to ten hours to pull a load of supplies and mining equipment up Hardscrabble Grade, the steep, 6-mile trail.

Today smooth country roads reach into the Bohemia mining country, wrapping around green hills and pastures where woolly sheep and multicolored cows graze peacefully in the sun. *Note:* Even though a shack may look long forgotten and deserted, it may actually be someone's headquarters for mining exploration or assessment work; the mines are on private land and are not to be disturbed by travelers. Check at the ranger station in Cottage Grove if you're interested in public gold-panning areas—there are several in the immediate area.

A wagon road was the first main route into the Row River area; it wound along the river through Culp Creek to ◆**Red Bridge,** a covered bridge built in 1879. In the surrounding Cottage Grove–Eugene–Springfield area, it's possible to explore nearly twenty of the fifty-three covered bridges still standing in the state. Calling forth a bit of horse-and-buggy nostalgia or images of kids with fishing poles and cans of worms, most covered bridges are under the protection of local historical societies. Although most are no longer for public use, a few do remain open to automobile traffic and, of course, to artists, photography buffs, and folks with fishing poles. In Cottage Grove the **Covered Bridge Festival** is celebrated in mid-September.

From exposed trusses and rounded portals, to Gothic-, portal-, or louvered-style windows, to tin or shingled roofs, the covered bridges in this area are more numerous than in any other section of the state; five are in the immediate Cottage Grove area, and four are still in the active use for automobiles, bicyclers, and hik-

Red Bridge

ers. The longest covered bridge in the state is **Office Bridge,** spanning 180 feet across a millpond off the North Fork of the Willamette River; the shortest, at just 39 feet, is **Lost Creek Bridge,** located in southern Oregon.

In the 1930s there were more than 300 covered bridges in the state, but by the 1950s their numbers had dwindled to fewer than 140. The **Covered Bridge Society of Oregon** is dedicated to preserving and restoring the remaining bridges and also promotes the study of the bridges' history and unique construction. A helpful map and brochure showing all fifty-three bridge locations in twelve different areas of the state can be obtained at the Cottage Grove Visitors' Center, 710 Row River Road (P.O. Box 587), Cottage Grove 97424; (541) 942–2411.

For easy hiking into meadows carpeted with alpine wildflowers in July and August, near Cottage Grove, try the ❖**June Mountain Trail,** the **Adams Mountain Trail,** or the **Hardesty Trail**—maps and information are available at the ranger station on Row River Road. Keep alert, too, for some of the forty kinds of edible wild berries that grow in the region. Tiny wild blackberries ripen in August, salal berries are abundant in forested areas, and the Oregon grape berries are plentiful in late summer and fall. All make delicious jams and jellies, and all were used by the Native American peoples as well.

In early spring you can see waves of blooming purple camas that carpet the swales along I–5 between Creswell and Cottage Grove. Long ago the Indians gathered the tiny bulbs of the purple camas for winter food and steamed them in large pits lined with heated rocks and wet grass, covered over with hides to hold in the heat.

In mid-July, Cottage Grove celebrates **Bohemia Mining Days** with a tour of historic homes, an old-timers' breakfast, fiddlers' contests, and the Grand Miners Parade down Main Street; the Prospector's Breakfast at the top of Bohemia Mountain usually ends the four-day celebration. You can also see Bohemia mining memorabilia at the **Cottage Grove Historical Museum,** housed in the circa 1897, octagonal, former church building located at Birch and H Streets. Call (541) 942–3963 for current hours.

By all means plan to stay overnight in Cottage Grove's covered bridge country, and for cozy accommodations check with the following friendly innkeepers: **The Ivanoff's Inn** located at 3101 Bennett Creek Road, (541) 942–3171; **River Country Inn** located at 71864 London Road, (541) 942–9334; **The Country House Bed & Breakfast** located at 30930 Camas Swale Road, (541) 895–3924; **Lily of the Field Bed & Breakfast** located at 35710 Ross Lane, (541) 942–2049; and **Apple Inn** located at 30697 Kenady Lane, (541) 942–2393. The Cottage Grove Visitors' Center can provide additional information as well.

Travel Planning Resources and Maps

Oregon Tourism Division, 775 Summer Street NE, Salem 97310; (800) 547–7842

Oregon Parks & Recreation Department, (503) 378–6305; for campground reservations, (800) 452–5687

U.S.D.A. Forest Recreation & Campgrounds Information, (503) 326–2877; for reservations, (800) 280–2267

National Park Service/Pacific Northwest Regional Office, Seattle, (206) 220–4000

Oregon Department of Fish and Wildlife, (503) 229–5403

Oregon Fishing Information, (800) ASK–FISH

Oregon State Marine Board, (503) 378–8587

U.S. Fish and Wildlife Service, (503) 231–6828

Oregon Guides and Packers Association, (541) 683–9552

Oregon Outdoors Association, (541) 747–9688

Snowmobile Activity Information, (541) 820–3366

U.S. Bureau of Land Management (BLM), (503) 952–6002

Flight Maps, Flight Seeing/Oregon Aeronautics Division, (503) 378–4880

Oregon highway, mountain pass, and road conditions, (503) 889–3999

INDEX

191

ACKNOWLEDGMENTS

Special thanks for the third edition of this book go to the following friends, innkeepers, historians, and fellow writers for providing information, helpful research assistance, and inspiration: Jack and Bea Rawls, Katrina and Doug Haines, Cynthia Withee, Melody and Bob Johnson, Sally-Jo Bowman, Terry Richards, Chantall Van Wey, and Marilyn McFarlane.

Thanks also to friendly staff members at visitor information centers throughout the state as well as friendly folks at regional offices and ranger districts, Bureau of Land Management (BLM), and USDA Forest Services.

ABOUT THE AUTHOR

Myrna Oakley has traveled the byways of the Northwest and western British Columbia since 1970, always with a camera in hand and an inquisitive eye for natural and scenic areas, as well as for wonderful inns, gardens, and places with historical character and significance. In this process she has developed an affinity for goosedown comforters, friendly conversations by the fire, and intriguing people who generally prefer to live somewhat off the beaten path.

In addition to *Oregon: Off the Beaten Path,* she has written *Public and Private Gardens of the Northwest* and *Bed and Breakfast Northwest.* She also teaches about the business of freelance writing, novel writing, and travel writing at Marylhurst College, near Portland.

ABOUT THE ILLUSTRATOR

Elizabeth Neilson Walker lives in Portland and operates her own graphic arts business. She also illustrates fiction and nonfiction books for children and adults. Her dream is to live in a beach house on the Oregon coast.